Biblical Introduction Series

THE PSALMS AND OTHER SACRED WRITINGS

THEIR ORIGIN, CONTENTS, AND SIGNIFICANCE

BY

FREDERICK CARL EISELEN
Professor of Old Testament Interpretation
in Garrett Biblical Institute

WIPF & STOCK · Eugene, Oregon

Wipf and Stock Publishers
199 W 8th Ave, Suite 3
Eugene, OR 97401

The Psalms and Other Sacred Writings
Their Origins, Contents, and Significance
By Eiselen, Frederick Carl
ISBN 13: 978-1-4982-1863-4
Publication date 3/31/2015
Previously published by Methodist Book Concern, 1918

The Bible text used in this volume is taken from the American Standard Edition of the Revised Bible, copyright, 1901, by Thomas Nelson & Sons, and is used by permission.

CONTENTS

CHAPTER		PAGE
	PREFACE	7
I.	HEBREW POETRY	9
II.	THE BOOK OF PSALMS	37
III.	THE WISDOM LITERATURE OF THE HEBREWS	81
IV.	THE BOOK OF PROVERBS	93
V.	THE BOOK OF JOB	123
VI.	THE SONG OF SONGS	163
VII.	THE BOOK OF RUTH	187
VIII.	THE BOOK OF LAMENTATIONS	197
IX.	THE BOOK OF ECCLESIASTES	211
X.	THE BOOK OF ESTHER	233
XI.	THE BOOK OF DANIEL	249
	APPENDIX TO CHAPTER XI	283
XII.	THE BOOKS OF EZRA AND NEHEMIAH	289
	APPENDIX TO CHAPTER XII	313
XIII.	THE BOOKS OF CHRONICLES	317
	INDEX	339

PREFACE

THE PSALMS AND OTHER SACRED WRITINGS represents Volume III in a series of books intended to furnish a scholarly, nontechnical Introduction to the entire Old Testament. Volume I has already appeared under the title THE BOOKS OF THE PENTATEUCH. The present volume discusses the origin, contents, and significance of the books included in the third division of the Hebrew Bible, known as *The Writings;* they are treated in the order in which they appear in the common editions of the Hebrew Bible. Volume II, which will be ready for publication in the near future, will deal with the remaining books of the Old Testament, forming the second division of the Hebrew Bible, and called by the Jews *The Prophets.*

For a statement of the aims and principles which guided the author and a description of the method of treatment, the reader may turn to the Preface of Volume I.

FREDERICK CARL EISELEN.

Evanston, Illinois.

CHAPTER I
HEBREW POETRY

CHAPTER I

HEBREW POETRY[1]

HEBREW poetry reaches back to the most ancient recollections of the people of Israel. As seems to have been the case with other nations of antiquity,[2] poetry was the form in which the earliest literary efforts of the Hebrews found expression; and even the earliest poetic efforts had to do with all conditions and experiences of life that yielded themselves to poetic treatment.

The Old Testament has preserved a large amount of this poetry, chiefly religious poetry; but there are references showing that much of it has been lost. For instance, reference is made to the *Book of the Wars of Yahweh*[3] and the *Book of Yashar*,[4] evidently the names of collections of songs and poems earlier than any of those now found in the Hebrew Scriptures.[5] Besides, there are allusions here and there to the existence of other poetic compositions[6] and to the use of songs at banquets and similar festal occasions.[7] Some poems and poetic fragments have been preserved in the so-called

---

[1] Since some of the most important books among the *Writings* are in poetic form, it seems desirable to devote a chapter to a discussion of the general characteristics of Hebrew poetry.

[2] C. F. Kent, *The Songs, Hymns, and Prayers of the Old Testament*, p. 3.

[3] Num. 21. 14.

[4] Josh. 10. 13; 2 Sam. 1. 18.

[5] F. C. Eiselen, *The Books of the Pentateuch*, pp. 259, 293, 294.

[6] For example, 1 Kings 4. 31-33.

[7] Gen. 31. 27; 2 Sam. 19. 35; Amos 6. 5; Isa. 5. 12; 16. 10, etc.

THE PSALMS AND OTHER SACRED WRITINGS

historical books.[8] The first specimen is the Song of Lamech, or of the Sword, in Gen. 4. 23, 24; but from there on poetic compositions appear again and again.[9] The prophetic books also contain many fine specimens of poetry, and frequently the prophets rise, in their discourses, to an elevated poetic style which cannot easily be distinguished from the poetry in the Psalter.[10] In addition to these poetic sections embedded in prose, there are five books in the Old Testament which consist entirely, or almost so, of poetic compositions. These are the books of Psalms, Proverbs, Job, Song of Songs, and Lamentations. The book of Ecclesiastes is a mixture of poetry and prose.

Essential Characteristics of Poetry. The English term "poesy" or "poetry," like its Greek original, ποίησις may be applied to all artistic literary productions in which the imagination plays an important part. Poetry in a wider sense, therefore, is not necessarily associated with verse or rime; it may find expression in prose, and, in point of fact, often has done so both in ancient and modern times. In the present discussion, however, the term is used in a narrower sense, poetry in form as well as in substance.

Poetry has been variously described or defined by modern literary critics. A convenient definition is that of Leigh Hunt, who says: "Poetry . . . is the utterance of a passion for truth, beauty, and power, embodying and illustrating its conceptions by imagination and fancy, and modulating its language on the principle of variety in

---

[8] From Genesis to Esther.
[9] See F. C. Eiselen, *The Books of the Pentateuch*, Chap. XVI.
[10] See G. B. Gray, *Commentary on the Book of Isaiah*, I–XXXIX sections 44-57, on "The Poetical Forms in the Prophetic Literature."

HEBREW POETRY

uniformity.[11] This definition recognizes three essential characteristics of all true poetry: (1) The substance is something that grips the emotions—it is the utterance of a passion for truth, beauty, and power. Poetry springs from quickened emotions; hence it arouses the emotions. (2) Its presentation is imaginative—literalism is discarded and imagination is given full sway in the presentation of the substance. (3) The inevitable result is the use of an emotional, exalted style, a style marked by the lively swing called rhythm.

The following lines from *In Memoriam* illustrate these three essential characteristics of true poetry:

> Perplexed in faith, but pure in deeds,
> At last he beat his music out;
> There lives more faith in honest doubt,
> Believe me, than in half the creeds.

The substance grips the deepest emotions—the struggle of a perplexed soul, the presentation is imaginative, the form of expression is rhythmical.

Rhythm in poetry may be defined as the harmonious repetition of fixed sound relations. These sound relations may be determined either on the basis of quantity or time; that is, the regulated succession of long and short syllables, or on the basis of accent or stress; that is, the regulated succession of accented and unaccented syllables. The units formed by each fixed group of sound relations are called feet, or meters, or measures. A method of emphasizing the rhythm, which may or may not accom-

---

[11] *Imagination and Fancy*, p. 1. Practically the same ideas are expressed by C. F. Kent, when he defines poetry as "the imaginative and rhythmic expression of the insight, the feeling, and the creative thought of an inspired soul" (*The Songs, Hymns, and Prayers of the Old Testament*, p. 3). Creative power, which Kent considers an essential element of all true poetry, is a sequel of the stirring of the emotions.

pany the use of the fixed sound relations, is the use of rime; that is, the correspondence in sound of the final syllables in the lines.

In ancient classical poetry—Sanskrit, Greek, and Latin—the rhythm is produced by the regulated succession of long and short syllables. Early poetry shows only isolated cases of rime, and these may be due to accident. As a common mark of poetry it seems to have been introduced by early Christian poets, and it reached a high degree of perfection in the twelfth and thirteenth centuries of the Christian era. In modern poetry rime is used extensively; it renders the rhythm more distinct and appreciable than the other methods by themselves could do. It is for this reason that in French, where the accents are so weak that verse without rime is almost indistinguishable from prose, poetry without rime has never been fully developed.

The regulated succession of long and short syllables, as a method of marking rhythm, has practically disappeared from modern Western poetry. The two methods commonly used are rime and the regulated succession of accented and unaccented syllables. Sometimes the two characteristics are found together. Frequently, however, rime is absent; in such cases the rhythm is marked solely by the regulated succession of accented and unaccented syllables, which form of poetry is known as "blank verse." Blank verse may be illustrated by these lines from the *Drama of the Exile:*

>If thou hadst gazed upon the face of God
>This morning for a moment, thou hadst known
>That only pity fitly can chastise,
>Hate but avenges.

The combination of the regulated succession of ac-

HEBREW POETRY

cented and unaccented syllables and rime is seen in the stanza from *In Memoriam*, quoted above.[12]

Characteristics of Hebrew Poetry. The ancient Hebrews were intensely religious, a characteristic shared by all Semites. The interest in religion furnished a vast amount of "emotional" material that yielded itself readily to poetic treatment. But leaving religion entirely out of consideration, the genius of the entire Semitic race, including the Hebrews, was emotional. "These peoples," says A. R. Gordon, "were all the children of passionate feeling. And the Hebrews shared to the full in the common race temperament. They loved intensely, and they hated intensely."[13] Thus, even apart from religion, the Hebrew spirit contained within itself the potentiality of great poetry. As orientals the Hebrews were richly endowed with the powers of imagination that are essential in the production of sublime poetic compositions. But wherever these two characteristics are present, rhythmic expression follows naturally and inevitably.[14]

Though the presence of poetry in the Old Testament has always been recognized by careful students, until modern times no one seemed to know what were the external marks that distinguished Hebrew poetry from

---

[12] In some instances, especially in the case of poetry intended to be sung, the "sound relations" are more or less vague; and it almost seems as if rime furnished the only external mark of poetry. Compare, for example, the stanza:

"Just as I am, without one plea,
But that thy blood was shed for me,
And that thou bidst me come to thee,
O Lamb of God, I come."

[13] *The Poets of the Old Testament*, pp. 1, 2.

[14] The influence of Semitic racial characteristics on the development of early Semitic poetry is fully discussed in G. A. Smith, *The Early Poetry of Israel*, especially Chapter II.

THE PSALMS AND OTHER SACRED WRITINGS

prose.[15] Indeed, it was not until 1753 that the study of Hebrew poetry was placed on a solid basis. The merit of discovering the chief characteristic of Hebrew poetry belongs to Bishop Robert Lowth, at the time professor of poetry at Oxford, who published in the year mentioned the results of his investigations in a book entitled *De Sacra Poesi Hebraorum Prælectiones Academicæ*. He pointed out that the rhythm of Hebrew poetry was not marked primarily by rime, nor the regulated succession of accented and unaccented syllables, nor the regulated succession of long and short syllables, but by the arrangement of the lines according to sense. This peculiarity he called "parallelism of members," by which he meant the parallel arrangement of two clauses of approximately the same length, the second of these sustaining a vital relation to the thought of the first line. For this parallelism of members it is not necessary to have agreement in thought; the parallelism may be in form only; in such cases the second line may express the very opposite thought, or may advance or otherwise complete the thought of the first line.

---

[15] The statements of ancient writers on the subject of Hebrew poetry were inspired more by a "desire to assimilate Hebrew poetry to the great productions of the classic nations with which they were familiar," than by an accurate knowledge of the facts. Thus Josephus states that Exod. 15 and Deut. 32 were written in hexameters, and he mentions the use of several other meters in the Psalms. Similar claims were made by Eusebius and Jerome; but a study of Hebrew poetry itself makes it clear that whatever elements of truth these statements may contain, they can in no sense be accepted as final. During the Middle Ages little advance was made toward an understanding of the form of Hebrew poetry: Christian interpreters were interested almost exclusively in the contents, and the Jewish rabbis, though some alluded incidentally to what were later found to be essential characteristics of Hebrew poetry, failed to carry their discoveries to their logical conclusions.

HEBREW POETRY

These differences did not escape Lowth, and in explanation of them he distinguished three types of parallelism:

(1) *Synonymous parallelism:* Parallel arrangement in which the second line contains a thought identical with or similar to the thought of the first line. For example,

> But his delight is in the law of Jehovah;
> And on his law doth he meditate day and night.[16]

Sometimes practically the same words are used in the two lines:

> For in a night Ar of Moab is laid waste, *and* brought to nought;
> For in a night Kir of Moab is laid waste, *and* brought to nought.[17]

(2) *Antithetic parallelism:* The thought of the first line is emphasized by calling attention to a contrast, the second line expressing the opposite thought. This kind of parallelism is used especially in gnomic or didactic poetry. For example,

> A wise son maketh a glad father;
> But a foolish son is the heaviness of his mother.[18]

(3) *Synthetic or constructive parallelism:* The second line contains neither a repetition of the thought of the first line, nor a contrast to it, but in various ways advances or completes it. There may be a simple completion of the thought; for example,

> Yet I have set my king   10
> Upon my holy hill of Zion.[19]

Or, the second line may furnish a comparison; for example,

> Better is a dinner of herbs, where love is,
> Than a stalled ox and hatred therewith.[20]

---
[16] Psalm 1. 2.
[17] Isa. 15. 1.
[18] Prov. 10. 1.
[19] Psalm 2. 6.
[20] Prov. 15. 17.

THE PSALMS AND OTHER SACRED WRITINGS

In other cases the second line supplies a motive; for example,

> Answer not a fool according to his folly,
> Lest thou also be like unto him.[21]

These are the three types of parallelism recognized by Lowth; and while it would be possible to make further subdivisions, for all practical purposes his classification is sufficient. It has become customary, however, to add at least one more type.

(4) *Climactic parallelism:* The first line leaves the thought incomplete; the second repeats certain words from it and then goes on to complete the thought; for example,

> Ascribe unto Jehovah, O ye sons of the mighty,
> Ascribe unto Jehovah glory and strength.[22]

The same phenomenon is known also as *Ascending Rhythm,* a designation used especially of the peculiar stairlike movement[23] found in some of the Pilgrim Psalms,[24] where an emphatic or significant word is carried over from one line or stanza to the next. For example,

> I will lift up mine eyes unto the mountains:
> From whence shall *my help* come?
> *My help* cometh from Jehovah,
> Who made heaven and earth.
> He will not suffer thy foot to be moved:
> *He that keepeth* thee will not *slumber.*
> Behold, he that *keepeth* Israel
> Will neither *slumber* nor sleep.[25]

---

[21] Prov. 26. 4.
[22] Psalm 29. 1.
[23] G. A. Smith calls it "Spiralism," *The Early Poetry of Israel,* p. 13.
[24] Psalms 120–134.
[25] Psalm 121. 1-4. The *italics*, not found in the American Revised Version, are introduced here to call attention to the significant expressions.

HEBREW POETRY

Bishop Lowth's theory that parallelism of members is the chief characteristic of Hebrew poetry is universally accepted. But it is not without its difficulties. After all, parallelism seems too narrow a term to fit all the facts. It is almost impossible to stretch its meaning sufficiently to satisfy all Old Testament poetry. Many of the stanzas are synthetic, and in these there is, strictly speaking, no parallelism at all. Nevertheless, with due recognition of the difficulties, parallelism of members as defined and described by Lowth must be regarded as a prominent factor in all Old Testament poetry.

Until recently it was thought that parallelism of members as a determining principle of poetic art was peculiar to the Hebrews, though incidentally it might be used by the poets of other nations and races. Later the discovery that the poetry of the Babylonians and Egyptians was constructed on the same principle, led to attempts to trace the origin of this parallelism to one or the other of these two civilizations with the assumption that the Hebrews derived it from them. It should be noted, however, that traces of the same kind of parallelism are found in the poetry of other ancient peoples; and that numerous modern illustrations can be found which cannot be explained as dependent on biblical poetry. True, modern classic poetry has largely discarded it, but popular poetry, and poetry imitating folk songs, still make use of it.[26]

Whatever, therefore, the influence of Babylon or Egypt on the development of Hebrew poetry may have been, the origin of parallelism as an essential factor in poetry must be sought, as first suggested by Herder, in the *"responsive* mode of primitive folk-song. . . . The

---
[26] Numerous illustrations of parallelism in popular poetry are given by G. A. Smith, *Early Poetry of Israel*, pp. 15, 16.

THE PSALMS AND OTHER SACRED WRITINGS

parallel lines, as it were, come dancing to meet each other, like the singing choruses that gave them form." [27] Speaking of the parallel lines, Herder says: "They sustain, uplift, and strengthen each other in their counsel or their joy. This result is obvious in songs of triumph. The effect aimed at through the mournful notes of sorrow, on the other hand, is that of the sigh or lamentation. As the very drawing of the breath seems to support and comfort the soul, so does the other half of the chorus share in our sorrow, becoming the echo, or, as the Hebrews say, the daughter of our expression of grief. In didactic odes the one line strengthens the other. It is as though the father spoke to his son, and the mother repeated his words. The counsel thus becomes so very true, cordial, and intimate. In love songs, again, we have sweet lovers' talk—a real interchange of hearts and thoughts. In fine, so simple a bond of family affection is formed between the two parallel expressions of feeling, that I may readily apply to them the words of the tender Hebrew ode (Psalm 133),*'Behold, how good and how pleasant it is for brethren to dwell together in unity'* . . ."[28] G. A. Smith explains the wide prevalence of parallelism in early poetry in these words: "The fact is, poetry was primitively the art of saying the same beautiful things over and over again in similarly charming ways, which rimed and sang back to each other, not in sound only but in sense as well. 'Deep calleth unto deep,' tree to tree, bird to bird, all the world over. The heart of the poet is full of such natural antiphons, he knows many metaphors for the thing which he loves or hates, and he will put

---

[27] A. R. Gordon, *The Poets of the Old Testament*, p. 14.
[28] J. G. von Herder, *Vom Geist der Hebraeischen Poesie*, in *Werke*, vol. xi, p. 237.

HEBREW POETRY

them over against each other; more careful at first that they are balanced in meaning than in rhythm, though as his art develops he will control this also to regularity. Like the musician (and the early poet always was a musician as well), he instinctively gives us variation upon variation of the same theme."[29]

Meter in Hebrew Poetry. The fact that practically all ancient and modern poetry outside of the Old Testament is constructed according to clearly defined systems of meter has inspired numerous efforts to discover a metrical system in Hebrew poetry. The theories proposed exhaust all the possibilities imaginable: some scholars have marked beats, some quantity, some accents; some have combined the first or second with the third; some have taken the syllable as the determining unit, some the word; some have built their theories upon the Hebrew text as it stands, others have taken all kinds of liberty with it.[30] As a result of these numerous and prolonged investigations, the confident assertion of Kuenen that Hebrew poetry is without meter may safely be displaced by the equally confident statement that Hebrew poetry is constructed according to a metrical system. Even as the text now stands a large portion of Hebrew poetry is fully metrical, while another large portion shows but few irregularities.

The determining factor in the Hebrew metrical system is, as was first suggested by Bellermann, the play of the *accent*. Moreover, as was discovered by Meier and Ley, the metrical movement is determined by the number of *accented syllables*, the number of unaccented syllables

---

[29] *Early Poetry of Israel*, p. 16.
[30] For an excellent discussion of the various theories proposed see W. H. Cobb, *A Criticism of Systems of Hebrew Meter*.

THE PSALMS AND OTHER SACRED WRITINGS

separating the accented syllables being immaterial; "as many may precede or follow the accented syllables as can be pronounced within a given duration of time." Bearing in mind the fundamental difference between the Hebrew and Greek metrical systems—the former being based on accent, the latter on quantity—the most common "foot" in Hebrew resembles the Greek anapæst (◡ ◡ —), from which the transition is easy to the iambus (◡ —) or to the pæon (◡ ◡ ◡ —).

The line, or *stichos*, found most frequently is one having three strong accents, but the line with four strong accents is not uncommon, and in poems picturing swift motion, there is a preference for lines with two accents.

A peculiar metrical grouping is found in the so-called *Ķînāh* verse. While studying the book of Lamentations, Lowth was impressed by the fact that "the verses are clearly longer by almost one half than those we usually meet elsewhere." Later De Wette noticed that each line was marked by a cæsura, corresponding both with the accent and the sense; and subsequently Keil pointed out that the Cæsura divided the line into unequal parts. Finally Professor Karl Budde, after an exhaustive investigation of the entire subject, set forth the true nature of the verse, to which he gave the name *Ķînāh*.[31] The Hebrew *Ķînāh* means "dirge" or "lamentation"; and the term was applied to this particular kind of verse because it was used "wherever poet or prophet fell into the dirge-note for the dead." Further study has shown, however, that its use is not restricted to the poetry of mourning. It seems that after it had once come to be recognized as a distinct measure it was used for the expression of intense feeling of every sort, be it joy or sorrow.

---

[31] *Zeitschrift fuer die Alttestamentliche Wissenschaft*, 1882, pp. 1ff.

HEBREW POETRY

The peculiarity of the *Ķînāh* verse consists in the fact that the line of more than ordinary extent is made up of two parts of unequal length, the ratio being ordinarily three accented syllables in the first part to two accented syllables in the second, but the ratio four to three and other irregularities are also found. The shortening of the second part gives a "limping" rhythm to the verse; it seems to die away and expire; hence its use in lamentations. Lam. 1. 1 may serve as an illustration, though the English translation makes no special attempt to reproduce the original rhythm:

How doth the city sit solitary—that was full of people!
She is become as a widow—that was great among the nations!
She that was a princess among the provinces—is become tributary!

The attitude of skepticism taken by some toward the question of a metrical system in Hebrew poetry may be traced to the presence of numerous irregularities even in poems in which the great majority of lines have the normal or expected number of accents. "A poem, the most of whose lines have three accents each, will be broken by several of two or four each; while sometimes a series perfectly regular in the proportion of their accents will be closed by a single longer line with an accent more than its predecessors. In the *Ķînāh* rhythm the normal proportion of three to two is not always observed; we find couplets of four to three and four to two."[32] The method adopted by some scholars, to establish regularity by wholesale emendations of the text, more or less arbitrary, does not increase confidence in their theories. Nevertheless, with full recognition of frequent irregularities, the presence of a metrical system in Hebrew poetry can no longer be doubted.

---

[32] G. A. Smith, *Early Poetry of Israel*, p. 12.

THE PSALMS AND OTHER SACRED WRITINGS

Many of the irregularities may be accounted for by corruption of the text. Such irregularities may easily be removed, and in many instances cautious emendations have greatly improved the rhythm. But in addition to irregularities due to carelessness in transmission, some may have been present from the beginning, due especially to two causes: (1) The dominant influence of the parallelism of members on the construction of the lines. "If parallelism be the characteristic and dominant form of Hebrew verse, if the Hebrew poet be so constantly bent on a rhythm of sense, this must inevitably modify his rhythms of sound. If his first aim be to produce lines each more or less complete in itself, but so as to run parallel to its fellow, it follows that these lines cannot be always exactly regular in length or in measure of time. If the governing principle of the poetry requires each line to be a clause or sentence in itself, the lines will frequently tend, of course within limits, to be longer or shorter, to have more or fewer stresses than are normal throughout the poem."[33] (2) Another cause may be found in what Smith calls "Symmetrophobia, an instinctive aversion to absolute symmetry," which may be traced in every form of Oriental art.

Poetic Units. In a sense the measure, or foot, discussed in the preceding paragraphs, is the smallest poetic unit in Hebrew, as in other poetry; but from the point of view of parallelism the smallest unit is the *line*, or *stichos*, or *verse*.[34] Upon an average the lines consist of seven or eight syllables, but they may be longer or shorter as

---

[33] G. A. Smith, *Early Poetry of Israel*, p. 17.
[34] Properly speaking, the verse is a single line, and the word is so used here; though common usage makes the verse a combination of lines.

HEBREW POETRY

the poet may desire; even within one and the same stanza the lines need not be of the same length, though ordinarily they are, at least approximately, of equal length.[35] When the line is much longer than seven or eight syllables it is commonly divided by a cæsura; for example:

> The law of Jehovah is perfect, restoring the soul:
> The testimony of Jehovah is sure, making wise the simple.
> The precepts of Jehovah are right, rejoicing the heart:
> The commandment of Jehovah is pure, enlightening the eyes.
> The fear of Jehovah is clean, enduring forever:
> The ordinances of Jehovah are true, *and* righteous altogether.[36]

The next larger unit in Hebrew poetry is the *stanza*, which consists of a combination of lines or *stichoi*. The stanza may be a *monostich*, that is, it may consist of one single line. These *monostichs*, found but rarely, are used to add emphasis to a thought, either at the beginning or at the close of a poem:

> I love thee, O Jehovah, my strength.[37]

Or,

> Jehovah shall reign forever and ever.[38]

By far the largest number of stanzas are *distichs*, or two-line stanzas:

> For Jehovah knoweth the way of the righteous;
> But the way of the wicked shall perish.[39]

---

[35] It is especially at the close of a strophe that sometimes a longer and heavier line occurs, similar to the "Schwellvers" in old German ballads; for example, Judg. 5. 3, 8, 10, 12, 19, 27; Deut. 32. 14, 24, 42, 43.
[36] Psalm 19. 7-9.
[37] Psalm 18. 1.
[38] Exod. 15. 18.
[39] Psalm 1. 6. For different types of distichs, see above pp. 17, 18, the paragraphs dealing with different kinds of parallelism.

THE PSALMS AND OTHER SACRED WRITINGS

There are also many stanzas consisting of three lines each, called *tristichs*. Here different types arise according to the relation in which the several lines stand to each other. Sometimes the three lines run parallel:

> But let all those that take refuge in thee rejoice,
> Let them ever shout for joy, because thou defendest them:
> Let them also that love thy name be joyful in thee.[40]

In other cases the first two lines are parallel, while the third completes the thought:

> The kings of the earth set themselves,
> And the rulers take counsel together,
> Against Jehovah, and against his anointed.[41]

In still other cases lines two and three are parallel, the two together continuing the thought of line one:

> Arise, O Jehovah; save me, O my God:
> For thou hast smitten all mine enemies upon the cheek bone;
> Thou hast broken the teeth of the wicked.[42]

Sometimes lines one and three are parallel; two being in the nature of a parenthesis:

> Answer me when I call, O God of my righteousness;
> Thou hast set me at large *when I was* in distress;
> Have mercy upon me, and hear my prayer.[43]

Still fairly common are the combinations of four lines, called *tetrastichs:*

> And he shall be like a tree planted by the streams of water,
> That bringeth forth its fruit in its season,
> Whose leaf also doth not wither;
> And whatsoever he doeth shall prosper.[44]

Here again different types arise, determined by the rela-

[40] Psalm 5. 11.
[41] Psalm 2. 2.
[42] Psalm 3. 7.
[43] Psalm 4. 1.
[44] Psalm 1. 3.

HEBREW POETRY

tion which the several lines sustain to each other.[45] Stanzas of five lines, *Pentastichs*, are rare in the Old Testament:

> God bringeth him forth out of Egypt;
> He hath as it were the strength of the wild-ox:
> He shall eat up the nations his adversaries,
> And shall break their bones in pieces,
> And smite *them* through with his arrows.[46]

Rarer still are the six-line stanzas, or *Hexastichs:*

> For though the fig-tree shall not flourish,
> Neither shall fruit be in the vines;
> The labor of the olive shall fail,
> And the fields shall yield no food;
> The flock shall be cut off from the fold,
> And there shall be no herd in the stalls.[47]

On the basis of more or less marked breaks in the development of the thought of a poem the stanzas may be grouped into *strophes*. Gnomic poetry, as found, for example, in the book of Proverbs, may exist without such grouping, for each couplet (stanza) may express a complete idea independent of its immediate context. However, in poetry that develops a theme at greater length, such as lyric poetry, strophic arrangement may be expected. And it is now almost universally admitted that Hebrew poets grouped their stanzas, with more or less consistency, into strophes. In some cases the close of

---

[45] In the passage quoted, Psalm 1. 3, line one is independent; the remaining three lines are parallel. For other types see Gen. 49. 7; Psalms 127. 1; 24. 12; 40. 17; Isa. 59. 8; etc.
[46] Num. 24. 8; for other types, as in the case of *tristichs* and *tetrastichs*, see Deut. 32. 14, 39; 1 Sam. 2. 10; Psalm. 39. 12; etc.
[47] Hab. 3. 17; for other types see Num. 24. 17; 1 Sam. 2. 8; Song of Songs, 4. 8.

groups of stanzas is marked by refrains;[48] Psalm 107 contains two distinct refrains;[49] in other poems the refrains appear in similar, though not identical, forms.[50] In Psalm 119 the strophic arrangement is indicated by the grouping of eight separate stanzas under each letter of the Hebrew alphabet. In many other instances, in which there is no formal indication of strophic arrangement, poems fall so naturally—logically and poetically—into groups of stanzas that there can be no doubt regarding intentional strophic arrangement.[51] In other poems breaks in the thought are not so easily seen, but in such cases also close examination reveals a development of thought which makes grouping into strophes at least possible.[52]

Since poems are of unequal length the number of strophes in different poems varies. There are a few short poems of only one strophe each.[53] The most frequent combination is the pair of strophes,[54] sometimes doubled, that is, four strophes;[55] eight or sixteen strophes are rare. In addition to these combinations the late Professor Briggs, who devoted many years to the study of Hebrew poetry, distinguished poems of three strophes and its

---

[48] For example, Psalm 46. 7, 11; it is not improbable that the same refrain was found originally after verse 3; compare also Amos 4. 6, 8, 9, 10, 11; Isa. 9. 12, 17, 21; 10. 4.
[49] Verses 6, 13, 19, 28 and 8, 15, 21, 31.
[50] Psalm 80; compare verse 3 with verse 7, with verse 19.
[51] Psalm 2 falls naturally into four groups: 1-3, 4-6, 7-9, 10-12.
[52] Diversity of opinion regarding the strophic arrangement of certain poems need not appear strange in view of the fact that in the large majority of cases the extent of the groups is not indicated in the text. Hence each investigator must be guided by his own judgment regarding the significant breaks in the thought of a poem.
[53] Psalms 133, 134.
[54] Psalm 1. 1-3, 4-6.
[55] Psalm 2. 1-3, 4-6, 7-9, 10-12.

multiples, six, nine, and twenty-four; also poems of five strophes and its multiples, ten, fifteen, and twenty. Poems of seven strophes are not common; poems of eleven and twenty-two strophes are confined to alphabetic poems.[56] The strophes vary in the number of lines and in the combination of kinds of parallelism. Strophes containing only one type of parallelism are not common, for such uniformity would tend to monotony. As to the number of lines in strophes,—there are strophes of two, three, four, five, six, seven, eight, nine, ten, twelve, and fourteen lines. Of these the two-line strophes are more appropriate in gnomic poetry; in lyric poetry four and six line strophes are the most common.

Artificial Devices. The Hebrew language, though in many respects poorer and less developed than the Indo-European languages, possesses certain characteristics which, in the hands of a true artist, may greatly enhance the power and æsthetic quality of poetry. Mention may be made, for instance, of the profusion of gutturals and sibilants, the frequent doubling of consonants and the great variety of vowel sounds; the almost complete absence of compounds and abstract terms—Hebrew words express concrete objects and actions rather than ideas—the wealth of synonyms and the richness of metaphors, the simplicity of construction of both words and sentences, with the verb the dominant element in the latter. The Hebrew poets seem to have been fully aware of the poetic possibilities inherent in their language, for they made the most of their opportunities. By a skillful mingling of appropriate consonants and vowels, by the careful selection of synonyms and metaphors, and by the effective

---

[56] C. A. Briggs, *The Book of Psalms*, I, pp. xlvff.; *The Study of Holy Scriptures*, pp. 398ff.

THE PSALMS AND OTHER SACRED WRITINGS

grouping of words and clauses, they produced results of high artistic merit. Assonance and alliteration, while not very common, are not unknown, and there are a few striking cases of paronomasia, or play upon words.[57] All these artistic devices, however, can be appreciated only by the student of Hebrew poetry in the original language.[58]

Rime, which, as has been stated, plays an important role in modern poetry, is used but rarely in Hebrew poetry. In one of the earliest poems preserved in the Old Testament, the Song of Lamech,[59] rime is found in the first four lines, each ending in the pronominal suffix of the first person, i. G. A. Smith has attempted to reproduce the rime in the following translation:

> Adah and Sillah, hear ye the voice of *me*,
> Lemekh's-wives, hearken the speech of *me*,
> For a man have I slain for a wound to *me*,
> And a youth for a blow to *me*.

Another illustration of rime may be seen in the riddle of Samson,[60] which is rendered by G. F. Moore:

> Out of the eater came something to *eat*
> And out of the strong came something *sweet*.

A few other cases are found in the Old Testament, but on the whole, rime is extremely rare in Hebrew poetry. Moreover, the means by which it is secured are few and simple. In the majority of cases it is formed by the

---

[57] For example, Gen. 9. 27, play on the name "Japheth"; Gen. 49. 16, on the name "Dan"; verse 19, on the name "Gad"; Deut. 33. 8, on the name "Meribah"; Judg. 5. 12, on the name "Deborah"; etc.

[58] For a fuller discussion of these artistic devices, see G. A. Smith, *Early Poetry of Israel*, Chapter I; compare also A. R. Gordon, *The Poets of the Old Testament*, pp. 1-8.

[59] Gen. 4. 23, 24.

[60] Judg. 14. 14.

HEBREW POETRY

repetition of the same pronominal suffix or the same plural ending; and in a few cases by the repetition of *ūn*, which is an unusual plural ending of the verb. There can be no question, therefore, that to the Hebrew poets it was more natural to produce "a parallel of meaning than a harmony of sound."

Of artificial devices for purposes of ornamentation, the most important is the alphabetic acrostic. The alphabetic psalms are 9-10, 25, 34, 37, 111, 112, 119, 145. Outside of the Psalter the alphabetic arrangement is used in the first four chapters of the book of Lamentations, and traces of it appear in Nah. 1. Sometimes each separate line begins with a different letter;[61] sometimes every two-line stanza begins with a different letter.[62] In Psalms 9-10, 37, two two-line stanzas are given to each letter, the characteristic letter standing at the beginning of the first of the four lines. In Psalm 119 each letter opens eight successive two-line stanzas. In Lam. 3 the three lines of each of the twenty-two stanzas begin each with the same letter. In Lam. 1, 2 every three-line stanza begins with a different letter.

Kinds of Poetic Composition. According to early Greek writers, the three principal kinds of poetic composition are epic, dramatic, and lyric poetry, and for the present discussion this classification is still adequate. Epic poetry is descriptive and is intended to be recited. It deals with external objects and events of which it gives a narrative in poetic form. The events portrayed may be partly real and partly fictitious, or all fictitious. Dramatic poetry is concerned with the reproduction of acts and events and is intended to be acted. Thus it makes

---
[61] Psalms 111, 112.
[62] Psalms 25, 34, 145; Lam. 4.

THE PSALMS AND OTHER SACRED WRITINGS

its appeal to the eye as well as to the ear. Its subdivisions are tragedy and comedy. Lyric poetry is subjective. It sets forth the inward occurrences of the poet's own mind: his feelings and reflections, his joys and sorrows, his cares and complaints, his aspirations and despairs, etc.

From the literature that has been preserved in the Old Testament it would seem that the Hebrews never created a verse epic, like the Iliad and Odyssey of Homer. Some of the prose narratives in the Old Testament, especially in the book of Genesis, are of an epic character, but, strictly speaking, the Old Testament contains no verse epic.[63] The drama, in the sense of a poetic composition intended to be acted, is also wanting in the Old Testament, and this lack the Hebrews seem to share with the rest of the Semitic peoples. The lack may be due to a certain onesidedness of disposition, a want of objectivity, on the part of the Semites.

On the other hand, dramatic form is a conspicuous element in Hebrew poetry. The book of Psalms and the prophetic literature contain many fine illustrations of dramatic arrangement. Psalm 24. 7-10, for instance, is dramatically arranged:

Chorus: { Lift up your heads, O ye gates;
And be ye lifted up, ye everlasting doors:
And the King of glory will come in.

Inquiry: Who is the King of glory?

Response: { Jehovah strong and mighty,
Jehovah mighty in battle.

Chorus: { Lift up your heads, O ye gates;
Yea, lift them up, ye everlasting doors:
And the King of glory will come in.

---

[63] According to present knowledge, the Babylonians alone among the Semites developed epic poetry.

HEBREW POETRY

Inquiry: Who is this King of glory?
Response: { Jehovah of hosts,
             { He is the King of glory.

In structure the book of Job is in the nature of a drama and may be termed a dramatic poem.[64] Its principal part consists of a series of dialogues between Job and his friends; other speakers are Elihu and Yahweh, and in the prologue "the Satan" is introduced as one of the speakers.[65] The Song of Songs also is interpreted by many scholars as a dramatic poem, whose object is the glorification of true human love. According to one view, two principal characters appear in the drama—Solomon and the Shulammite maiden, according to another view three persons take the principal parts—Solomon, the Shulammite, and her shepherd lover.[66]

By far the largest part of Hebrew poetry is lyric in character. Lyric poetry seems to have been the earliest development of literature, and the Hebrew poets seem to have been content with its cultivation in all its varieties. In large measure this may have been due to the fact that the genius of the ancient Hebrews was preeminently subjective. As a result Hebrew poets found it difficult to adjust themselves to the presentation, in poetic form, of the emotions, thoughts, and actions of others, as both epic and dramatic poetry require. It was their own thoughts and emotions for which they endeavored to find forms of expression. In lyric poetry proper, the poet seeks to give expression to his own emotions and experiences: his joys or sorrows, his cares or complaints, his aspiration or despair; or he reproduces in words the impressions which

---
[64] But see below, p. 131.
[65] See below, Chapter V.
[66] See below, Chapter VI.

THE PSALMS AND OTHER SACRED WRITINGS

nature and history have made upon him or upon those whom he represents.

By the side of lyric poetry proper the Hebrews developed to a high degree of perfection the thought-lyric or gnomic poetry. This kind of poetry does not express the author's experiences or emotions, but his thoughts and observations on human life and society, or generalizations respecting conduct and character.[67] Only a few specimens of secular gnomic poetry are preserved in the Old Testament; the finest of which is the Fable of Jotham.[68] Its religious and ethical types are found chiefly in the wisdom literature—represented by some of the Psalms, the books of Proverbs, Job, and Ecclesiastes.

The line between the two kinds of lyric poetry cannot always be clearly drawn. Sometimes a lyric poem assumes a gnomic or didactic tone; on the other hand, a poem which on the whole is gnomic may in parts rise to a lyric strain. In Psalm 25, for example, verses 1 and 2 are lyric:

> Unto thee, O Jehovah, do I lift up my soul.
> O my God, in thee have I trusted,
> Let me not be put to shame;
> Let not mine enemies triumph over me.

Verse 3 assumes the character of thought-lyric:

Yea, none that wait for thee shall be put to shame:
They shall be put to shame that deal treacherously without cause.

Secular Poetry. The Old Testament being preeminently a book of religion, it is only natural that almost all poetry in it should be of a religious nature. It contains secular poetry only in the sense that a few poems center around secular themes; but even some of these are

---

[67] See below, Chapter III.
[68] Judg. 9. 8-15.

HEBREW POETRY

permeated by an intense religious spirit. The following secular poems or fragments of poems are embodied in the Pentateuch and the book of Joshua:

Gen. 4. 23, 24, The Song of Lamech, or, of the Sword.
Gen. 49. 2-27, The Blessing of Jacob.
Exod. 15. 1-18, The Triumph Song over the Destruction of the Egyptians.
Num. 21. 14, 15, The Song concerning the Boundary Line between Israel and Moab.
Num. 21. 17, 18, The Song of the Well.
Num. 21, 27-30, The Song Commemorating Israel's Victory over Sihon.
Deut. 33. 2-29, The Blessing of Moses.
Josh. 10. 12, 13, The Standing Still of Sun and Moon.[69]

Outside of these books the following secular poems may be noted:

Judg. 5. 2-31, The Song of Deborah.
Judg. 9. 8-15, The Fable of Jotham.
Judg. 14, 15 (*passim*), Riddles and Proverbs of Samson.
1 Sam. 18, 7, The Greeting of David by the Women.
2 Sam, 1. 19-27, The Lament of David over Saul and Jonathan.
2 Sam. 3. 33, 34, The Lament of David over Abner.

Psalm 45 may have been originally a secular poem; if so, it was changed subsequently into a religious psalm. The Song of Songs may have been intended originally to represent a collection of secular love poems.[70]

---

[69] For a discussion of these poems, see F. C. Eiselen, *The Books of the Pentateuch*, Chapter XVI.

[70] See below, Chapter VI. Allusions to secular songs sung at banquets and other festal occasions occur in a number of places; see, for example, Gen. 31. 27; 2 Sam. 19. 35; Amos 6. 5; Isa. 5. 12; 16. 10; 24. 9; Job 21. 12; Psalm 69. 12; etc.

CHAPTER II

THE BOOK OF PSALMS

CHAPTER II

THE BOOK OF PSALMS

Title. The first book in the collection of *Writings*, in the ordinary Hebrew Bible, is the book of Psalms. The book itself furnishes no title for the collection of psalms as a whole; nor is such title found anywhere else in the Old Testament. The nearest approach to it occurs in Psalm 72. 20, "The prayers[1] of David the son of Jesse are ended." The singular of the same word "prayer" appears as the title of Psalms 17, 86, 90, 102, 142, and would be appropriate in many other cases; indeed, all the psalms glow with the spirit of prayer, if prayer is interpreted in a broad sense as any turning of the heart to God in supplication, reverence, or praise. The later Jews gave to the book the title *sēpher tehillīm*, "book of praises," which title was known also to the early church fathers. The singular noun *tehillāh*, "praise" or "praise-song," which has furnished this appropriate title for the entire book, is found in the Hebrew text as the title of only one psalm.[2]

The usual Septuagint title is βίβλος ψαλμῶν, *bíblos psalmōn*, "book of psalms,"[3] rendered in the Vulgate, *Liber psalmorum*. In the *Codex Alexandrinus* the title ψαλτήριον, *psaltērion*—the name of a stringed instrument[4]—is substituted for the usual Septuagint title. The latter

---
[1] Hebrew, *tephillōth;* singular, *tephillāh*.
[2] Psalm 145.
[3] The ψαλμός is primarily a song sung to the accompaniment of stringed instruments.
[4] Perhaps the same as the frequently mentioned Hebrew *nebhel*.

39

THE PSALMS AND OTHER SACRED WRITINGS

is used in the New Testament in Luke 20. 42 and Acts 1. 20. The English titles, *Book of Psalms* and *Psalter*, are the equivalents of the two Septuagint headings.

Number and Division. Both the Hebrew Bible and the Septuagint give the total number of psalms as 150, though the two recensions show differences in the arrangement of the individual psalms:

Hebrew	Septuagint
1-8	1-8
9, 10	9
11-113	10-112
114, 115	113
116	114, 115
117-146	116-145
147	146, 147
148-150	148-150

However, there are early traditions, embodied in the Talmud and some early MSS., which show that this number was not always accepted as definitely fixed.[5] Moreover, internal evidence makes it doubtful that the collection contains exactly one hundred and fifty separate poems. It seems that in some cases what was originally one poem has become divided into two,[6] while in other cases two poems originally separate have been united into one.[7]

---

[5] The Palestinian Talmud, *Sabbath* XVI, 1, gives the number as one hundred and forty-seven, "corresponding to the one hundred and forty-seven years of our father Jacob."

[6] Psalms 9 and 10, for example, were originally one poem, as is shown by the continuation of the same acrostic scheme throughout both psalms; so also Psalms 42 and 43, as appears from the recurrence of the same refrain in 42. 5, 11 and 43. 5.

[7] This is clear in the case of Psalm 108, which consists of two psalms or fragments of psalms, 57. 7–11 + 60. 5–12; in other instances internal evidence points in the same direction; for example, Psalm 19 = 1–6 + 7–14; Psalm 24 = 1–6 + 7–10; Psalm 27 = 1–6 + 7–14; Psalm 36 = 1–4 + 5–12.

THE BOOK OF PSALMS

The Septuagint arrangement was adopted in the Vulgate and in the early English translations based upon the latter; but the English translations made directly from the Hebrew follow the arrangement in the Hebrew Bible. The Septuagint contains one additional psalm, but makes the definite statement that it is not to be considered a part of the canonical book. Its title reads: "This psalm was written by David with his own hand, though *it is outside of the number,* when he fought in single combat with Goliath." The contents show this extra psalm to be unworthy of being classed with the others, for it consists almost entirely of prose sentences taken, with slight variations, from the books of Samuel.[8]

The book of Psalms in its present form is divided into five books, a division recognized in the American Revised Version: I, 1-41; II, 42-72; III, 73-89; IV, 90-106; V, 107-150. While this division is not original and does not mark successive steps in the formation of the psalter,[9] it is very old. A Midrash[10] on the Psalms, which undoubtedly embodies pre-Christian traditions, opens with a glowing comparison between the lawgiver and the king, the five books of the Torah and the five books of the Psalms, the blessing of Moses and the blessing of David. The Septuagint also recognizes the fivefold division, which may indicate that it was known at least as early as the second century B. C.[11] The Midrash passage suggests

---

[8] For a translation of the psalm, see Hastings's *Dictionary of the Bible,* vol. iv, p. 146.
[9] See further below, pp. 64ff.
[10] A Midrash is in the nature of a homiletical commentary.
[11] On the basis of the literary parallel between 1 Chron. 16. 8, 36 and the doxology closing Book IV, Psalm 106. 47, 48, it is sometimes claimed that the chronicler knew the division; but this is doubtful, for verses 47, 48 may have been a part of Psalm 106 before the division was

THE PSALMS AND OTHER SACRED WRITINGS

the reason for the fivefold division: it was to make the hymn book of the temple service, which contained the response of the people, correspond to the lawbook, which contained the expression of the divine will.

The close of each of the five books is marked by a doxology, which either was a part of the last psalm in the group or was added at the time the division was made. These doxologies are found in 41. 13; 72.18, 19; 89.52 and 106. 47, 48. Since Psalm 150 was in the nature of a doxology it was considered a suitable close of the fifth book; hence no special doxology was added.

Psalm Titles. Many of the psalms have superscriptions or titles. These are of three kinds, referring (1) to the musical setting of the psalm, (2) to its authorship or composition, and (3) to the historical circumstances giving rise to it. The musical notes are manifold and the terms used are frequently obscure; hence an adequate discussion is possible only in connection with a detailed study of individual psalms; but the other two kinds of statements deal with the origin of the psalms, and therefore cannot be passed over in the study of questions of Introduction. The following authors are named in the psalm titles:

1. Moses (Psalm 90)   Total, 1
2. David (Book I, 37: 3-9, 11-32, 34-41;
        Book II, 18: 51-65, 68-70;
        Book III, 1: 86;
        Book IV, 2: 101, 103;
        Book V, 15: 108-110, 122, 124, 131, 133, 138-145) Total, 73
3. Solomon (72, 127)   Total, 2

---

introduced. The artificial character of the division appears clearly in the case of Books IV and V. Psalm 107, which opens Book V, goes naturally with Psalms 105 and 106, which close Book IV. The fact that the number of psalms in Book IV is the same as in Book III also suggests that the break was made arbitrarily at the close of Psalm 106.

THE BOOK OF PSALMS

4. Asaph (50, 73-83)   Total, 12
5. Sons of Korah (42, 44-49, 84, 85, 87, 88)   Total, 11
6. Ethan, the Ezrahite (89)   Total, 1
7. Heman, the Ezrahite (88), ascribed also to the Sons of Korah.
Total number of psalms ascribed to an author in the title   100

One hundred psalms, therefore, out of one hundred and fifty, are ascribed to some author. Seventy-three of these—that is, less than one half—bear the name of David. Nevertheless, David being looked upon as the founder of temple psalmody,[12] in the course of time all the psalms in the collection came to be credited to him.[13]

What is the significance and value of these titles? If their testimony could be accepted as authoritative, the further study of the authorship of the psalms with titles would be a simple matter; but unfortunately a closer investigation of the psalms and their superscriptions has convinced practically all modern scholars that the titles cannot be followed implicitly:

(1) Even the Hebrew MSS. are not in complete agreement; for example, in several important MSS. Psalms 66 and 67 are also ascribed to David.

(2) In many instances the Septuagint—or, at least, some important MSS. of the Septuagint—is not in agreement with the tradition embodied in the Hebrew title. For example, (*a*) David is not given as the author of Psalms 122, 124, 131, 133. (*b*) Solomon is not given as the author of Psalm 127. (*c*) The following fourteen psalms are credited to David: 10, 33, 43, 67, 71, 91, 93-99, 104. (*d*) The following psalms are ascribed to Haggai and Zechariah: 138, 146-148. (*e*) To Jeremiah is ascribed Psalm 137.

---

[12] 1 Chron. 23. 5; 25. 1-7.

[13] See the quotation from the Babylonian Talmud, *baba bathra*, 14b, 15a, in F. C. Eiselen, *The Books of the Pentateuch*, p. 86.

THE PSALMS AND OTHER SACRED WRITINGS

(3) To judge from the ancient versions much liberty was taken with the psalm titles, especially by adding to them. Even the Septuagint contains such additions; for example, Psalm 27 is said to have been written by David "before his anointing"; Psalm 96, "when the house was being built after the captivity"; Psalms 76 and 80 are said to refer to "the Assyrian." In the Syriac translation this tendency is carried to greater extremes. There the title of Psalm 73, for example, reads: "Composed by Asaph from memory about the death of Absalom. Besides, a confession of human infirmity; also concerning the prosperity of the ungodly and the longsuffering of God." These additions continued to be made until a rather late period, as may be seen, for example, from the reference in the title of Psalm 1 to the beatitudes in the Gospel of Matthew. It may be safe to infer from the lack of care in the transmission of the titles, and from the liberties taken with them until after the opening of the Christian era, that the post-Old Testament Jews and the early Christians did not look upon these titles as integral parts of the psalms.

(4) It is practically certain that the titles did not originate with the authors of the psalms themselves. In some instances, at least, they seem to have been taken almost verbatim from the books of Samuel. It is interesting to compare, for example, Psalm 18. 1 with 2 Sam. 22. 1; Psalm 34. 1 with 1 Sam. 21. 13; Psalm 51. 1 with 2 Sam. 12. 1ff.; Psalm 52. 1 with 1 Sam. 22. 9; Psalm 54. 1 with 1 Sam. 23. 19; etc.

In addition to these four considerations, which are not without weight, two others may be mentioned that seem to be even more conclusive against the absolute reliability of the testimony of the psalm titles:

THE BOOK OF PSALMS

(5) The contents of some of the psalms show that they belong to a historical situation other than that indicated in the titles. Thus Psalm 122 cannot come from the time of David, because it presupposes the existence of the temple, and the expression in verse 5, "the thrones of the house of David," implies that the dynasty of David has occupied the throne for some time. Psalms 20, 21 are not prayers of a king for his people, but prayers of subjects for their king. Psalm 59 evidently refers to enemies of the nation and not to David's persecution by Saul. In many other cases it is difficult, if not impossible, to harmonize the circumstances reflected in the text with the situation referred to in the superscription.

(6) At other times the language is inconsistent with the period to which the title assigns the psalm. Psalm 139, for instance, contains so many Aramaisms and other linguistic peculiarities that on the basis of its language alone it must be regarded as one of the latest psalms in the entire collection. Davidic authorship, therefore, is an impossibility. Similarly, Psalms 103, 122, 144 and others must, for the same reason, be assigned to late dates.

In the light of these facts, what is the significance of the psalm titles? They occupy very much the same position as the subscriptions to some of the New Testament epistles, which name the place in which the writer lived, or the persons through whom the letter was sent, or both.[14] These subscriptions are not a part of the original text, but they embody early traditions, which may or may

---

[14] For example, "The Second Epistle to the Corinthians was written from Philippi, by Titus and Lucas." These subscriptions are found in the Authorized Version, but are omitted from the American Revised Version.

THE PSALMS AND OTHER SACRED WRITINGS

not be correct. In a similar manner, the psalm titles did not originate with the authors of the psalms; they too embody early traditions, though, perhaps, farther removed from the time of composition than is the case with the New Testament epistles. No evidence is available for determining the time of their addition; internal evidence, however, shows that in many cases they are altogether uncritical in character.

What, then, should be the attitude of the modern student toward these titles? There are always three stages in the use of tradition: (1) At first tradition is accepted as equivalent to history. (2) When the discovery is made that tradition is unreliable in certain details a tendency arises to reject tradition entirely as fictitious. (3) Usually further study brings about a reaction: the wholesale rejection is seen to be unwarranted; then tradition is carefully tested, and an attempt is made to discover and use the historical nucleus that may have given rise to the tradition.

Each of these three conflicting attitudes has or has had its advocates in the case of the psalm titles. There have been and still are those who accept them as absolutely reliable, though perhaps no living Old Testament scholar belongs to this class. Others reject them entirely, while there are many who believe that they contain an historical nucleus and who insist that it is the duty of the modern student to discover that nucleus and to use it for what it may be worth. The last appears to be the only safe and sane attitude. The psalm titles cannot be disposed of as a whole; they cannot be accepted or rejected as a whole; they must be examined separately, and their acceptance or rejection must be determined by the results of the examination. In other words, the psalm titles may be used as starting points; it may even be proper to start with a presumption in their favor; only if the facts revealed by fair and unbiased study cannot be harmonized with them should they be given up. In cases in which the evidence is not decisive, at least the possibility of the titles being correct may be admitted.

Date and Authorship. The attitude with reference to the date and authorship of the psalms is determined largely by the attitude toward the psalm titles. It is possible, therefore, to distinguish two extreme positions, with many modifications between the two. At one end is the older view which, following the traditions embodied in the titles, ascribes to David seventy-three psalms and twenty-seven others to the authors whose names they bear,[15] leaving the authorship of the "orphans," that is,

[15] This view, as the whole discussion of the question of authorship on the basis of the psalm titles, rests upon the interpretation of the expressions "of David," "of Asaph," etc., as implying authorship. It is not impossible, however, that in some cases at least, these phrases were not intended to indicate authorship at all. In some instances the Hebrew preposition *le* may have been used with the meaning "belonging to," that is, implying possession rather than authorship. Thus the psalms credited to the sons of Korah may have been derived from a collection in the possession of the Levitical family bearing that name during the period of the second temple. It can hardly be assumed that the psalms were the product of joint authorship on the part of members of the Korah family. In the same way, the psalms ascribed to Asaph, Ethan, and Heman may have been derived from collections in the possession of families or guilds bearing the names of these men. Similarly, the expression "of David," as found in the psalm titles at the present time, may have been used to suggest that the psalms so marked were taken from a collection bearing the title "Psalms of David," perhaps because the nucleus of the collection was thought to be Davidic. In other cases the phrase may be used with the meaning, "suitable for David," that is, a psalm befitting the character or circumstances of David. In either case, the interpretation implying authorship would be due to a later misunderstanding of an ambiguous Hebrew phrase.

THE PSALMS AND OTHER SACRED WRITINGS

the psalms without indication of authorship, unsettled. Some extend the tradition so as to ascribe all the psalms to David. The other extreme is advocated by Wellhausen, Cheyne, Duhm, and other scholars. "Since the Psalter belongs to the Hagiographa," says Wellhausen, "and is the hymn book of the congregation of the second temple . . . the question is not whether it contains any postexilic psalms, but whether it contains any preexilic psalms."[16] Cheyne maintains that the whole psalter, with the possible exception of parts of Psalm 18, is postexilic.[17] And Duhm goes even farther and considers it an open question whether any of the psalms are as old as the Persian period. He assigns most of them to the century beginning with the Maccabean uprising and ending with the death of Alexander Jannæus, B. C. 78.[18]

Now the question of date and authorship is, perhaps, less important in the case of the Psalms than in the case of the prophetic books or other Old Testament writings. A psalm retains the power of carrying the devout reader into the very presence of God, no matter by whom or

---

[16] The argument of Wellhausen, though in reality the outgrowth of his idea regarding the development of Hebrew religion, is apparently based on the fact, which cannot be denied, that the psalter was the hymn book of the second temple. But a moment's thought will show that this does not prove that all the psalms were composed during the postexilic period. Such inference rests upon a confusion of composition with compilation. It might be asserted with equal propriety that all the hymns in a modern hymnal were written at the time the book was compiled or in the immediate past. This is not true of any modern hymnal, and there is no good reason for believing that it was so in the case of the ancient Jewish hymnal that has been preserved in the Psalter.

[17] *The Origin and Contents of the Psalter*, p. xxxi. In his *Introduction to the Book of Isaiah*, p. III, he says: "No part of the Psalter has yet been shown to have a preexilic basis."

[18] *Die Psalmen,* in *Kurzer Hand-Commentar*, pp. xixff.

THE BOOK OF PSALMS

under what circumstances it was written. In the words of W. T. Davison: "The universality and, if one may say so, the timelessness of the Psalter are amongst its prominent characteristics. The personal elements which the psalms contain are soon lost in the impersonal, the finite in the infinite. The singer seldom lingers long amidst the streets of the city, within the limits of a single nation or country, among the fields and homesteads; he soon wings his flight into the upper air, from whence the whole familiar landscape dwindles to a mere speck. The psalmist, of all men, is alone with God and his own soul."[19]

Nevertheless the determination of date and authorship is of interest and value even in the case of the psalms. In the first place, some of the psalms are the outgrowth of definite historical situations; these must remain more or less unintelligible unless their historical background can be determined, which implies a fixing of the date. Again, though all the psalms breathe a living faith in Yahweh, they differ in religious and ethical conception. The right devotional use of the psalms depends upon a proper appreciation of these varying religious and ethical conceptions; but this in turn depends upon the discovery of their approximate dates. The investigation of date and authorship, therefore, is not without significance for a comprehensive study of the development of Hebrew religion, theology, and ethics.

Davidic Psalms. The question of authorship, however, retains its chief interest on account of the alleged connection of King David with so many of the psalms. Are there good reasons for believing that any of the psalms came from him, or at least from his age? Argu-

---
[19] *The Praises of Israel*, p. 31.

THE PSALMS AND OTHER SACRED WRITINGS

ments in favor of Davidic authorship may now be considered:[20]

First place may be given to certain *a priori* arguments:

(1) The history of the Hebrew nation begins with an outburst of song. The deliverance at the Red Sea was celebrated, according to Exod. 15, with a song. Though this song, in its present form, contains indications of a later date, it is generally admitted that it embodies some very early elements.[21]

(2) The Song of Deborah,[22] one of the finest specimens of Hebrew poetry, is almost universally accepted as practically contemporaneous with the events portrayed. "The contemporary character of the Song," says G. A. Smith, "is clear, and is generally recognized; it can be denied only by ignoring the evidence of the language and perverting that of the substance and spirit of the poetry . . . Whoever was its author, the Song springs to us from the heart of the time."[23]

(3) In 2 Sam. 1. 17 the lament over Saul and Jonathan[24] is credited to David. There is nothing in this psalm, historical, literary, or linguistic, that militates in any way against Davidic authorship. C. F. Kent uses these strong words: "This is one of the most beautiful elegies in the Old Testament and beyond reasonable doubt comes from Israel's greatest king."[25]

There are, then, preserved in the Old Testament at

---

[20] The present discussion must, in the nature of the case, confine itself to general considerations; in order to reach entirely satisfactory conclusions each psalm must be examined separately.
[21] F. C. Eiselen, *The Books of the Pentateuch*, pp. 258, 259.
[22] Judg. 5.
[23] *The Early Poetry of Israel*, pp. 81, 82.
[24] Verses 19-27; compare also the lament over Abner, 2 Sam. 3. 33, 34.
[25] *The Songs, Hymns, and Prayers of the Old Testament*, p. 71.

THE BOOK OF PSALMS

least three pieces of poetry which cannot well be dated subsequently to the age of David,[26] and one of these bears the name of David himself. These poems offer conclusive evidence that the art of poetic composition was sufficiently developed in the days of David to warrant the assignment of other poems to that age. True, the lament differs in its religious tone from the psalms ascribed by tradition to David; but this is to be expected, since a dirge over a fallen hero is not the same as a psalm; and yet even the lament shows that the warrior king of Israel was capable of exquisite tenderness and sympathy. Is it thinkable that a poet with the genius of the author of the lament should sing but once? Is it probable that a nation capable of producing these gems should during all these centuries produce nothing else worthy of preservation? Is it reasonable to believe that the Greeks, Babylonians, Egyptians, and other peoples of antiquity sang to their gods, but that Israel's saints, with their sublime faith in Yahweh, remained silent? If these questions are answered in the negative, then either it must be assumed that all the sacred lyrics of ancient Israel were lost or it must be admitted that some of them may have been preserved in the sacred literature of this the most religious people of the ancient world.

(4) It may further be noted that Hebrew tradition as reflected in the Old Testament credits David with unusual musical skill: in 1 Sam. 16. 18 mention is made of his skill upon the harp, and 2 Sam. 23. 1 describes him as the "sweet psalmist of Israel."[27] At a later time the Chronicler narrates that David introduced stringed instru-

---

[26] To these might be added Gen. 4. 23, 24; Num. 21. 17, 18; and perhaps Gen. 49.
[27] Literally, "pleasant in the psalms of Israel."

THE PSALMS AND OTHER SACRED WRITINGS

ments into the service of the sanctuary to accompany the psalms sung there.[28] Even more significant is the offhand reference in Amos 6. 5, "that invent for themselves instruments of music, like David,"[29] which could have no meaning to the prophet's hearers unless David's reputation was widely known. Thus it would seem that in the days of Amos, only about two centuries after the death of David, he enjoyed the reputation of having been a skilled musician. The *a priori* evidence, therefore, allows the possibility of David having written psalms. More than this can rarely be demonstrated by arguments of this kind.

The *external* evidence, which may be considered next, includes all definite ascriptions of psalms to David. Here belong, then, in the first place, the psalm titles crediting psalms to the shepherd king of Israel. Though these titles cannot be accepted at their face value,[30] is it not reasonable to suppose that they contain an element of truth, that they grew out of an historical kernel? Outside of the book of Psalms only one psalm is ascribed directly to David: 2 Sam. 22. 1 makes him the author of the psalm contained in the rest of the chapter, which is essentially identical with Psalm 18. If the statement in 2 Sam. 22. 1 could be accepted as contemporaneous evidence, the authorship of at least one psalm would be fixed, and it might serve as a criterion by which to judge others. But unfortunately this cannot be done; the closing chapters of Second Samuel, chapters 21-24, are generally considered a kind of appendix added at a later time; hence the assertion in 2 Sam. 22. 1 has not the force of con-

---
[28] 1 Chron. 23. 5; 2 Chron. 29. 25.
[29] Margin, "like David's."
[30] See above, p. 43.

THE BOOK OF PSALMS

temporaneous testimony. At the same time the date of the addition cannot be placed so late as to rob the statement of all value. This being the extent of the external evidence, the question remains undecided.

In the absence of decisive external evidence the matter under consideration, which is the presence of Davidic psalms in the Psalter, must be settled, if at all, on the basis of *internal* evidence, that is, evidence furnished by the individual psalms themselves. This kind of evidence may be arranged under four heads: (1) Historical allusions or references in the psalms; (2) religious and theological ideas expressed and reflected; (3) the relation of a psalm to other writings whose dates are known; (4) language and style. The proper, scientific use of this evidence is not always an easy task. In some cases the historical allusions are so clear and pointed, as, for instance, in Psalms 122 or 137, that it is quite easy to draw definite conclusions, but in many more cases the data are few and indecisive. Great caution must be exercised in the use of the argument based upon the differences in religious and theological ideas.[31] In the first place, the successive stages in the religious and theological development of the Hebrews are not easily separated. Moreover, the development of Israel's religion was not in a perfectly straight line; it proceeded, rather, in zigzag fashion, now an advance, now a relapse, followed by another advance. As a result it is at times difficult to decide whether a passage reflects a certain stage in the religious development when it was reached in the course of the first advance, or during the subsequent relapse or during the second advance. Once more, cognizance must be taken of the unusual spirits. Even if the general course of the

---
[31] F. C. Eiselen, *The Books of the Pentateuch*, p. 215.

THE PSALMS AND OTHER SACRED WRITINGS

religious development can be determined, there are always some men in advance of their age, while others lag behind. Who can be certain that a given psalm was not written by a man representing one or the other of these classes?

Difficulties present themselves also in any attempt to determine priority in the case of two seemingly related passages. And in the few cases in which a conclusion may be reached with any degree of certainty, only the earliest possible date of the dependent passage can be fixed, which may leave a leeway of several centuries. Linguistic and stylistic data are almost always inconclusive, especially when considered by themselves. In a few cases, it is true, they are so striking that the composition containing them can be assigned to an early or a late date, with a good deal of assurance; but in the majority of cases language and style must be considered unsafe criteria, for (1) language and style are as much a matter of temperament and training as of date, and (2) the possibility always exists that verbal changes may have been made so as to accommodate the language of an early poem to later usage. All this simply shows that the greatest caution must be exercised in the use of the internal evidence.

When, now, the bearing of the internal evidence on the question under discussion is considered, it is found, as has already been pointed out,[32] that the historical allusions in some of the psalms and the linguistic characteristics of others make it necessary to set aside the testimony of the titles and deny the psalms to David. Similarly, the fact that the eighty-sixth psalm, for example, gives evidence of literary dependence on other psalms, some of them certainly later than the time of David, prevents the accept-

---
[32] See above, p. 45.

ance of the testimony of the title in that case. In still other instances the religious and theological ideas undoubtedly point to a late date.[33]

On the other hand, there remain some psalms in which the most careful application of the criteria indicated can discover nothing that militates against Davidic authorship. In such cases those who, nevertheless, insist on a late date raise two more general objections: (1) The claim is made that the David of the historical books moves on too low a religious and ethical plane to permit the belief that he wrote any of the psalms in the Psalter. (2) Moreover, it is asserted that spiritual religion of the high type reflected in the psalms was not known as early as the time of David. However, neither of these objections is conclusive. The first rests upon an inadequate estimate of David's character. The warrior king of Israel was not without faults; indeed, at times he sank to a very low level. But when this admission is made, attention may be directed also to the bright side of his character; he possessed such virtues as courage, generosity, moderation, and justice in high degree, and even the oldest elements in the books of Samuel portray him as a man who, in spite of all his shortcomings, deeply and genuinely feared Yahweh. His religious instincts may have found expression chiefly in external forms, and his ideals may have been below New Testament standards, or even below the standards of later generations in Israel; nevertheless, the dominating principle of his life was to do the will of Yahweh as he understood it. More cannot be said of anyone; and he who lives thus may well be called a man after God's own heart. The manifoldness of David's character and personality is admirably de-

---
[33] For example, Psalm 139.

THE PSALMS AND OTHER SACRED WRITINGS

scribed by Edward Irving in these words: "His harp was full-stringed, and every angel of joy and sorrow swept over the chords as he passed; but the melody always breathed of heaven. And such oceans of affection lay within his breast as could not always slumber in their calmness. For the hearts of a hundred men strove and struggled together within the narrow continent of his single heart; and will the scornful men have no sympathy for one so conditioned but scorn him, because he ruled not with constant quietness the unruly host of diverse natures which dwelt within his single soul?"[34] With this more adequate view of David's personality it becomes quite possible to believe that in some of the loftier moments of his life and experience he gave expression to his confidence, his penitence, his hopes, his aspirations, and other emotions in words of song for which his poetic genius qualified him so well.

The other objection also lacks sufficient justification. That the religion and ethics of the Hebrews developed from a lower to a higher level is undoubtedly true; but this idea may easily be carried beyond proper bounds, and it is carried farther than the facts warrant by those who assert that the eighth-century prophets are the discoverers or founders of spiritual religion in Israel. The ideals reflected in the utterances of these prophets imply a long previous religious history, "such as leaves abundant room for Davidic psalms two hundred years before." Moreover, the presence of great souls, in advance of their age in spiritual vision, must always be reckoned with.[35] Hence, even if the age of David had been on too low a plane to give expression to its religious emotions in the

---

[34] *Works*, vol. i, p. 416.
[35] See above, p. 54.

THE BOOK OF PSALMS

words of songs now in the Psalter, David still might have been a writer of psalms, because he might have surpassed his contemporaries in depth of religious experience and clearness of spiritual insight. And even if it should be insisted that his life as a whole did not rise to a sufficiently high level, another fact must be considered, especially notable in persons of highly poetic temperament, namely, that at times such persons seem to rise above themselves, to heights which at other times are far beyond them. Why may not David have had moments of spiritual elevation when he burst into song of matchless sweetness and beauty?

In the very nature of the case conclusions reached by these lines of argument never can have the certainty of mathematical demonstration. "In the quest for Davidic psalms," says J. E. McFadyen, "we can never possibly rise above conjecture."[36] Assertions must always remain in the realm of probability, though at times probability may amount to practical certainty. Summarizing, then, the results of this part of the investigation, it may be safe to draw the following conclusions—everything else must remain more or less uncertain: (1) It cannot be established with absolute certainty that David wrote any psalms. (2) In view of the unquestioned poetic genius of David, his intense devotion to Yahweh, and the peculiar circumstances of his life, which yielded themselves to poetic treatment, it is not improbable that he wrote some psalms. (3) Since David was the great national hero of Israel, who lived continuously in the hearts and minds of his countrymen, it is not likely that all such psalms

---

[36] *Old Testament Introduction*, p. 248; compare also G. B. Gray, *Critical Introduction*, p. 138.

THE PSALMS AND OTHER SACRED WRITINGS

would be lost. (4) Some of the psalms credited to David in their titles are appropriate in his lips.[87]

Preexilic Psalms. Notwithstanding the opinion of a few recent writers that practically all the psalms are postexilic, there can be little doubt that the Psalter contains numerous preexilic psalms and fragments of psalms, even though it may not be possible to *prove* beyond question the date of any psalm. The incidental reference in Amos 5. 23 to music and singing in connection with the worship of Yahweh suggests that religious songs or psalms were known and used at least as early as the

---

[87] There exists much difference of opinion regarding the number of Davidic psalms even among those scholars who believe that David wrote some of the psalms in the Old Testament. The great Franz Delitzsch assigned forty-four psalms to David. It should be remembered, however, that during the later years of his life this scholar took more advanced views on numerous Old Testament questions; and it is not impossible that, had he revised his Commentary, the number would have been reduced. Ewald specified seventeen psalms or parts of psalms as Davidic. Koenig, a very cautious scholar, is content to say "a number of psalms, among them 3, 4, 6, 7, 8, 11, 15, 18, 23, 29, 30, 32." Schultz at one time attributed to David ten or twelve psalms, but later reduced the number to one, Psalm 18. Driver does not care to commit himself: "A *non liquet* must be our verdict. It is possible that Ewald's list of Davidic psalms is too large; but it is not clear that none of the psalms contained in it are of David's composition." Baethgen, the author of the best modern commentary on the Psalter in German, is in doubt, but thinks that some may be ascribed to David, among them 3, 4, 18. C. A. Briggs has this to say: "Psalm 18 in its original form was probably Davidic, and possibly Psalm 7 and Psalm 60 (in part)." W. H. Bennett reaches the following conclusion: "In most of the Davidic psalms the internal evidence, as far as it goes, is unfavorable to Davidic authorship; and, with the exception of 18, never amounts to anything like a proof of authorship by David." From these statements it appears that Psalm 18 is considered Davidic by practically all scholars who defend the Davidic authorship of any psalms; others frequently ascribed to him by modern scholars are 3, 4, 6, 7, 15, 19. 1–6, 24. 7–10, 29, 32.

eighth century B. C. If this was the case at the local sanctuaries in the northern kingdom, is there any reason to doubt that similar songs were in use at the temple in Jerusalem? That such songs were used in the southern kingdom is further shown by the allusion—again purely incidental and therefore the more significant—in Psalm 137. 4 to "songs of Zion" and "songs of Yahweh." Is it not natural to suppose that these were the psalms, perhaps already combined in a small collection, used in the temple service? Moreover, at least some of the so-called royal psalms, for example, Psalms 20 and 21, are most naturally referred to the time when a king still sat upon the throne, in other words, to the preexilic period. The fact that there is no other mention of psalms in the preexilic literature leads Cornill to ask the question: "If Israel had psalms in the period before the exile, is it thinkable that all the historians and prophets of preexilic times, as if by agreement, should pass by the psalms and consistently ignore this most precious gem of the spiritual possessions of Israel?"[38] But it is at least equally difficult to suppose that during all these centuries the worship of Yahweh was carried on without hymns and sacred songs. "When we remember," says J. E. McFadyen, "that for nearly two centuries before the exile great prophets had been working—and we cannot suppose altogether ineffectually, for they had disciples—it is difficult to see why, granting the poetic power which the Hebrews had from the earliest times, pious spirits should not have expressed themselves in sacred song, or why some of these songs may not be in the Psalter."[39]

---

[38] *Einleitung in das Alte Testament*, p. 220.
[39] *Old Testament Introduction*, p. 249.

THE PSALMS AND OTHER SACRED WRITINGS

These early songs may not have been preserved exactly in their original form; for evidently the songs of Israel passed through successive editings and combinations before they reached their final form in the present book of Psalms;[40] and a comparison of modern hymns as they appear in different collections shows how easily and naturally sacred songs come to be modified from time to time. But by the application of proper methods of criticism it is possible to separate the early elements from later additions; and when the process of separation is completed it will be found that the present Psalter contains much that may have arisen during the preexilic period.[41]

Maccabean Psalms. Does the Psalter contain psalms that originated during the Maccabean period? As has been stated, Duhm is inclined to assign most of the psalms to the century following the Maccabean uprising;[42] and though in this extreme position he is not followed by scholars in general, many believe that there are a few psalms in the collection which can best be interpreted upon a Maccabean background. The psalms generally regarded as Maccabean are 44, 74, 79, and 83, because "they speak of a desolation of the temple in spite of a punctilious fulfillment of the law, a religious persecution, a slaughter of the saints, a blasphemy of the holy name." It is further claimed that "no situation fits these circumstances so completely as the persecution of the Jews by Antiochus Epiphanes in B. C. 168, and these psalms

---

[40] See further below, pp. 64ff.
[41] C. A. Briggs assigns twenty-seven psalms or fragments of psalms to the period of the monarchy; see list below, p. 63.
[42] See above, p. 48; also R. A. Kennett, article "Psalms," in *Encyclopædia Britannica*, 11th ed.

THE BOOK OF PSALMS

betray many remarkable affinities with passages in the first book of Maccabees."[43]

The presence of Maccabean psalms in the Psalter is not inconsistent with what we know of the history of the Old Testament canon. If the book of Daniel, written in the same period, found a place in the canon, why might not a few psalms be equally fortunate; especially since these might be inserted even after the completion of the collection as a whole? Moreover, the "Psalter of Solomon," a collection of poems reflecting the troubles and sorrows of the persecution under Pompey,[44] and the "Odes of Solomon,"[45] are in themselves evidence that the Jews continued to compose psalms for some time after the Maccabean era.

On the other hand, the marked difference in spirit between these two collections and the biblical Psalter points to a long interval between the writing of the Psalms in the biblical collection and those in the extra-biblical books. In the same direction points the testimony of Ecclesiasticus, written about B. C. 180, which shows familiarity with many of the psalms. According to Schechter, there are more than seventy parallels between Ecclesiasticus and the Psalter; and the impression made upon Schechter by the character of these parallels was "that of reading the work of a postcanonical author who already knew his Bible and was constantly quoting it."[46]

---

[43] J. E. McFadyen, *Old Testament Introduction*, p. 251. Bennett and Adeney, *A Biblical Introduction*, pp. 145-147; Driver, *Introduction to the Literature of the Old Testament*, p. 387. It is worthy of note that these psalms are not included by Briggs in his list of Maccabean psalms; see below, p. 64.

[44] B. C. 63-48.

[45] These come from about the middle of the first century A. D.

[46] *The Wisdom of Ben Sira*, p. 26.

THE PSALMS AND OTHER SACRED WRITINGS

Of the psalms generally assigned to the Maccabean era the author of Ecclesiasticus seems to have known Psalms 44 and 74;[47] which would exclude them from the list of Maccabean psalms. If, therefore, these psalms reveal any Maccabean elements, the latter must be regarded as later interpolations in the psalms coming from an earlier date. Briggs gives a list of eight psalms or fragments of psalms as coming from the Maccabean era;[48] but Fullerton has shown that at least one of these was known to the author of Ecclesiasticus.[49] It is clear, therefore, that the matter of Maccabean psalms in the Psalter is one on which dogmatic assertions cannot be made. The whole situation may be summed up in these words: "The existence of Maccabean psalms cannot be categorically denied. But the question should at least be handled with caution, and such psalms sought only in the latest sections of the Psalter."[50]

Dates of Individual Psalms. Attempts have been made to fix at least approximately the dates of all the psalms, but the results are more or less uncertain. The fact that a given psalm fits into a certain period is no proof that it comes from that period; it might perhaps be fitted with equal ease into some other age. Only if the occasion in question is the *only one* to which the terms of the psalm are applicable can certainty be reached; and such cases are rare, if they can be discovered at all. It is perfectly safe to assert that here again conclusions

---

[47] Compare Ecclus. 46. 11 with Psalm 44. 18, and Ecclus. 36. 6ff. with Psalm 74. 9ff.
[48] See below, p. 64.
[49] *Biblical World*, September, 1910, and succeeding numbers.
[50] A. R. Gordon, *The Poets of the Old Testament*, p. 114; compare also H. T. Fowler, *A History of the Literature of Ancient Israel*, pp. 376–378; E. Sellin, *Einleitung in das Alte Testament*, pp. 112, 113.

THE BOOK OF PSALMS

never rise above probability and in many cases not above possibility. In general, all that can be said is that the psalms originated during the centuries beginning with David and ending with the Maccabean era.

C. F. Kent states his conclusions regarding the dates of psalms in these words: "The three great crises that have left their indelible stamp upon the Psalter are (1) the destruction of Jerusalem in 586, (2) the seventy years of discouragement and petty persecution which followed the disillusionment of those who rebuilt the second temple, and (3) the bitter Maccabean struggle. The brighter, more joyous periods were (1) the few short years between B. C. 520 and 516, when the temple was being rebuilt, (2) the period of hopefulness and rejoicing following the work of Nehemiah in 445, (3) the comparatively calm though less joyous Greek period, and (4) the confident, exultant, warlike age inaugurated by the brilliant victories of Judas Maccabeus."[51]

The chronological arrangement of the psalms proposed by C. A. Briggs after a study of the Psalter continuing during forty years may serve as an illustration of the various attempts along that line:

I. The period of the early monarchy, that is, before Jehoshaphat: 7, 13, 18, 23, 24b, 60a, 110.............. 7
II. The middle monarchy: 3, 20, 21, 27a, 45, 58, 61......... 7
III. The late monarchy: 2, 19a, 28, 36a, 46, 52, 54, 55, 56, 60b, 62, 72, 87..................................... 13
IV. The period of the exile: 42-43, 63, 74, 77a, 79, 81b, 82, 84, 88, 89b, 90, 137, 142........................... 13
V. The early Persian period (Haggai and Zechariah): 4, 6, 9-10, 11, 12, 14 (=53), 16, 17, 22, 25, 31, 32, 34, 35, 37, 38, 39, 41, 57a, 59, 64, 69a, 70 (=40b), 75, 76, 78, 80, 83, 101, 109a, 140, 143, 144a.................... 33

---

[51] *The Songs, Hymns, and Prayers of the Old Testament*, p. 44.

THE PSALMS AND OTHER SACRED WRITINGS

VI. The middle Persian period (Ezra-Nehemiah): 5, 8, 15, 26, 29, 30, 40a, 47, 51, 57b, 65, 66a, 69b, 138, 139a, 141.. 16
VII. The late Persian period: 27b, 36b, 44, 48, 49, 50, 68, 81a, 85, 89a, 102a... 11
VIII. The early Greek period: 93 + 96-100, 66b, 67, 73, 86, 91, 95, 108, 145................................... 9
IX. The later Greek period: 1, 19b, 24a, 71, 77b, 89c, 92, 94, 103, 139c, 144b, 119, 120, 121, 122, 123, 124, 125, 126, 127, 128, 130, 131, 132, 133, 134, 104, 105, 106, 107, 111, 112, 113, 114, 115, 116, 117, 135, 136, 146, 148, 150...... 42
X. The Maccabean period: 33, 102b, 109b, 118, 139c, 129, 147, 149.. 8

Total number of Psalms.........................[52]159

Compilation of the Psalter. The Psalter has rightly been called the hymn book of the second temple. Whatever differences may exist between it and a modern hymn book—and they are many, since the Psalter contains many poems which in no sense can be called hymns—the growth of the Psalter resembles that of a modern hymnal. "A true hymn book," says W. T. Davison, "is not made, it grows."[53] In a similar manner the Psalter has reached its present form as the result of natural growth or development. It may not be easy to trace in detail all the stages of development, but careful study may make it possible to discover at least the more important steps in its formation. W. R. Smith gives the following account of the process which he thinks resulted in the present book of Psalms:[54]

---

[52] The total 159 instead of 150 is due to the breaking up of several psalms into two or more originally independent psalms; on the other hand, some psalms now separate are thought to have been originally parts of one single psalm.

[53] *The Praises of Israel*, p. 10.

[54] Article "Psalms," in *Encyclopædia Britannica*, 9th ed.; *The Old Testament in the Jewish Church*, Chapter VII.

THE BOOK OF PSALMS

I. The formation of the *first* Davidic collection, with a closing doxology, Psalms 1-41[55]—about the time of Ezra-Nehemiah.
II. The formation of a *second* Davidic collection, with a doxology and subscription, Psalms 51-72—during the fourth century, B. C.
III. The formation of a twofold Levitical collection,[56] a Korahite collection, Psalms 42-49, an Asaphic collection, Psalms 50, 73-83—between B. C. 430 and 330.
IV. An Elohistic redaction[57] and combination of II and III—during the third century B. C.
V. The addition to IV of a non-Elohistic supplement and doxology, Psalms 84-89.
VI. The formation of another collection, which was later added to I + V, Psalms 90-150.

According to this scheme, the completed Psalter would have consisted in the beginning of three originally independent collections, the first, Psalms 1-41; the second, Psalms 42-89; the third, Psalms 90-150. This threefold division would be earlier than the later fivefold division, which has come down to the present.[58]

In support of this theory of W. R. Smith, at least in its general positions, attention may be directed to the following facts:

---

[55] Here as in the other cases the original collection may not have contained every psalm now found there; individual psalms may have been added subsequently; in this group, for instance, Psalms 1 and 2 seem to have been prefixed at a later time.

[56] John P. Peters has suggested that the original Korahite collection was the hymn book of the sanctuary at Dan, the Asaphic collection that of the sanctuary at Bethel; see "The Sons of Korah," in *Essays in Modern Theological and Related Subjects*, pp. 41-47; *The Religion of the Hebrews*, p. 168; compare H. T. Fowler, *History of the Literature of Ancient Israel*, pp. 133-136. If this suggestion is correct, the psalms in both collections must have originated in the northern kingdom; and both collections must have originated before B. C. 722.

[57] That is, a redaction in the course of which the divine name "Yahweh" was uniformly changed to "Elohim."

[58] Book I, 1-41; Book II, 42-72; Book III, 73-89; Book IV, 90-106; Book V, 107-150; see above, p. 41.

THE PSALMS AND OTHER SACRED WRITINGS

1. The three divisions reveal differences in regard to titles. In division I all the psalms have titles except 1, 2, 10, 33. Psalms 1 and 2 seem to have been added to the collection at a later time, perhaps as a suitable introduction to the completed Psalter; Psalm 10 was originally a part of Psalm 9, and is so preserved in the Septuagint.[59] Psalm 33 is credited to David in the Septuagint, but it, too, may be a later addition. "Psalm 33," says Kirkpatrick, "appears to be of distinctly later date, inserted as an illustration of the last verse of Psalm 32."[60] In division II all psalms have titles except 43 and 71. Psalm 43 was originally a part of Psalm 42; Psalm 71 is without title for reasons unknown. In division III few psalms have titles.

2. The three divisions differ in alleged authorship. In division I all psalms with titles are ascribed to David. Division II contains psalms ascribed to different authors; including the supplement there are 19 psalms of David, 12 of Asaph, 11 of the sons of Korah, 1 of Solomon, 1 of Heman, the Ezrahite, also ascribed to the Sons of Korah, 1 of Ethan, the Ezrahite, and 4 are anonymous. Division III contains 1 psalm of Moses,[61] 15 of David, practically all of them bearing marks of a late date, and 1 of Solomon; all the others are anonymous. These facts may suggest that at first a Davidic collection was formed; when in time this proved insufficient, another collection was made, probably out of smaller groups that had been gathered since the formation of the first collection. In the course of time the two collections proved inadequate; then a third was made, again probably out of smaller

---
[59] See above, p. 40.
[60] *Commentary on the Psalms*, p. liv.
[61] Perhaps suitable for Moses's character and circumstances; compare Psalm 102, "of the afflicted."

groups, one of which, the Pilgrim Psalms,[62] may still be recognized.

3. The three divisions differ in character. In the words of Kirkpatrick: "Speaking broadly and generally, the psalms of the first division are personal, those of the second division, national, those of the third, liturgical."[63] No doubt there are numerous exceptions to this rule, but on the whole the characterization is correct: Personal prayers and thanksgivings are found chiefly in the first part; petitions in times of national calamity or thanksgivings in times of national prosperity, in the second; while the third consists largely of psalms of thanksgiving and praise intended primarily for use in the temple service.

4. A more striking difference may be seen in the use of the divine names. In division I Yahweh occurs 272 times, Elohim alone only 15 times. In division II, excepting the supplement, Psalms 84-89, Yahweh occurs 43 times, while Elohim is found 200 times; in the supplement Yahweh appears 31 times, Elohim 7 times. In division III Yahweh is used almost exclusively, 339 times, the only exceptions being Psalms 108 and 144; and of these Psalm 108 is composed of fragments of two psalms in division II, in which Elohim predominates.

It may not be easy to determine the full significance of this difference, but there can hardly be a doubt that, in part at least, it must be traced to editorial activity. It has been suggested that the preponderance of Elohim over Yahweh in division II is due to a preference on the part of the authors of the psalms in this group for Elohim; but this explanation is inadequate, as appears from the

---
[62] Psalms 120-134.
[63] *Commentary on the Psalms*, p. lviii.

fact that two psalms that are found in division I with the name "Yahweh" are repeated in the second division with a change of the divine name to "Elohim."[64] Editorial activity alone can account for changes in other instances: Psalm 50. 7 is taken from Exod. 20. 2; several verses in Psalm 68 from Num. 10 and Judg. 5; Psalm 71. 19 from Exod. 15. 11, and in each case "Yahweh" is changed to "Elohim." Sometimes the change has been made at the cost of clearness. In Exod. 20. 2, for instance, occurs the expression, "I am Yahweh, thy Elohim,"[65] which is intelligible; Psalm 50. 7 reproduces this in greatly weakened form as "I am Elohim thy Elohim."[66] Whatever the reason for the alteration may have been, and whatever the full significance of the differences between the several divisions in the use of the divine names may be, the facts enumerated seem to warrant the inference that at one time three distinct groups of psalms made up the Psalter as a whole.

5. That there must have been different collectors and collections is made very probable also by the fact already mentioned that one and the same psalm appears in different parts of the book. Psalm 53, in division II, is the same as Psalm 14, in division I; Psalm 70, in division II, is the same as Psalm 40. 13-17, in division I; and Psalm 108, in division III, is the same as Psalm 57. 7-11 and 60. 5-12, in division II. Is it probable that one and the same collector would insert a psalm twice in the same collection? On the other hand, if the present Psalter is the result of compilation from earlier smaller collections, the repetition could easily be explained, for one and the

---

[64] Psalm 14 = 53; 40. 13–17 = 70; in the latter the change is not carried through consistently.
[65] Revised Version, "I am Jehovah thy God."
[66] Revised Version, "I am God, *even* thy God."

THE BOOK OF PSALMS

same psalm might be found in more than one of the smaller collections used and thus reappear in different parts of the larger compilation. Summing up the evidence, it would seem that as the first step individual psalms were brought together to form small collections; these small collections were combined into three larger collections, which, in turn, were united into one book. Then, at a later time, this book was divided, after the analogy of the *Torah*, into five books, in which form the Psalter has come down to the present.

Date of Compilation. The dates of the several collections cannot be definitely determined. Probably none of the larger collections, and perhaps none of the smaller collections, were made until after the restoration, when the temple service was arranged according to a more systematic and elaborate ritual. That the Psalter existed practically in its present form when the Septuagint translation was made has been stated;[67] but while the beginning of that translation, the translation of the Pentateuch, can be assigned approximately to the middle of the third century B. C., it is more difficult to fix the time of its completion. The Law, the Prophets, and some of the Writings existed in a Greek translation as early as 132 B. C., for the Prologue to the book of Ecclesiasticus, written in that year, alludes to the existence of three divisions of the Jewish canon of Sacred Scripture in a Greek translation. Since the Psalter appears to have been received as canonical among the first of the Writings, it is not improbable that the Septuagint translation of the Psalms was in existence at that time. If so, the formation of the Hebrew collection must be dated at least a generation earlier. The period between B. C. 450 and

---

[67] See above, p. 41.

THE PSALMS AND OTHER SACRED WRITINGS

150, therefore, may be considered the age of compilation, during which the several collections of psalms were made and combined; this, however, does not exclude the possibility that even after B. C. 150 individual psalms may have been added to the collection.

Chiefly on the basis of the musical notes in the psalm titles C. A. Briggs suggests the following stages in the process of compilation:[68]

I. Toward the close of the early Persian period, before Nehemiah, a collection of choice poems was made, entitled *Miktamim,* that is, golden poems.

II. In the late Persian period another collection was formed, entitled *Maskilim,* that is, religious meditations.

III. At approximately the same time the first Davidic collection was edited as a prayer book for use in the synagogues, the editor drawing his material largely from the two collections named.

IV. A short time later the Psalms of the sons of Korah were compiled.

V. During the early Greek period the Psalter of Asaph was formed in Babylonia.

VI. A little later an edition of hymns for use in the synagogues was prepared in Palestine, entitled *Mizmorim,* or Psalms. The compiler embodied psalms contained in the earlier collections and added directions for their musical rendering; hence it may be called "the Psalter of the Director."

VII. During the middle Greek period the Elohim Psalter was formed in Babylonia for synagogue use there.

VIII. During the same period a collection of *Hallels* or Songs of Praise, was made for the temple service; this received additions during the Maccabean period.

IX. Still in the middle Greek period a collection of songs was made for the use of pilgrims on their way to the great feasts.

X. After the rededication of the temple in B. C. 165 the present Psalter was prepared, combining psalms appropriate for use in the temple and in the synagogue, and making use of all the earlier collections. The first part was based on the Palestinian Director's Psalter, and was made to

---

[68] *Commentary on the Book of Psalms,* vol. i, pp. lxff.

embody chiefly psalms from the Davidic Psalter. The Babylonian Elohistic Psalter was placed next and to it Psalms 84-89 were added as a supplement. The third part was arranged around the Hallel and Pilgrim collections, to which were added the remaining psalms of the Director's Psalter and other appropriate psalms, chiefly of a late date.

XI. Toward the close of the second century B. C. the final editor divided the Psalter into one hundred and fifty psalms and five books, in accord with the fivefold division of the Law.

Principle of Arrangement. In former times various fanciful meanings were read into the arrangement of the psalms.[69] As a matter of fact, no precise rules seem to have been followed: A certain broad outline of chronological order is perhaps discernible; at any rate, the earliest psalms are found chiefly in the first division, those composed in the middle period in the second division, and the latest in the third division, but there are numerous exceptions to this rule. Sometimes the topical principle seems to have been followed; that is, psalms dealing with the same subject-matter are placed together. At other times similarity in title may have exerted an influence; for instance, *Maskil* is found in Psalms 42-45 and 52-55; *Miktam* in Psalms 56-60. In other instances the presence of "catchwords" may have determined the order. It has been suggested, for example, that Psalms 1 and 2 were placed together because of such words as "way" in 1. 1 and 2. 12, or "meditate" in 1. 2 and 2. 1. But the indications are not sufficiently numerous to permit the formulation of any fixed theory regarding the principle or principles underlying the arrangement of the psalms in their present order.

Classification according to Subject-Matter. A clas-

---

[69] For illustrations, see W. T. Davison, *The Praises of Israel*, pp. 23ff.

THE PSALMS AND OTHER SACRED WRITINGS

sification of the psalms according to subject-matter is almost an impossibility, because in many cases psalms present a mixed character. "We find rapture blend with pleading, or the night of sorrow lose itself in the morning of joy, mood succeeding mood and experience passing into experience more rapidly than the sunshine and rain that blend and pass in the sweet confusion of an April morning. The rehearsal of God's mighty acts, which one generation tells to another, suddenly breaks away into penitence for national sin, or an outburst of thanksgiving which abundantly utters the memory of his great goodness." But with full recognition of the difficulty of the task and of the fact that any classification will be open to more or less criticism, a classification along broad lines may prove suggestive:

I. PSALMS NOT REFLECTING A SPECIFIC HISTORICAL SITUATION

1. *Hymns* in praise of God as creator, governor, and protector of the world and his people, suggested by the contemplation of his manifestations in nature, history, and personal experience. For example, Psalm 8, God's glory manifested in the creation of man; Psalm 19. 1-6, God's glory manifested in the heavens; Psalm 29, God's glory manifested in the thunderstorm; Psalm 33, God's glory manifested in his moral attributes, in creation, in his government, in the choice of Israel. To the same general class belong Psalms 36, 65, 66, 76, 92, 103, 104, 107, 145-147. Similar in tone are Psalms 24. 7-10, 47, 67, 93, 96-100, 111, 113, 115, 117, 118, 134-136, 148-150; but these differ from the preceding in that they contain invocations of a liturgical character.

2. *Experiences,* that is, psalms embodying the religious

THE BOOK OF PSALMS

emotions arising from the poet's intimate fellowship with God, expressing confidence, resignation, spiritual yearning, joy in God's presence, etc. Such experiences are reflected in Psalms 16, 23, 26, 27, 42, 43, 62, 63, 84, 91, 101, 121, 127, 128, 130, 131, 133, 138, 139. To the same group may be assigned the eulogies of the Law of Yahweh in Psalms 19. 7-14 and 119. In some psalms promises of confidence for the future are added to the expressions descriptive of present conditions; in others, petitions that Yahweh will judge the wicked who are trying to injure the psalmist; here belong Psalms 9, 10, 11, 12, 14, 52, 53, 58, 64, 75, 82.

3. *Reflections:* (1) On God's moral government of the world—he blesses the righteous and punishes the wicked, Psalms 1, 34, 37, 90, 112. (2) The same, with a pronounced didactic purpose—the author seeks to harmonize the apparent inequalities of life with his belief in God's moral government of the world, Psalms 49 and 73. (3) On the character and service acceptable to God, Psalms 15, 24. 1-6, 32, 50.

II. Psalms Reflecting a Specific Historical Situation

1. *Personal Psalms,* that is, psalms reflecting the personal condition of the psalmist, either as an individual or as a representative of the God-fearing community. (1) Petitions for help in sickness, persecution, or other trouble, or for forgiveness of sin, often accompanied by expressions of assurance that the prayer will receive an answer, Psalms 3-7, 13, 17, 22, 25, 28, 31, 35, 38, 39, 40. 11-17, 41, 51, 54-57, 59, 61, 69, 70, 71, 77, 86, 88, 109, 120, 140-143. (2) Thanksgivings for deliverance wrought, Psalms 18, 30, 40. 1-10, 116, 144.

THE PSALMS AND OTHER SACRED WRITINGS

2. *National Psalms,* that is, psalms reflecting conditions in the holy city, or the religious community, or the nation. (1) Complaints of national oppression or disaster, Psalms 44, 60, 74, 79, 80, 83, 85, 94, 102, 123, 137. (2) Thanksgivings received or promised, Psalms 46, 48, 68, 108, 114, 124-126, 129; with special reference to Zion, Psalms 87, 122. (3) Retrospect of the national history, with special reference to the lessons deducible from it, Psalms 78, 81, 95, 105, 106.

3. *Royal Psalms,* that is, psalms centering around an historical or ideal ruler, embodying thanksgiving, good wishes, promises, prayers for his preservation, etc., Psalms 2, 20, 21, 45, 72, 89, 110, 132.[70]

The Speaker in the Psalms. Many recent writers have expressed the opinion that in most of the psalms, if not in all, the speaker who uses the pronoun of the first person singular is not an individual but the religious community—either coextensive with the nation or a party within it. The "collective" view is not a new discovery, for it is reflected in the Septuagint and in the writings of the early church fathers, who interpreted the *I* of the psalms allegorically as the voice of the Christian Church; it was also advocated by some of the most eminent Jewish scholars of the Middle Ages, among them Raschi, Ibn Ezra, and Kimchi. Through the influence of Luther and Calvin the "individual" interpretation prevailed; but as early as the sixteenth century the Protestant commentator Rudinger again favored the collective view. It was revived and expanded in the nineteenth century by Hengs-

---

[70] For other classifications, see J. E. McFadyen, *Old Testament Introduction,* pp. 240, 241; Bennett and Adeney, *A Biblical Introduction,* pp. 148, 149; Driver, *Introduction to the Literature of the Old Testament,* pp. 368, 369.

tenberg, Reuss, Olshausen and Stade, and notably by Rudolf Smend, who, as the result of a detailed study of each individual psalm, reached the conclusion that the *I* is invariably not an individual, but the community expressing itself as a personified unit.[71] He was followed in large part by W. R. Smith and by Cheyne, who asserts that to a considerable extent the psalmists speak, not as individuals, but in the name of the Church-nation.[72]

Meanwhile the individual interpretation has not lacked defenders. Many scholars have insisted that the men named have carried the collective tendency too far and that the individual note is much more prominent than they are willing to admit. The leader in this reaction was Duhm;[73] but most recent commentators[74] agree with him in holding that many of the psalms reflect the experiences of individuals.

The principal argument in favor of the collective view may be stated in these words: The Psalter being the hymn book of the postexilic community, it is not probable that hymns included in the collection should be based upon individual experience; it is much more likely that they should be the outgrowth of community experience. Moreover, the experiences and emotions reflected in the psalms assume greater significance if they are interpreted as the expressions of the pious community—or of the pious in the community—which was conscious of its intimate relationship with God and of the enmity existing between it and the surrounding nations, or between the

---

[71] Article "Ueber das Ich der Psalmen," in *Zeitschrift fuer die Alttestamentliche Wissenschaft*, 1888, pp. 49ff.
[72] *The Historical Origin and Religious Ideas of the Psalter*, p. 261.
[73] *Die Psalmen*, in *Kurzer Hand-Commentar, passim*.
[74] Beer, Baethgen, Gunkel, Davies, Briggs, etc.

THE PSALMS AND OTHER SACRED WRITINGS

faithful and the faithless within the community. Furthermore, the argument continues, the community interpretation removes, or at least lessens, some difficulties which the individual interpretation cannot explain. Attention is called, for example, to the imprecatory psalms, that is, psalms filled with a spirit of hatred and vindictiveness, and containing prayers for God's curse to fall upon the enemies of the psalmist,[75] or to psalms in which far-reaching consequences are attached to the deliverance of the poet.[76] It is on the basis of these considerations that the conclusion is reached that the voices heard in the psalms are the voices not of individuals but of the community expressing its thankfulness, its faith, its complaints, its despair, and similar emotions.

What are the facts in the case? The use of the pronoun of the first person plural in twenty-seven psalms would seem to indicate that in these psalms at least the poet's interest is primarily in the experiences and emotions of the community.[77] In twenty-five psalms the pronoun of the first person is sometimes in the singular and sometimes in the plural, while the contents show that in some of these twenty-five psalms the primary interest is decidedly in the experiences of the community.[78] In addition, there are twenty-four psalms, chiefly calls to praise God for his goodness or reflections on the character of the service and worship acceptable to God, the contents

---

[75] Psalms 7, 35, 69, 79, 83, 109, 137, etc.
[76] For example, Psalms 22, 40.
[77] Psalms 21, 33, 46, 47, 48, 50, 60, 65 (in verse 3a the Septuagint and Vulgate read "us" for "me"), 67, 79, 80, 81, 90, 95, 98, 99, 100, 105, 113, 115, 117, 124, 126, 132, 136, 144, 147.
[78] Psalms 8, 17, 22, 40, 44, 59, 62, 66, 68, 71, 74, 75, 78, 84, 85, 89, 94, 103, 106, 116, 118, 122, 135, 137, 141.

THE BOOK OF PSALMS

of which make it clear that the author is not exclusively concerned with the experiences of individuals.[79] It would seem, therefore, that in about one half of the psalms the community interest is more or less dominant. The other half, referring to the speaker in the first person singular, might, on first sight, be thought to describe individual experiences and emotions. But the case is not quite so simple; for one of the psalms using consistently the singular pronoun interprets that singular pronoun as referring not to an individual but to the community or the nation.[80] Which immediately raises the question, To what extent is this usage adopted in other psalms? Are there other psalms in which the pronoun of the first person, though in the singular, refers not to an individual but, as in Psalm 129, to the community? Now, the personification of the nation as an individual, which underlies this usage, is not uncommon in the Old Testament; hence from the standpoint of the language alone no objection can be raised to the community interpretation.

But the final decision must rest not upon such general considerations but upon a careful examination of each individual psalm. Such examination must not forget the fact that in lyric poetry the poet, even when describing his own experiences and emotions, frequently writes with his eyes and mind on the people about him, and consequently so generalizes his expressions that others, in similar circumstances, may feel that he is their spokesman, and are led to appropriate his words as expressive of their own sentiments. Thus an individual psalm may from the very beginning, without the slightest editorial changes,

---

[79] Psalms 1, 12, 14, 15, 19, 24, 29, 34, 72, 76, 82, 93, 96, 97, 107, 112, 114, 125, 127, 133, 134, 148, 149, 150.
[80] Psalm 129. 1.

possess traits fitting it for community use. In other cases expressions that appear to support the community interpretation may be due to later attempts of adapting an originally individual psalm to community use in the temple service.

The conclusions reached by most of the scholars who have taken the trouble to subject the individual psalms to a careful, detailed investigation point to the presence in the Psalter of a greater number of community psalms than was formerly recognized on the basis of the use of the plural pronoun. On the other hand, they show with equal definiteness that the community tendency has been carried too far and that the interpretation of every single psalm as descriptive of community experiences is without warrant. Clearly, some of the psalms were written without any thought of community experience or community use in the temple, but for the sole purpose of expressing the poet's own individual experience and emotion.

Devotional Value. The book of Psalms has fittingly been called the heart of the Old Testament or of the Bible as a whole. "What the heart is in man," says Johannes Arndt, "that is the Psalter in the Bible." The Psalter does, indeed, sustain a close relation to all parts of the Old Testament. The divine manifestations which receive more objective treatment elsewhere are here viewed subjectively in their bearing and effect upon the personal experience of the author or of those in whose name he speaks. The moral law and the ritual as a means of approaching God are glorified, the lessons of history are appropriated and made a matter of personal experience, and the passion for truth and righteousness as preached by the prophets finds an even more vital expression in the words of the psalmists. There are also some psalms

THE BOOK OF PSALMS

which reflect the influence of the wisdom movement, both in its practical and in its speculative aspects.

The psalms grip the heart because they are the expressions of the deepest feelings of the human heart; they are the outpourings of human souls in closest fellowship with God, giving without restraint expression to the most various emotions, hopes, desires, and aspirations; there are no other literary compositions capable of creating the same intense atmosphere of religious thought and emotion. And because they are so true to human nature and experience they may be used at all times and in all places to express the various emotions of joy, sorrow, hope, fear, anticipation, etc., even of persons who live on a higher spiritual plane than did the authors. "What is there," says Richard Hooker, "necessary for man to know which the psalms are not able to teach? Heroical magnanimity, exquisite justice, grave moderation, exact wisdom, repentance unfeigned, unwearied patience, the mysteries of God, the sufferings of Christ, the terrors of wrath, the comforts of grace, the works of Providence over this world, and the promised joys of that world which is to come, all good necessarily to be either known, or done, or had, this one celestial fountain yieldeth. Let there be any grief or disaster incident to the soul of man, any wound or sickness, named for which there is not in this treasure house a present comfortable remedy at all times to be found."[81]

The variety of moods and experiences reflected in the psalms is well brought out in the following words of Luther: "Where can one find nobler words of joy than the psalms of praise and thanksgiving contain? In these thou mayest gaze into the heart of all the saints, as into

[81] *Ecclesiastical Polity*, V, 37. 2.

THE PSALMS AND OTHER SACRED WRITINGS

lovely pleasure gardens, or into heaven itself, and see how fine, pleasant, delightsome flowers spring up therein from all manner of beautiful, gladsome thoughts of God because of his goodness. And, again, where canst thou find deeper, more plaintive and heart-moving words of sorrow than in the psalms of lamentation? There, too, thou mayest look into the heart of all the saints—but as into death, or hell itself. How dark and gloomy all things are when the heart is troubled by the sense of the wrath of God! And so also when they speak of fear or hope, they use words that no painter could approach in coloring, or even an orator like Cicero in vividness of description."[82] But in spite of this great variety of moods there is one bond that unites them all into one living unity, namely, a sublime faith in Yahweh, the God of Israel. This variety on the one hand and essential unity on the other are the qualities that have given to the book such unique place in the religious life of individuals and of the church. With full justice says Perowne: "No single book of Scripture, not even the New Testament, has, perhaps, ever taken such hold on the heart of Christendom. None, if we dare judge, unless it be the Gospels, has had so large an influence in molding the affections, sustaining the hopes, purifying the faith of believers. With its words, rather than their own, they have come before God. In these they have uttered their desires, their fears, their confessions, their aspirations, their sorrows, their joys, their thanksgivings. By these their devotion has been kindled and their hearts comforted. The Psalter has been in the truest sense the prayerbook of both Jews and Christians."[83]

---
[82] *Preface to the Psalter.*
[83] *Commentary on the Psalms,* vol. i, p. 18.

CHAPTER III

THE WISDOM LITERATURE OF THE HEBREWS

CHAPTER III

THE WISDOM LITERATURE OF THE HEBREWS

THE wisdom literature of the Hebrews corresponds to the philosophic literature among other peoples. Philosophy, in the narrower sense of the term, which has been defined as "human speculation in pursuit of abstract truth and systematized thoughts constructed on a basis of metaphysics and ruled by strict laws of reasoning," had no existence among the Hebrews. A process of thinking free from presuppositions was unknown to them, for two fixed points were accepted without question by all Hebrew thinkers, or at least by those whose efforts have been preserved in the Old Testament: (1) The existence of a personal God, and (2) the reality of a divine revelation. Accordingly, the primary aim of Hebrew philosophic thought was simply to understand adequately the contents of these two truths, to define them more clearly, and to apply them to the problems of daily living.

But while it is hardly correct to speak of philosophic literature among the Hebrews or in the Old Testament, the latter contains a type of literature which presents at least attempts at philosophizing and which is clearly distinguished from the other kinds of literature found there —prophetic, priestly, devotional, and historical. The central theme of the prophetic literature is the obligation to serve Yahweh alone and no other God; the priestly literature concerns itself chiefly with the ritual and other formal expressions of religion; the devotional literature, rep-

THE PSALMS AND OTHER SACRED WRITINGS

resented chiefly by the Psalter, contains expressions of religious emotion; and the historical literature portrays the movements of God in human history. The wisdom literature occupies itself with the universal moral and religious principles that are applicable to all human life. To this literature belong three or four Old Testament books—Proverbs, Job, Ecclesiastes, and, according to one interpretation, the Song of Songs; it includes also a number of psalms,[1] and some traces of the wisdom strain are found in other Old Testament books.[2]

The Aim and Function of the Wise Men. The origin of the wisdom literature may, in the last analysis, be traced to human need. The hearts and consciences of some men may be reached by an authoritative command in the name of some one in whom they have confidence; others are influenced by way of their æsthetic sensibilities through the ritual and other beautiful forms of religion; the dormant emotions of some may be roused by an account of the personal experiences of other men; but there always have been and always will be those whose intellects must be carried, at least in part, before appeals to heart and conscience can prove effective. These different means of approach were tried among the Hebrews during Old Testament times: The prophet came with the authoritative "Thus saith Yahweh," it was the task of the priest to make the appeal of the ritual effective, the psalmist gave expression to personal experience, and the wise man made his appeal to the intellect. Certainly, at times the prophet might assume the role of a priest or *vice versa,* or the psalmist might fall into the strain of

---
[1] For example, Psalms 1, 8, 15, 19, 29, 37, 49, 50, 73, 90, 92, 103, 104, 107, 139, 147, 148.

[2] Judges, Habakkuk, Malachi; see further, below, pp. 89ff.

the wise man, or other interchanges of a similar nature might take place; nevertheless, certain Old Testament passages make it clear that the wise men formed a distinct class of religious workers in Israel during a long period of the nation's history.[3]

The wise men, like the prophets, were men who knew God intimately, and who as the result of this vital fellowship with God were able to comprehend truth hidden from the minds of other men; then, like the prophets, they sought to impress their convictions upon their contemporaries. However, they differed from the prophets in two important respects: (1) While the prophets were orators making their appeals principally at great public gatherings, the wise men seem to have done their teaching in private; they addressed themselves to small groups or to individuals. (2) The prophets ordinarily made their appeals directly to the heart and conscience; the wise men were equally desirous of reaching the conscience and of influencing conduct, but they accomplished their ultimate aim in a roundabout way. They addressed themselves to those whose intellects needed to be carried before their consciences could be touched; hence they sought first of all to clear away the intellectual difficulties or to present the reasonableness of their cause; then they drove home the truth to the conscience or allowed it to make its own appeal. The prophets commanded, they might or might not argue the case; the wise men commanded but rarely, and when they did so they were careful to give a reason for the command. Ordinarily, they were satisfied with counseling, reasoning, arguing, making the appeal only by implication. The prophet would have said to the indolent man: "Thus saith Yahweh, Go to work,

---
[3] For example, Jer. 18. 18; Prov. 1. 6; 22. 17; 24. 23; Job 15. 18.

THE PSALMS AND OTHER SACRED WRITINGS

thou sluggard"; the method of the wise man is illustrated in Prov. 24. 30-34:

> I went by the field of the sluggard,
> And by the vineyard of the man void of understanding;
> And lo, it was all grown over with thorns,
> The face thereof was covered with nettles,
> And the stone wall thereof was broken down.
> Then I beheld, and considered well;
> I saw, and received instruction:
> Yet a little sleep, a little slumber,
> A little folding of the hands to sleep;
> So shall thy poverty come as a robber,
> And thy want as an armed man.

False Wise Men. By the side of the wise men whose sayings and writings were considered worthy of a place in the canon there was a class of "false" wise men, corresponding to the false prophets and faithless priests against whom the true Yahweh prophets hurled such severe denunciations. The information regarding these "false" wise men is limited; however, there probably were two classes of "false" wise men as there were two classes of "false" prophets:[4] (1) The mercenary wise men, that is, men who did not hesitate to twist or pervert commonly accepted moral principles if they thought it to their own advantage to do so; (2) the unspiritual, though honest, wise men; that is, men who may have been capable, sincere, and conscientious, but who lacked spiritual insight; hence their advice was determined by narrow, worldly, and political considerations and not by religious conviction.[5] The counterfeit wise men received the severest

---
[4] See F. C. Eiselen, *Prophecy and the Prophets*, p. 28.
[5] It is not impossible that the reputation for unusual wisdom enjoyed by Solomon rested upon the possession of this kind of natural sagacity rather than of the wisdom that has its source in the fear of God and finds expression in high ethical instruction.

THE WISDOM LITERATURE OF THE HEBREWS

condemnation from the Yahweh prophets. Isaiah, for example, pronounced a terrible woe upon those "that are wise in their own eyes and prudent in their own sight";[6] and Jeremiah classed such wise men with the false prophets and the insincere priests.[7]

Growth of the Wisdom Movement. The Israelites, like other peoples, began to reflect on general questions affecting life as soon as they attained to a sufficiently settled mode of living to permit them to think of anything beyond the supply of the absolute necessities of life. The earliest reflections of this kind usually find expression in popular proverbs or parables or fables, which reflect, ordinarily in a one-sided and superficial way, everyday common-sense experience and observation.[8] In the beginning of the movement the term "wisdom" was without religious content; it was used to denote "the faculty of acute observation, shrewdness in discovery or device, cleverness of invention."[9] The religious leaders of Israel did not hesitate to take advantage of this method of teaching; but, in the nature of the case, their wisdom sayings are permeated by a higher religious and ethical spirit. The wisdom reasoning and method are

---

[6] Isa. 5. 21; the preceding verse may refer to the same class of wise men.

[7] Jer. 8. 8–13.

[8] This early stage of the wisdom movement is reflected, for example, in proverbs such as are found in 1 Sam. 10. 12; 2 Sam. 5. 8; 20. 18; Jer. 31. 29; in a more elaborate form in the fable of Jotham, Judg. 9. 8–15.

[9] Compare the wise woman of Tekoa, 2 Sam. 14. 2ff.; the wise judgment of Solomon, 1 Kings 3. 16–28; and his readiness to answer hard questions and solve riddles, 1 Kings 10. 1ff.; the skill of Joseph in interpreting dreams, Gen. 41. 39; the fame of Edom, Jer. 49. 7; Obad. 8; the wise men of Egypt, Gen. 41. 8; Exod. 7. 11; 1 Kings 4. 30; Isa. 19. 11, 12; the wise men of the east, 1 Kings 4. 30, 31.

THE PSALMS AND OTHER SACRED WRITINGS

reflected in some prophetic parables;[10] but these are directed against particular cases of sin, they are not reflections on life in general.

The wisdom movement proper, as illustrated in the Old Testament, found expression at first in very simple form. The wise men accepted the fundamental religious verities proclaimed by the prophets; they considered it their task to apply these truths to the details of everyday life, and to instruct their contemporaries in that application. Their work was necessary and of the greatest importance, for they pointed out constantly and persistently that religion cannot be separated from life. In discharging this self-imposed duty the ancient wise men were dealing with persons the great majority of whom were little removed from the childhood stage in things religious and ethical; hence they must put even the profoundest truths in the simplest possible form. They must, as far as possible, abstain from speculation, and confine themselves to simple, practical precepts which might be expected to appeal to the practical common sense of the ordinary hearer. "The great desire of the sages," says Marshall, "was to reduce the lofty, theistic morality which underlies Mosaism to brief, pithy sayings, easily remembered and readily applicable to the everyday life of every man."[11] Out of consideration for the limitations of their hearers they used not the language and style of the philosopher, but the simple, forceful style of the poet. The book of Proverbs is a collection of such simple, practical, wisdom sayings dealing with the ordinary affairs of common men.

In the course of time more serious tasks demanded the

---

[10] For example, the parable of Nathan, 2 Sam. 12. 1-7; the parable of the vineyard, Isa. 5. 1-7; the parables of Ezekiel, Ezek. 16, 17, 23.
[11] *Job and His Comforters*, p. 4.

THE WISDOM LITERATURE OF THE HEBREWS

attention of the wise men; for it became incumbent upon them to attempt, by speculation or otherwise, a solution of the more perplexing problems of life, though, in the nature of the case, the demand for the more simple sayings of these moral guides did not cease. The speculative wisdom of the Hebrews, like all their thinking, is theistic, for it starts from the presupposition that there is a personal God. Some traces of speculation are found in the book of Proverbs, especially in the first nine chapters. It may be seen also in some of the so-called historical books. In the book of Judges, for example, expressions like these are used again and again: "The children of Israel did evil. . . .He delivered them in the hands of . . . They cried unto Yahweh. . . . He raised them up a deliverer." The repetition of this formula throughout the narrative indicates that the author attempted to supply a theistic philosophy of the history during the period of the Judges. He was familiar with the events of history, and the question suggested itself, What is the reason for the regular succession of adversity and prosperity? He gave the answer, on the basis of a vital faith in Yahweh the God of Israel, in the simple formula to which reference has been made.

Speculative wisdom is found also in the prophetic books. A philosophy of calamity, for example, is suggested in the question of Amos: "Shall evil [calamity] befall a city, and Jehovah hath not done it?"[12] The same prophet indulges in speculation when he explains famine, drought, blasting and mildew, pestilence, and other natural calamities as punishments for Israel's disobedience and attempts to bring the people to their

---

[12] Amos 3. 6.

senses.[18] Another specimen of well-sustained speculation is offered by Hab. 1. 1 to 2. 5. Habakkuk beholds on every side wickedness and violence, and apparently Yahweh is doing nothing to punish the evildoers. Since the prophet believes Yahweh to be a holy and righteous God, he feels perplexed, and the question arises in his mind, How can Yahweh justify his indifference in the presence of widespread wickedness and violence? Current events offer a solution: Yahweh is not indifferent; the well-deserved judgment is about to be executed by the all-victorious Chaldeans. This answer, however, instead of relieving the situation, only increases the prophet's perplexity: How can a holy God use an impure and godless agent like the Chaldeans for the execution of his divine purpose? To which comes the reply: The wicked Chaldeans, though temporarily exalted, will meet certain doom; the righteous Israel, though temporarily afflicted, will live forever.

Amos and Isaiah philosophized regarding calamities of various kinds; the explanation these prophets offered was that Yahweh sends them as punishment for sin. Habakkuk wrestled with the problem created by the apparent inequalities of life—the wicked prosper while the righteous are oppressed. How can this condition of affairs be harmonized with the belief that this world is governed by a holy and righteous God? The prophet solved the problem by the assertion that the exaltation of the wicked and the affliction of the righteous are only temporary; in the end the wicked will be destroyed and the righteous will be exalted. The passages considered thus far look at the problems in their national bearings, not in their individual aspects; the perplexity arose from national ex-

---

[18] Amos 4. 6-11; compare also Isa. 9. 8-21.

THE WISDOM LITERATURE OF THE HEBREWS

periences and the solution has to do with changes affecting the nation. This national emphasis is due to the fact that during the greater part of the national life the nation as a whole, or the righteous nucleus within the nation, filled the horizon of the religious thinkers of Israel. The prophets Jeremiah and Ezekiel were the first to emphasize the significance of the individual in religion and ethics;[14] and from their time onward attention came to be focused upon the fortunes of individuals; consequently, problems seen previously only in their national bearings came to be recognized as equally troublesome when created by the experiences of individuals. The sufferings of godly individuals and the prosperity of wicked individuals demanded explanation.

In Mal. 2. 17 to 4. 3 the inequalities of life are considered, though not exclusively, in their individual aspects. Malachi and the religious thinkers of his age were confronted by two serious problems. There was, first of all, widespread religious indifference and skepticism, due in large measure to the nonfulfillment of prophecies previously delivered.[15] The people were sorely disappointed, and many began to ask, Why do the promises made to the fathers remain unfulfilled? What has become of the divine interest in us or the divine care for us? But if Yahweh cannot or will not do anything for us, why continue to waste our sacrifices and offerings in his service? These national disappointments were troublesome enough; but the saints in the community who would retain their faith in Yahweh were confronted by another difficulty. According to popular ideas piety should invariably be followed by prosperity, impiety by adversity. Now, there

---
[14] F. C. Eiselen, *Prophecy and the Prophets*, pp. 159-162, 219.
[15] F. C. Eiselen, *Prophecy and the Prophets*, p. 276.

had grown up in Jerusalem, during the first half of the fifth century B. C., a group of godless nobles who by the use of unscrupulous means succeeded in accumulating immense fortunes, which enabled them to live in luxury and splendor, while their victims, many of them God-fearing and upright, were reduced to abject poverty. Small wonder that the question arose in many quarters, Where is the God of justice?[16] or that many who, perhaps, never had attained a strong, living faith gave way to a temper of moroseness, skepticism, and even positive hostility to Yahweh. Malachi, in attempting to explain the problems, followed in the footsteps of his predecessors. The nonfulfillment of the prophetic promises he traced to the sinfulness of the people, not to the unwillingness or inability of Yahweh to bless his chosen people;[17] and he promised that the present inequalities of life would be straightened out when Yahweh would appear in judgment.[18]

In addition to these and similar illustrations of "wisdom" speculation, the Old Testament contains two books that are devoted entirely to this kind of speculation, the books of Job and Ecclesiastes. The first named deals with the age-long problem of suffering, especially the suffering of the righteous man, while Ecclesiastes considers the perplexities of life in general.

---
[16] Mal. 2. 17.
[17] Mal. 3. 7–12.
[18] Mal. 3. 13 to 4. 3.

CHAPTER IV

THE BOOK OF PROVERBS

CHAPTER IV

THE BOOK OF PROVERBS

Name. The Massoretic title of the book of Proverbs is מִשְׁלֵי שְׁלֹמֹה,[1] *Mishelē Shelōmōh*, that is, Proverbs of Solomon, which is translated in the Septuagint, παροιμίαι Σαλομῶντος,[2] *Paroimiai Salomōntos*; in the Vulgate, *Liber Proverbiorum*. The book is an anthology of Hebrew and Jewish proverbial literature, but its contents are by no means confined to sayings that are commonly known as proverbs. The Hebrew word, מָשָׁל, *māshāl*, frequently translated "proverb," means in reality "representation" or "similitude"; that is, "a statement not relating solely to a single fact, but *standing for* or *representing* other similar facts. The statement constituting the *māshāl* may be one deduced from a particular instance, but capable of application to other instances of a similar kind, or it may be a generalization from experience, such as in the nature of the case admits of constantly fresh application. The *māshāl* is by usage limited almost entirely to observations relative to human life and character, and is expressed commonly in a short, pointed form."[3] The *māshāl*, therefore, may be in the nature of a fable, parable, proverb, riddle, moral or political maxim, satire, philosophical or speculative sentence; and, as a matter

---
[1] Usually abridged to מִשְׁלֵי, *mishelē*, by the later Jews.
[2] *Codex Vaticanus* omits Σαλομῶντος.
[3] S. R. Driver, *Introduction to the Literature of the Old Testament*, p. 394.

of fact, all these forms are found in the book of Proverbs.[4]

Contents and Outline. With the exception of chapters 1-9 the book of Proverbs does not submit itself readily to detailed analysis or outline, for chapters 10-31 consist almost wholly of disconnected sayings; only occasionally kindred sayings are gathered in groups of two or more couplets, while in a few cases successive stanzas begin with the same letter of the Hebrew alphabet.[5] On the whole, the description of the book as a "forest of proverbs" is not inappropriate.

The book of Proverbs consists of eight parts of unequal length, with a general heading. Seven of the eight constitute the collection of proverbs, one, the first, seems to have been prefixed at a later time as a suitable introduction to the entire collection.

Preface: THE NATURE AND OBJECT OF PROVERBIAL WISDOM (1. 1-6)

I. THE PRAISE OF WISDOM (1. 7 to 9. 18)

1. Warning against crimes of violence (1. 7-19).
2. Wisdom's denunciation of those who despise her (1. 20-33).
3. The pursuit of wisdom as the road to virtue and the fear of God (2. 1-22).
4. Blessings of piety and the value of wisdom (3. 1-20).
5. Wisdom a protection (3. 21-26).
6. Liberality and integrity (3. 27-35).
7. A father's counsel (4. 1 to 5. 6).
8. Fidelity to the marriage relation (5. 7-23).
9. Folly of becoming surety for another (6. 1-5).
10. Advice to the sluggard (6. 6-11).

---

[4] The *Hebrew and English Lexicon* edited by Brown, Driver, and Briggs gives the following meanings of *māshāl*: (1) *Proverbial saying*, brief, terse sentence of popular sagacity; (2) *Byword*; (3) *Prophetic, figurative discourse*; (4) *Similitude, parable*; (5) *Poem*, of various kinds; (6) *Sentences of ethical wisdom*.

[5] For example, 20. 7-9; 22. 2-4; but this peculiarity may be purely accidental.

THE BOOK OF PROVERBS

11. Various forms of wrongdoing (6. 12-19).
12. Warning against adultery (6. 20-35).
13. Warning against the wiles of the harlot (7. 1-27).
14. Wisdom's call (8. 1-36).
15. Wisdom and folly contrasted (9. 1-18).

II. PROVERBS OF SOLOMON (10. 1 to 22. 16)
A collection of miscellaneous aphorisms on life and conduct.

III. WORDS OF THE WISE (22. 17 to 24. 22)
Practical precepts in the form of maxims and proverbs.

IV. ADDITIONAL SAYINGS OF THE WISE (24. 23-34)
Appendix to III, and similar to it.

V. ADDITIONAL PROVERBS OF SOLOMON (25. 1 to 29. 27)
Appendix to II; consisting for the most part of short sayings like those in II.

VI. THE WORDS OF AGUR (30. 1-33)
A series of epigrams dealing with the divine transcendence and with various human characteristics.

VII. THE WORDS OF KING LEMUEL (31. 1-9)
A series of maxims in which Lemuel is warned by his mother against sensuality and indulgence in wine, and exhorted to care for the poor.

VIII. AN ANONYMOUS ALPHABETIC ACROSTIC (31. 10-31)
Description of a virtuous and capable housewife.

Each of the eight divisions has characteristics of its own, which is in itself evidence that they did not all originate at the same time or were written by the same individual. Division I is in the nature of a hortatory introduction to the proverbs in 10. 1ff. The wise man—who probably had before him the rest of the book, or at least the more important parts of it—speaking as a father, warns his son or disciple against the temptations and dangers to which he will be exposed, invites him to listen to the precepts he is about to utter, and urges upon him the claims of wisdom to be his friend and guide. The

THE PSALMS AND OTHER SACRED WRITINGS

wrongs against which he utters the most persistent warnings are crimes of violence and unchastity, but other forms of wrongdoing are not overlooked. One of the most beautiful passages in the whole book, if not in the entire wisdom literature, is chapter 8, which portrays wisdom as calling to men and offering to them herself and her gifts as a priceless boon. "The unity of thought and efficiency operative in the world is here abstracted from God, the actual operator, and presented as a *personal* agent, the first-born child of the Creator, standing beside him and giving effect to his creative design, afterward, in history, inspiring kings and princes with their best thoughts, delighting in the sons of men (verse 31), and promising abundant reward to those who will commit themselves to her guidance. The representation in 3. 19, 20; 8. 22ff. is the prelude of the later doctrine of the Λόγος."[6]

In literary form this section differs greatly from the rest of the book. It consists not, like the succeeding chapters, of disconnected proverbs, but of continuous, well-developed proverbial discourses. The style is flowing and in the nature of "rich rhetorical prose rather than of finely polished poetry."[7] The hortatory element is so pronounced that Delitzsch and others have directed attention to striking similarities in tone, purpose, warmth of feeling, and even expression between these chapters and the book of Deuteronomy. "As Deuteronomy would have the rising generation lay to heart the Mosaic *Tōrāh,* so here the author would impress upon his hearers the *Tōrāh* of wisdom."

---
[6] S. R. Driver, *Introduction to the Literature of the Old Testament,* p. 396.
[7] A. R. Gordon, *The Poets of the Old Testament,* p. 268.

THE BOOK OF PROVERBS

Division II constitutes the main body of the book. It consists of a series of loosely connected proverbs, each proverb consisting of two lines,[8] each line, as a rule, of three or four words. In the first few chapters[9] antithetic parallelism is used almost exclusively, but in the remaining chapters the other types, synonymous and synthetic or constructive parallelism, are not uncommon. No clear or well-defined plan of arrangement is discernible;[10] in some instances, however, proverbs centering around the same subject or containing the same characteristic words seem to be grouped together.[11]

Though division II contains some religious proverbs, on the whole the generalizations are drawn from secular life. The religious proverbs emphasize the divine sovereignty,[12] the service acceptable to God,[13] the reward of the righteous and the punishment of the unrighteous— always in this world.[14] There are frequent contrasts between the wise and the foolish, the rich and the poor, the diligent and the slothful, the reverent and the scoffer. Wealth as such is declared to be an advantage,[15] but man

---

[8] The Hebrew text shows only one exception, 19. 7, which has three lines, but this has arisen from a corruption of the text; the Septuagint has preserved in the place of verse 7c a complete couplet. With this change the total number of proverbs in division II becomes 376.

[9] Chapters 10 to 15.

[10] Ewald subdivided the section into five parts, with new beginnings at 10. 1; 13. 1; 15. 20; 17. 25; 19. 20.

[11] 10. 6-7, 11-12, 14-15, 16-17, 18-19; 12. 5-7; 15. 8-9; 16. 12-15; 18. 6-7, etc.

[12] 15. 3, 11; 16. 2, 4, 9; 17. 3; 19. 21; 20. 12, 24; 21. 2, 30, 31; 22. 2, etc.

[13] 11. 1, 20; 12. 22; 15. 8, 9, 26; 16. 5, 6; 17. 15; 20. 10, 23; 21. 3, 27, etc.

[14] 10. 2, 3, 6, 7, 25, 27, 30; 11. 4, 5, 6; 15. 16, 29, etc.

[15] 10. 15; 13. 8; 14. 20, 24; 19. 4; 22. 7.

THE PSALMS AND OTHER SACRED WRITINGS

is warned against putting his trust in it,[16] and the assertion is made that riches wrongly acquired profit nothing.[17] Care for the poor is a special sign of piety.[18] Children are instructed to respect and obey their parents,[19] and parents, to use their authority over the children;[20] a good wife is pronounced a blessing from God,[21] but a bad one a curse.[22] The king is regarded with awe and reverence,[23] and, in general, is referred to in terms of praise and admiration.[24] National prosperity, like individual prosperity, is the reward of righteousness.[25] Pride is a source of much trouble;[26] the folly of becoming surety for another is emphasized;[27] and numerous proverbs deal with the right and wrong use of speech.[28]

The opening verses of division III are in the nature of an introduction, in which the author, perhaps the compiler of the collection, states, in the first person, the purpose of the proverbs which follow and invites attention to the admonitions contained therein. In subject-matter this section is similar to the preceding, but the hortatory tone is much more prominent; as a result this part of the book is "less a collection of individual proverbs than a body of maxims in which proverbs are inter-

---

[16] 11. 28.
[17] 10. 2.
[18] 14. 31; 17. 5; 19. 17.
[19] 13. 1; 15. 5; 19. 26; 20. 20.
[20] 13. 24; 19. 18; 22. 6, 15.
[21] 12. 4; 18. 22; 19. 14.
[22] 11. 22; 19. 13; 21. 9, 19.
[23] 16. 14, 15; 19. 12; 20. 2.
[24] 14. 28, 35; 16. 10, 12, 13; 20. 8, 26, 28; 21. 1; 22. 11.
[25] 14. 34.
[26] 13. 10; 16. 18, 19; 21. 4.
[27] 11. 15; 20. 16; compare 6. 1-5.
[28] 10. 11, 13, 14, 18-21, 31, 32, etc.

THE BOOK OF PROVERBS

woven, addressed with a practical aim[29] to an individual,[30] and worked up usually into a more or less consecutive argument." The purpose and aim naturally affect the literary form. Two-line proverbs, or distichs, are rare,[31] and there is only one tristich;[32] generally four lines, that is, a tetrastich or two distichs, are given to the development of an idea, the second half emphasizing it by means of repetition, or furnishing a reason, or suggesting a purpose, or in some other way completing the thought.[33] Frequently the theme is developed at even greater length; there are some pentastichs[34] and hexastichs,[35] a heptastich,[36] and an octastich,[37] and in one case a short poem is given to the presentation of one theme.[38]

Division IV, with the title, "These also are *sayings* of the wise," is an appendix to division III, which it resembles, both in contents and literary form: a hexastich,[39] a distich,[40] a tristich,[41] a tetrastich,[42] and a decastich,[43] in which the parable of the sluggard is developed.

---

[29] Compare, for example, the warnings against becoming surety for another, 22. 26, 27; excessive indulgence, 23. 1–3; pursuit of riches, 23. 4, 5; gluttony and drunkenness, 23. 20, 21, 29–35.

[30] Compare the expression "my son" in 23. 15, 19, 26; 24. 13, 21, which is very common in division I, but used only once in division II, 19. 27.

[31] 22. 28; 23. 9; 24. 7–10.

[32] 22. 29.

[33] 22. 22–23, 24–25, 26–27; 23. 10–11, etc.

[34] 23. 4–5; 24. 13–14.

[35] 23. 1–3, 12–14, 19–21, 26–28; 24. 11–12.

[36] 23. 6–8.

[37] 23. 22–25.

[38] 23. 29–35.

[39] 24. 23–25.

[40] Verse 26.

[41] Verse 27.

[42] Verses 28, 29.

[43] Verses 30–34; see above, p. 86.

THE PSALMS AND OTHER SACRED WRITINGS

Division V bears the title, "These also are proverbs of Solomon, which the men of Hezekiah king of Judah copied out."[44] Evidently, therefore, it is intended to be understood as an appendix to division II. But while there are some resemblances between it and the main collection of "Proverbs of Solomon," in other respects it exhibits marked differences. Since division II covers practically all human interests, it is only natural that, on the whole, the subject-matter of the appendix should be the same: there are a few religious proverbs,[45] the fool[46] and the sluggard[47] are condemned, and agricultural industry is inculcated.[48] As in division II, the address "my son" occurs but once;[49] two-line proverbs are much more common than in divisions III and IV, but the longer forms, unknown in II, are also found; there are several tristichs[50] and tetrastichs,[51] at least one pentastich[52] and a decastich.[53] A favorite type of proverb, exceedingly rare in division II, is the so-called comparative proverb, in which a truth is illustrated from nature or human life; sometimes the comparison is expressed; at other times the particle of comparison is omitted.[54] The grouping of individual proverbs seems to be determined at times, as in division II, by the presence of characteristic words

---

[44] 25. 1.
[45] 29. 13, 25, 26.
[46] 26. 1, 3–12; 27. 22.
[47] 26. 13–16.
[48] 27. 23–27.
[49] 27. 11.
[50] 25. 8, 13, 20; 27. 10, 22; 28. 10.
[51] 25. 4–5, 9–10, 21–22, etc.
[52] 25. 6–7.
[53] 27. 23–27.
[54] 25. 3, 11, 12, 14, 18, 19, 20, 23, 26, 28; 26. 3, 7, 9, 11, 14, 17, 21, 23; 28. 3, 15, etc.

THE BOOK OF PROVERBS

or expressions;[55] on the other hand, the grouping according to subject-matter is carried much farther.[56] The king is a prominent figure,[57] but, on the whole, he is not spoken of as highly and favorably as in II. The collection as a whole leaves the impression that the conditions reflected are different from those presupposed in 10. 1 to 22. 16.

Division VI is full of difficulties. It bears the title, "The words of Agur the son of Jakeh; the oracle"; which is followed by the additional introductory statement, "The man saith unto Ithiel, unto Ithiel and Ucal."[58] The latter part of this introduction is both awkward and obscure; it becomes smoother reading if, with the margin of the Revised Version, it is joined to verses 2-4 as a part of the speaker's utterance, and translated, with slight alteration of the text: "I have wearied myself, O God, I have wearied myself, O God, and am consumed: For I am more brutish...." The word translated "oracle," in the first part of the title, also creates difficulty. It is introduced very abruptly and is commonly used only of prophetic utterances; hence most modern scholars believe that it should not be translated at all, but should be understood as a proper name, the home of Agur, and should be rendered "of Massa."[59] The same change should, perhaps, be made in 31. 1. If so, the proverbs in divisions VI and VII may have been of non-Jewish origin, and may have been later adapted by the

---
[55] 25. 8-9, 11-12; 26. 1-2.
[56] The king, 25. 1-7; fools, 26. 3-12; the sluggard, 26. 13-16; flattery, 26. 23-26, 28, etc.
[57] 25. 1-7; 28. 2, 12, 15, 16, 28; 29. 2, 4, 14, 16.
[58] 30. 1.
[59] The name is used in Gen. 25. 14 of a district in Arabia. Another emendation giving the reading "the proverb writer" is less probable.

THE PSALMS AND OTHER SACRED WRITINGS

editor to Jewish modes of thinking. Nothing is known of Agur or Jakeh, or of Lemuel in 31. 1.

It is by no means certain that the heading should be made to include the whole of chapter 30; perhaps only verses 1-6, or, at the most, verses 1-9 are to be regarded as the words of Agur, not in their original form but as worked over by a pious Jew. It is even possible that only verses 2-4 are to be interpreted as the utterance of Agur, in which he asserts that it is impossible to know God; verses 5 and 6 might then be regarded as a rebuke and contradiction of this skeptical statement by a pious Jew, who, in verses 7-9, utters a prayer that he may never be tempted to lose faith in his God.

If verses 10-33 are separated from the preceding section, they must be regarded as an anonymous collection of nine groups of proverbs, each describing some quality or character in terms of either warning or commendation. In most of the proverbs the number *four* is conspicuous; four marks of a wicked generation,[60] four insatiable things,[61] four wonderful things,[62] four intolerable things,[63] four things little but wise,[64] four stately things.[65]

Division VII is entitled "The words of king Lemuel; the oracle which his mother taught him."[66] The verses contain warnings against debauchery and injustice and an exhortation to care for the poor and needy.

---
[60] 30. 11-14.
[61] Verses 15, 16.
[62] Verses 18-20.
[63] Verses 21-23.
[64] Verses 24-28.
[65] Verses 29-31.
[66] This should be rendered, with margin Revised Version, "The words of Lemuel king of Massa, which his mother taught him." Compare 30. 1.

THE BOOK OF PROVERBS

The closing division[67] is an anonymous alphabetic acrostic in praise of a virtuous and capable housewife. It consists chiefly of two-line stanzas in which synonymous parallelism predominates.

Date and Authorship. The critical questions regarding the origin of the book of Proverbs are similar to those regarding the origin of the Psalter. The latter is a collection of groups of psalms credited to various authors; similarly, the book of Proverbs is a collection of groups of wisdom sayings ascribed in their titles to different authors. Leaving aside the introduction, chapters 1-9, the book claims to contain proverbs of Solomon,[68] words of the wise men,[69] and words of Agur and Lemuel.[70] The titles indicating authorship were added by late editors; hence there exists the same uncertainty as in the case of the psalm titles, and their value can be determined only by a careful investigation of all available evidence.

Following the statement in 1. 1, and with complete disregard of the other titles, the traditional view has been that Solomon is the author of all the proverbs. Support for this view was found in 1 Kings 4. 29-34, a passage celebrating Solomon's wisdom, especially in verse 32, which states that the wise king "spake three thousand proverbs; and his songs were a thousand and five." The wisdom of Solomon was as manifold as that reflected in the proverbial literature; it was partly practical,[71] partly philosophical,[72] in part it lay in the region of natural

---
[67] 31. 10-31.
[68] 10. 1; 25. 1.
[69] 22. 17; 24. 23.
[70] 30. 1; 31. 1.
[71] For example, 1 Kings 3. 16-28.
[72] 1 Kings 4. 31.

THE PSALMS AND OTHER SACRED WRITINGS

history,[73] and in part it consisted of the ability to solve riddles or answer hard questions.[74]

Modern scholarship, practically without exception, has given up the traditional view for the following reasons: (1) The titles themselves recognize diversity of authorship; (2) the differences in character between the several collections point in the same direction; (3) proverbs are repeated in whole or in part, not only in different divisions, but within the same division of the book, which would be difficult of explanation on the assumption that the entire book is the work of a single author.[75] But, granting diversity of authorship, may the two divisions said to contain proverbs of Solomon[76] be ascribed to the wise king of Israel? This question also is answered in the negative by modern scholars: (1) Though the nature of the Solomonic proverbs is not indicated in 1 Kings 4. 32, the context suggests that they consisted of comparisons between men and trees or animals, which is not true of many of the proverbs in the Solomonic collections. (2) The frequent repetitions within the first collection credited to Solomon suggest that it contains proverbs coming from different periods and authors; and is not the product of a single individual. (3) The character and contents of many proverbs make it impossible to assign them to King Solomon. One would hardly expect the advice regarding proper behavior in the presence of a king[77] to come from one who himself was a king; indeed, all the proverbs

---

[73] 1 Kings 4. 33.
[74] 1 Kings 10. 1.
[75] Compare 14. 12 with 16. 25; 10. 1 with 15. 20; 10. 2 with 11. 4; 14. 31 with 17. 5, etc.
[76] 10. 1 to 22. 16; 25. 1 to 29. 27.
[77] 23. 1–3; 25. 6, 7.

centering around the king receive a more natural interpretation as expressing the sentiment of the people concerning the king than as reflecting the feeling of a king concerning himself or other kings. Similarly, proverbs depreciating wealth, or condemning excessive taxation, or praising monogamy, do not sound natural in the mouth of Solomon.[78] These considerations have convinced modern scholars that even the two collections ascribed to Solomon in their titles cannot come from him in their entirety.

On the other hand, the sweeping assertion of Smend that "Solomon has no connection whatever with the canonical proverbs"[79] is without warrant. A. B. Davidson gives a much truer interpretation of the facts when he writes: "Much may be referred to the age of Solomon, particularly the sayings in chapters 10-22, though much even in this division may be later."[80] In other words, the situation is much the same as in the case of Davidic psalms:[81] (1) It cannot be established with absolute certainty that Solomon wrote any of the proverbs contained in the book of Proverbs. (2) In the light of the statements in 1 Kings 4. 29-34 it is not improbable that he was an author of proverbial sayings. (3) Since Solomon continued to live in the minds of the people as the wise king *par excellence,* it is not probable that all such proverbs would be lost. (4) Some of the proverbs in the collections bearing his name are not inappropriate in his lips. But even admitting that some of the proverbs

---

[78] Consider, for example, 13. 1; 15. 16; 18. 22; 19. 13, 14; 21. 31; 22. 14; 29. 4 in the light of Solomon's life and character as portrayed in 1 Kings 1-11.
[79] *Alttestamentliche Religionsgeschichte,* p. 510.
[80] *The Book of Job,* p. lxx.
[81] See above, p. 57.

THE PSALMS AND OTHER SACRED WRITINGS

may come from Solomon, there is no way of separating these Solomonic proverbs from others originating during subsequent generations and centuries. The tradition ascribing all the proverbs to Solomon, reflected in 1. 1, is due to a tendency noticeable also in the case of the laws and the psalms, of ascribing late institutions and literary productions to early heroes: Moses, the typical representative of law, was credited with all Jewish law; David, the typical representative of psalmody, was credited with all the psalms; in like manner Solomon, the typical representative of wisdom, was credited with the whole proverbial literature.[82]

The difficulties in the way of determining the dates of individual proverbs are as great and troublesome as in the case of the psalms. Perhaps the only assertion that can safely be made is that it is quite impossible to determine definitely the date of a single proverb. The tendency at the present time is to assign practically all the proverbs in their present form[83] to the late postexilic period, between Job and Ecclesiasticus, that is, between about B. C. 400 and 180. In support of this contention attention is directed to the following data: (1) The tacit assumption of monotheism throughout the book, which, it is claimed, cannot belong to the preexilic or even the early postexilic period.[84] (2) The absence of characteristic national traits. The only national element is the mention of sacrifice. On the other hand, significant terms, like Israel, Israel's covenant with Yahweh, temple, priest, or prophet, are completely ignored. There is also a significant broadening of the term "law," so as to

---
[82] See F. C. Eiselen, *The Books of the Pentateuch*, p. 87.
[83] It is admitted that some may rest upon simpler, preexilic sayings.
[84] See Ezek., Chapters 6, 8, 23, etc.; Zech., Chapter 13; Job 31. 26, 27.

THE BOOK OF PROVERBS

include the teaching of the wise men, not only the direct commandments of Yahweh. "This non-national form of thought," says Toy, "belongs to a sort of culture which did not exist among the Jews till they were scattered throughout the world and came under Persian and Greek influence."[85] (3) The social life depicted is that of the later period: monogamy is taken for granted;[86] agricultural pursuits occupy a relatively insignificant place; chief attention is given to city life with its special occupations and temptations; the vices condemned are those prevalent in the cities of the later age; the system of education reflected is more advanced than that of Deut. 6; the relation between king and subjects is not that of the earlier Old Testament books but of later, post-Old Testament writings. (4) The philosophic conceptions belong to the time when the Jews came into contact with the non-Semitic world, more especially with Greek thought and civilization: The practical identification of virtue with knowledge; the exaltation and personification of wisdom, which is credited with all the functions which elsewhere in the Old Testament are ascribed to Yahweh himself;[87] the expression of skepticism in 30. 2-4 finds parallels only in other postexilic wisdom books. (5) The very existence of a separate class of wise men, such as the wise men of Proverbs are said to have been, points to a late date. The words "wise" and "wisdom" are used in other Old Testament books, but there they refer to mechanical or artistic skill,[88] cleverness in ordinary

---

[85] *The Book of Proverbs*, p. xxi.
[86] Polygamy existed and was regulated by law during the earlier centuries, Deut. 21. 15-17; Lev. 18. 18.
[87] See especially Chapter 8, in which wisdom is said to control all human society and to have been present at the creation of the world.
[88] Exod. 35. 10; Isa. 40. 20; 1 Chron. 22. 15.

THE PSALMS AND OTHER SACRED WRITINGS

affairs,[89] political sagacity,[90] magical or prophetic knowledge,[91] or general intelligence.[92] In Proverbs and the other wisdom books the terms relate to a definite class of teachers "whose function is the pursuit of universal moral and religious wisdom—men who, unlike the prophets, lay no claim to supernatural inspiration, but make their appeal simply to human reason." Jer. 9. 23 is quoted to show that down to the close of the national history of Judah the wise men were looked upon with suspicion by the Yahweh prophets; the change in character and position reflected in the wisdom books must have taken place subsequently to the time of Jeremiah, which throws the legitimate wisdom activity into the postexilic age. (6) The proverb writers appear to have known the Law and the Prophets[93] in completed form.[94] (7) The literary form of the proverbs in the book of Proverbs is artistically superior to that of the proverbs known to be early.[95] (8) A comparison with the other wisdom books,[96] both as to language and thought, favors a late postexilic date for the book of Proverbs.[97]

But these arguments are by no means conclusive: (1) It is true that the earliest dogmatic statements of mono-

---

[89] 2 Sam. 13. 3; 14. 2.
[90] Gen. 41. 33; Deut. 1. 13; Isa. 3. 3; 19. 11; Jer. 8. 9; Ezek. 27. 8; 28. 4; Esth. 1. 13.
[91] Exod. 7. 11; Dan. 5. 11.
[92] Hos. 14. 9; Isa. 11. 2.
[93] That is, the first two divisions of the Old Testament canon.
[94] 28. 4-9; 29. 18.
[95] 1 Sam. 10. 12; 24. 13, 14; 1 Kings 20. 11; Jer. 31. 29, etc.
[96] The canonical books of Job and Ecclesiastes, and the non-canonical Ecclesiasticus and Wisdom of Solomon.
[97] C. H. Toy, *The Book of Proverbs*, pp. xixff. G. B. Gray, *A Critical Introduction to the Old Testament*, pp. 144ff.; A. R. Gordon, *The Poets of the Old Testament*, pp. 259ff.

theism are found in Isa. 40ff., but it is also a fact that monotheism is at least implied in much of the Old Testament literature from the eighth century onward.[98] (2) The absence of national traits may be accounted for by the aim of the wise men. The standpoint of the pre-exilic prophets was primarily national, hence they could not avoid referring to national beliefs and national institutions; the Old Testament narrators, both prophetic and priestly, were under the same necessity. But the wise men, who were dealing primarily with the practical, everyday affairs and needs of individuals, could accomplish their purpose, either before or after the exile, without reference to the broader national interests and institutions. The wise men undoubtedly considered their teaching the truth of Yahweh, hence there could be no objection to calling their utterances *Tōrāh*.[99] (3) The social conditions reflected in Proverbs were not unknown before the exile. Since the proverbial teaching was intended primarily for popular guidance, what is more natural than the implication that monogamy is the normal type of marriage relation? Polygamy never was widespread among the common people. The eighth-century prophets reveal the same familiarity with city temptations and city vices as do the writers of the proverbs. The book of Proverbs has nothing to say about a system of education. The difference in the portrayal of the relation between king and subject is easily accounted for by the peculiar purpose of the wise men. (4) Philosophizing is confined almost entirely to chapters 1-9, which, no doubt, are late; but the late date of these chap-

---

[98] Compare F. C. Eiselen, *The Minor Prophets*, pp. 205, 206, 211.
[99] F. C. Eiselen, *The Books of the Pentateuch*, pp. 43, 44.

THE PSALMS AND OTHER SACRED WRITINGS

ters does not establish the same late date for the entire book. (5) The incidental reference to the wise men in Jer. 18. 18 seems to show that a class of professional wise men, ranking with the prophets and the priests, was recognized at least as early as the days of the prophet Jeremiah. The existence of "false" wise men[100] no more disproves the existence of a class of legitimate wise men than the existence of false prophets and faithless priests disproves the existence of legitimate prophets and priests; on the contrary, it tends to establish it. (6) The passages referred to do not prove that the Law and the Prophets were known in their completed form. All the expressions used can be explained on the assumption of a knowledge of legal and prophetic teaching such as might be had by any God-fearing Hebrew as early as the eighth century. (7) Who can substantiate the claim that the literary form of the proverbs in the book of Proverbs was unknown during the preexilic period? (8) The significance of language and style has been differently estimated. There are undoubtedly some late features, but they are not sufficiently numerous to throw light on the dates of any considerable number of proverbs. Nor are the resemblances in thought with the other wisdom books of such a character that definite conclusions respecting dates can be drawn from them.[101] All this simply means that the arguments in favor of a postexilic date for virtually all the proverbs can in no sense be regarded as conclusive.

But as it is impossible to prove the postexilic origin of the proverbs, it is equally difficult to prove their pre-

---
[100] See above, p. 86.
[101] Again, with the exception of Chapters 1-9, which are among the latest portions of the book.

THE BOOK OF PROVERBS

exilic date. True, there are the titles in 10. 1 and 25. 1,[102] but they, like the psalm titles, cannot be accepted as final authority. Some have argued that the frequent references to the king imply the origin of the royal proverbs while the Hebrew monarchy was still in existence. If it could be shown that the wise men always had in mind a king of Israel or Judah, this contention might have some weight, but evidently the outlook of the wise men is broader, they are thinking of kings in general, of kings as a part of human society; and kings continued to play an important role in society long after the fall of Judah in B. C. 586. That the argument is of little or no value is further shown by the fact that Ecclesiastes and Ecclesiasticus, both written in the late postexilic period, contain numerous references to kings similar to those in Proverbs.[103] Attention has also been called to proverbs which seem to reflect the spirit and moral fervor of preexilic prophecy, proverbs which place the emphasis not on ritual or sacrifice but on character and conduct.[104] But the proverbial literature being professedly interested in life and conduct above everything else, could there have been any other emphasis during the postexilic era? An

---

[102] It is worthy of note that the Chronicler, who seems to relate of his heroes all that is noteworthy, mentions no such literary activity on the part of King Hezekiah. The question may well be asked: "Were Hezekiah's copyists a real literary guild of the eighth century, or a reflection back to that period from the postexilic period, the period of the scribes and of the wise, just as certain guilds of singers seem to have traveled back from postexilic times to the age of David purely in the imagination of the Chronicler (1 Chron. 25)?"

[103] Compare Prov. 14. 28, 35; 16. 10, 12–15; 19. 12; 20. 2, 8, 26, 28; 21. 1; 22. 11, 29; 24. 21; 25. 2, 3, 5, 6; 29. 4, 14; 30. 28–31; 31. 3, 4 with Eccl. 4. 13–16; 5. 9; 8. 2–4; 10. 16, 17, 20 and Ecclesiasticus 7. 4, 5; 8. 2; 10. 3.

[104] For example, 15. 8; 16. 6; 21. 3, 27.

THE PSALMS AND OTHER SACRED WRITINGS

argument for a preexilic date has also been seen in the fact that the whole of the book of Proverbs reflects the same view of prosperity and adversity that is advocated by the friends of Job, a view that was first seriously affected by the individualism of Jeremiah and Ezekiel. But it is evident from Mal. 2, 17ff. that this view persisted far into the postexilic period, and from John 9. 2 that it had not fully disappeared in the days of Jesus. Language and style, while not conclusive in themselves, make it possible to assign some of the proverbs to the preexilic period, but others reveal such late features that they must be considered postexilic.

This discussion shows how difficult it is to fix the dates of the individual proverbs. The traditional view cannot be maintained, but though there is abundant evidence to prove the presence of postexilic proverbs in the book, there is equally good reason for believing that some are of preexilic origin. Perhaps, as in the case of the psalms, the facts justify only a general statement to the effect that the proverbs are the outgrowth of Hebrew and Jewish life and thought, beginning with Solomon[105] and ending about B. C. 200. The formation, about B. C. 180, of a new collection of proverbial sayings in Ecclesiasticus, instead of an enlarged edition of Proverbs, suggests that at that time Proverbs was considered a finally closed book; hence it is not probable that any considerable number of proverbs originating later than B. C. 200 were embodied in the canonical book of Proverbs.[106]

The attempt to determine the dates of the several col-

---

[105] It is not impossible that even some pre-Solomonic proverbs may have been preserved.

[106] This does not exclude the insertion of individual proverbs by later copyists or editors.

THE BOOK OF PROVERBS

lections and of the book as a whole is beset with similar difficulties. On the basis of the present arrangement the following table may be offered as indicating the successive steps in the formation of the book of Proverbs; though, in the nature of the case, there is abundant room for differences of opinion:

I. Formation of a collection of wisdom sayings called "Proverbs of Solomon,"[107] probably a compilation of earlier smaller collections.
II. Formation of an anonymous collection of "Sayings of the Wise Men,"[108] embodying miscellaneous proverbs.
III. Addition of a brief appendix[109] to the "Sayings of the Wise Men."
IV. Combination of II and III with I.
V. Formation of a second collection entitled "Proverbs of Solomon,"[110] which was added to IV.[111]
VI. Prefixing of a comprehensive introduction[112] to I-V.
VII. Addition of three or four short appendices, the words of Agur,[113] an anonymous collection,[114] the words of Lemuel,[115] and an alphabetic acrostic.[116]
VIII. Prefixing of a prologue[117] by the final editor, referring to the entire book as "Proverbs of Solomon."[118]

If the statement in 25. 1 could be accepted at its face value—and there are many who believe that there is no

---

[107] 10. 1 to 22. 16.
[108] 22. 17 to 24. 22.
[109] 24. 23–34.
[110] 25. 1 to 29. 27.
[111] The wording of the title in 25. 1 implies that the compiler, or at least the author of the title, was familiar with the first Solomonic collection.
[112] 1. 7 to 9. 18.
[113] 30. 1–9.
[114] 30. 10–33.
[115] 31. 1–9.
[116] 31. 10–31.
[117] 1. 1–6.
[118] 1. 1.

THE PSALMS AND OTHER SACRED WRITINGS

good reason for questioning its accuracy[119]—the date of chapters 25 to 29 would be fixed during the reign of Hezekiah; then 10. 1 to 22. 16 might be assigned to the early part of the eighth or the closing years of the ninth century, before the rise of the evils condemned by the eighth century prophets; between the two, some time during the eighth century, the "words of the wise," in 22. 17 to 24. 34 would have been compiled. The introduction in 1. 7 to 9. 18, on account of its resemblances to Deuteronomy,[120] might be assigned to the closing years of the monarchy, between the reform movement under Josiah in B. C. 621 and the exile. The three or four short appendices, which give every evidence of being among the latest portions of the book,[121] and the prologue might have been added after the exile.

But can the present arrangement be regarded as indicative of successive steps in the formation of the book of Proverbs? A cautious and conservative scholar like A. B. Davidson feels perfectly free to disregard it, and he argues strongly in favor of the priority of chapters 25 to 29 over 10. 1 to 22. 16, as well as over the other divisions of the book;[122] and other scholars share this opinion. The principal support for this position is found in the more regular and highly polished form of the proverbs in 10. 1 to 22. 16 as compared with those in chapters 25 to 29. The less regular, but more forceful

---

[119] See. for example, S. R. Driver, *Introduction to the Literature of the Old Testament*, p. 407; but see above, note 102.

[120] See above, p. 98.

[121] The thought and form of chapter 30, the Aramaic elements in the language of the sayings of Lemuel, and the acrostic arrangement of the closing section all favor a late date.

[122] Article "Proverbs" in *Encyclopædia Britannica*, 9th ed.

THE BOOK OF PROVERBS

and epigrammatic proverbs in the latter section, Davidson concludes, are more nearly what early, popular proverbs may be expected to be than the more regular proverbs in 10. 1 to 22. 16, which presuppose an advanced stage of literary culture and a long development of the art of proverb-making. If, now, chapters 25 to 29, the earliest collection, belong to the age of Hezekiah, the dates of practically all the other sections demand readjustment.

However, just as the testimony furnished by the present arrangement of the book is inconclusive, so little weight can be attached to the chronological statement in 25. 1.[123] Hence the whole question regarding the dates of the several collections and of the book as a whole must be determined on the basis of internal evidence. Now, it has been pointed out[124] that every collection contains some features which may be interpreted as pointing to a late date, while at least the larger sections contain other elements which seem to favor an early date.[125] In other words, whatever the number of preexilic proverbs embodied in the several collections may be, these collections appear to have been compiled during the postexilic period. This is the view of most recent writers. A good summary of the whole matter is given by C. H. Toy in the following paragraph: "Out of certain current collections of aphorisms were first put together our subsections chapters 10 to 15, 16 to 22. 16, 25 to 27, and 28, 29,

---

[123] See above, p. 113.
[124] See above, pp. 108ff.
[125] In the introduction, 1. 7 to 9. 18, the resemblances to Deuteronomy, which are thought by many to favor an early date, soon after the reform movement under Josiah, are counterbalanced, for example, by the personification of wisdom in Chapter 8, which is an advance over Job 28, and is closely akin to Ecclesiasticus 24 and to the still later Wisdom of Solomon.

THE PSALMS AND OTHER SACRED WRITINGS

and from these by different editors the sections 10. 1 to 22. 16 and 25 to 29 were made, the editor of the latter being aware of the existence of the former. The two may have reached substantially their present form between B. C. 350 and B. C. 300, the second a little later than the first. During the next half-century the section III (22. 17 to 24)[126] was produced, and a book of aphorisms was formed by combining II[127] and IV[128] and inserting III between them; it is not apparent how this position came to be assigned III, but, as 25. 1, ('these also are proverbs of Solomon') seems to presuppose 10. 1 ('proverbs of Solomon'), and III is referred not to Solomon but to the 'sages,' it is likely that it was added after II and IV had been combined; it is possible, however, that it was first attached to II, the collection IV, with its title unchanged, being then added. The opening section (omitting 6. 1-19; 9. 7-12) may have been composed about the middle of the third century B. C., and was combined by its author (or by some contemporary editor) with II-IV; the introduction (1. 2-7) is couched in the technical terms of the schools, and is probably the work of the author of the section; he seems also to have prefixed the general title (1. 1). The additions to the section (6. 1-19; 9. 7-12), which resemble III, V,[129] and II, may be due to the final redactor, or to a very late scribe. Finally, the work was completed by the addition of the fragments contained in chapters 30, 31, the completion falling in the second century B. C. Succeeding copyists introduced into the text a number of errors,

---

[126] Including sections II and III in the table given above, p. 115.
[127] 10. 1 to 22. 16.
[128] Chapters 25 to 29.
[129] Chapters 30, 31.

THE BOOK OF PROVERBS

not only in words and phrases but also in arrangement of lines and couplets."[130]

The history of the book as outlined by Toy differs slightly from that suggested in the table on p. 115; but this simply shows that the data are not sufficiently numerous or definite to warrant dogmatic assertions regarding details. If, therefore, anyone should feel that the conclusions here set forth are too definite or specific, he may content himself with the general statement that the book of Proverbs reached its final form about B. C. 200, and that it embodies several collections of wisdom sayings formed at earlier periods, some of them containing pre-exilic material.

Significance and Value. The charge has been brought against the book of Proverbs that it is not truly religious, that it moves on a lower plane and contemplates lower aims than do the other books of the Old Testament. But this estimate of the book is altogether inadequate. That there are differences between it and other books in the Old Testament canon may be admitted, but these differences are due not to a lack of spiritual insight or moral fervor, but to differences in aim and purpose. Neither the authors of the individual sayings, nor the compilers of the several collections, nor the editor of the book in its final form, were interested primarily in prophetic discourses or religious lyrics; their concern was with those simple precepts of life which, because of their very simplicity, are ever needed for the proper guidance of men. There are two phases of religion, the one internal, the religious experience, the other external, the religious life. The two belong together, but at times the first, at other

---

[130] *The Book of Proverbs*, p. xxx.

THE PSALMS AND OTHER SACRED WRITINGS

times the second, may be emphasized. The authors, adapters, and compilers of the wisdom sayings in the canonical book of Proverbs placed the emphasis on life and conduct. They sought to teach the most difficult of all lessons—how to practice religion, how to overcome the temptations, and to discharge the duties of everyday life. Hence, "Guide to the happy or successful Life" would be an appropriate title for the book.

The teaching of the wise men rests upon a religious basis. Their religion may not rise to a New Testament level, but in this they resemble other Old Testament writers; their conceptions of reward and punishment may be crude and materialistic, but this point of view they share with all the saints of Israel whose vision was confined to this world. But with all these shortcomings, their teaching is inspired by a firm belief in the existence of a personal, righteous God and his rule over the world, and in the other great verities taught by the prophets. Far from disregarding religion the writers of proverbs sought to make it the controlling motive of life and conduct. As a result a healthy, religious spirit pervades the book from beginning to end; and, in addition, there are numerous passages which give definite expression to the lofty religious conceptions of the wise men.[131]

Nevertheless, as is natural in a book seeking to influence conduct, greater stress is laid upon ethics, the practice of religion. No interest or relation of life seems to have escaped the attention of these keen observers of human nature and life. Precepts are given concerning ordinary, everyday conduct,[132] the relation of men to

---
[131] For example, 3. 5–7; 16. 3, 6, 9; 23. 17, etc. The creed of the wise men is summed up in the expression, "Fear of Yahweh."
[132] For example, 10. 4; 11. 28; 12. 10; 14. 3.

THE BOOK OF PROVERBS

their fellows,[133] domestic relations and domestic happiness,[134] national life and the proper attitude toward governmental authority,[135] as well as concerning all other relations of life. The ideals of the authors are admirably expressed in these words of W. T. Davison: "For the writers of Proverbs religion means good sense, religion means mastery of affairs, religion means strength and manliness and success, religion means a well-furnished intellect employing the best means to accomplish the highest ends. There is a healthy, vigorous tone about this kind of teaching which is never out of date, but which, human nature being what it is, is only too apt to disappear in the actual presentation of religion in the church on earth."[136] These ideals receive almost endless application to the problems of daily life in a manner that must and does commend these forceful sayings even to-day to the universal moral instincts of mankind. Hence no one can question the justice of McFadyen's remark: "A book so rich in moral precept and religious thought may well claim to have fulfilled its program: 'to give prudence to the simple, to the young man knowledge and discretion.' 1. 4." [137]

---
[133] For example, 11. 1; 14. 21; 17. 5.
[134] For example, 6. 20–22; 18. 22; 31. 10–31.
[135] For example, 14. 34, 35; 16. 12–15.
[136] *The Wisdom Literature of the Old Testament*, p. 134.
[137] *Old Testament Introduction*, p. 263.

CHAPTER V

THE BOOK OF JOB

CHAPTER V

THE BOOK OF JOB

Name. The name of the hero[1] of the book of Job is in the Massoretic text, אִיּוֹב, Iyyōbh, in the Septuagint, Ἰώβ, Iōb, in the Vulgate, Job. The etymology of the word is doubtful. A favorite interpretation regards it as a passive formation of a verb meaning "to be hostile," with the meaning "object of enmity"; but in reality no satisfactory explanation has been found, and the meaning of the word remains uncertain. There is no connection between this man and the Job in Gen. 46. 13 or Jobab in Gen. 36. 13; but the Job mentioned in Ezek. 14. 14, 20 is undoubtedly identical with the hero of this book.[2]

Contents and Outline. The book of Job, in form a

---

[1] No claim is made anywhere in the book that Job is the author. A few writers have assigned the book to him, for instance, Carpzov.

[2] It is worthy of note that the genuine Septuagint translation of the book, recovered during the latter part of the nineteenth century from a Coptic version, is shorter than the Hebrew text by nearly four hundred lines. The ordinary editions of the Septuagint, as well as the majority of MSS., contain not this text but the Hexaplar text of Origen, that is, the Greek text constructed by this early church father on the basis of the several Greek translations available in his day. Though he indicated by means of critical marks the changes he proposed in the Septuagint text, the critical signs have not been preserved with any kind of care; hence it is exceedingly difficult to determine from Origen's text the original form either of the Septuagint translation or of the underlying Hebrew text. The origin of the differences between the Hebrew and the genuine Septuagint translation is not clear. At first sight it might seem that the latter had preserved a more original form of the book, but this is by no means certain; and the omissions do not remove the difficulties presented by the Hebrew text.

drama, relates how Job, a man perfect even in the sight of God, was suddenly overtaken by a series of distressing calamities, which finally caused him to curse the day of his birth and to cry out for death. All this is contained in the first three chapters. The rest of the book, with the exception of a brief epilogue narrating the restoration of Job to health, prosperity, and happiness, reports the debates between Job and other speakers to which his outburst is said to have given rise. The book falls into five parts of unequal length: I. The prologue,[3] written in prose. The Satan, or "adversary," is permitted by Yahweh to test Job's righteousness by depriving him of his wealth and children, and by afflicting him with a loathsome disease. Job remains faithful. II. Debate between Job and his three friends.[4] Three friends of Job come to comfort him; moved by their unspoken sympathy, he breaks forth in a passionate cry, cursing the day of his birth and praying for death. This outburst gives occasion to the friends to speak, and thus opens the debate. There are three cycles of speeches;[5] in the first two each of the three friends speaks and Job replies to each; in the third, according to the present arrangement of the book, Zophar is absent, but Job speaks three times. III. The speeches of Elihu.[6] Elihu, a young man who is represented as a bystander, has listened to the debate and, vexed with both Job and his friends, steps forward to set both sides right. IV. The speeches of Yahweh and Job's submission.[7] When Elihu ceases, Yahweh intervenes and answers Job out of the whirlwind. The answer consists of two parts,

[3] 1. 1 to 2. 10.
[4] 2. 11 to 31. 40.
[5] Chapters 4–14; 15–21; 22–31.
[6] Chapters 32–37.
[7] 38. 1 to 42. 6.

THE BOOK OF JOB

each followed by a few words from Job. The aim of Yahweh's speeches is to bring Job, who has shown himself impatient and rebellious, back into a right attitude of mind toward his God. This is accomplished, for Job admits the folly of his doubts and solemnly retracts his hasty and ill-considered words. V. The epilogue,[8] written in prose. Job, restored to a right attitude of heart and mind, receives the divine commendation, while his friends are condemned for their foolish utterances. Then he is blessed with a prosperity twice as great as he enjoyed before.

I. THE PROLOGUE—JOB'S TEST AND FAITHFULNESS (1. 1 to 2. 10)
1. Job's uprightness (1. 1-5).
2. Job's first test and his faithfulness (1. 6-22).
3. Job's second test and his faithfulness (2. 1-10).

II. DEBATE BETWEEN JOB AND HIS THREE FRIENDS (2. 11 to 31. 40)
1. Introduction (2. 11 to 3. 26).
    (1) Coming of the three friends (2. 11-13).
    (2) Job's passionate cry for death (3. 1-26).
2. First cycle of speeches (4. 1 to 14. 22).
    (1) Speech of Eliphaz—No man just in the sight of God (4. 1 to 5. 27).
        (a) Security of the righteous (4. 1-11).
        (b) God's righteousness, man's unrighteousness, (4. 12 to 5. 7).
        (c) Submission and penitence to be followed by restoration (5. 8-27).
    (2) Reply of Job—Renewal of complaint and prayer for death (6. 1 to 7. 21).
        (a) Job's intolerable wretchedness (6. 1-13).
        (b) Disappointment over the attitude of his friends (6. 14-23).
        (c) Appeal for fair treatment (6. 24-30).
        (d) Wearisomeness of life (7. 1-10).
        (e) Challenge of God, prayer for death (7. 11-21).

---
[8] 42. 7-17.

- (3) Speech of Bildad—Appeal to tradition (8. 1-22).
  The experience of generations proves the justice of God; the righteous prosper while the wicked are destroyed.
- (4) Reply of Job—The divine government of the world an unfathomable mystery (9. 1 to 10. 22).
  - (a) Job's helplessness in the presence of God's infinite might (9. 1-21).
  - (b) God's responsibility for the prevailing situation: good and bad suffer alike (9. 22-24).
  - (c) God's unfair treatment of Job (9. 25-35).
  - (d) God's present attitude incomprehensible (10. 1-17).
  - (e) Plea for brief respite before death (10. 18-22).
- (5) Speech of Zophar—Impossibility of deceiving an all-wise God (11. 1-20).
  - (a) Rebuke of Job's challenge of the divine righteousness (11. 1-6).
  - (b) God's wisdom, man's blindness (11. 7-12).
  - (c) Exhortation to repentance (11. 13-20).
- (6) Reply of Job—Traditional doctrines not in accord with the facts of life (12. 1 to 14. 22).
  - (a) Job's insight not inferior to that of his friends (12. 1 to 13. 2).
  - (b) Worthlessness of the friends' defense of God (13. 3-12).
  - (c) New challenge of God (13. 13-28).
  - (d) Frailty and brevity of human life (14. 1-12).
  - (e) Hopelessness of Job's condition (14. 13-22).

3. Second cycle of speeches (15. 1 to 21. 34).
  - (1) Speech of Eliphaz—The awful fate of the wicked (15. 1-35).
    - (a) Rebuke of Job's presumptuousness (15. 1-16).
    - (b) Evil conscience and speedy destruction of the wicked (15. 17-35).
  - (2) Reply of Job—Reassertion of his innocence (16. 1 to 17. 16).
    - (a) Reproach of the heartlessness of his friends (16. 1-5).
    - (b) Job's sorrowful condition: forsaken by God and men (16. 6-17).
    - (c) The witness in heaven (16. 18 to 17. 9).
    - (d) Death the only hope of deliverance (17. 10-16).

THE BOOK OF JOB

- (3) Speech of Bildad—The lot of the sinner in life and death (18. 1-21).
  - (a) Condemnation of Job's rejection of friendly counsel (18. 1-4).
  - (b) Calamity in life and dishonor after death the lot of the wicked (18. 5-21).
- (4) Reply of Job—Cry for sympathy and light (19. 1-29).
  - (a) Protest against the reproaches of his friends (19. 1-6).
  - (b) Job's sufferings: despised by God and man (19. 7-20).
  - (c) Appeal to the friends (19. 21-22, 28-29).
  - (d) Appeal to the divine vindicator (19. 23-27).
- (5) Speech of Zophar—Affliction the result of sin (20. 1-29).
  Speedy overthrow of the wicked; if he prospers, it is only for a little while; he will soon be overtaken by misery and shame (like Job).
- (6) Reply of Job—Arraignment of the justice of God's government of the world (21. 1-34).
  The wicked prosper and die in peace; the friends in asserting the contrary pervert the truth.

4. Third cycle of speeches (22. 1 to 31. 40).
   - (1) Speech of Eliphaz—Job's condition due to his sin (22. 1-30).
     - (a) Job's sins the cause of his affliction (22. 1-5).
     - (b) Enumeration of Job's alleged sins (22. 6-20).
     - (c) Exhortation to repentance (22. 21-30).
   - (2) Reply of Job—There is no evidence of a Divine Providence (23. 1 to 24. 25).
     - (a) Job's yearning for access to God (23. 1-7).
     - (b) Reassertion of his innocence (23. 8-17).
     - (c) God's indifference to wickedness (24. 1-25).
   - (3) Speech of Bildad—Man's inferiority to God (25. 1-6).
   - (4) Reply of Job—The friends have obscured the issue (26. 1-14).
     He acknowledges the divine greatness but suggests by implication that the real point at issue is the divine justice.
   - (5) Final words of Job to his friends (27. 1 to 28. 28).
     - (a) Reaffirmation of his innocence (27. 1-6).
     - (b) Mental condition and material ruin of the wicked (27. 7-23).

(c) The wisdom of God unattainable by man (28. 1-27).
(d) The fear of God the chief duty of man (28. 28).
(6) Job's final survey of his case (29. 1 to 31. 40).
(a) Job's former prosperity (29. 1-25).
(b) Job's present humiliation and wretchedness (30. 1-31).
(c) Integrity of Job's entire life (31. 1-40).

III. SPEECHES OF ELIHU (32. 1 to 37. 24)

(Introductory—Cause of Elihu's interference, 32. 1-5).
1. Introduction—Elihu's vexation with Job and his friends; he desires to express his own opinion (32. 6-33).
2. Disciplinary purpose of affliction (33. 1-33).
3. Defense of the justice of God (34. 1-37).
4. Condemnation of Job's presumptuousness and self-righteousness (35. 1-16).
5. God's providential dealings with men (36. 1 to 37. 24).
   (1) Affliction an evidence of the divine goodness: it is sent for purposes of warning and purification (36. 1-15).
   (2) Exhortation to patient submission (36. 16-23; 37. 14-24).
   (3) God's unsearchable greatness (36. 24 to 37. 13).

IV. SPEECHES OF YAHWEH AND JOB'S SUBMISSION (38. 1 to 42. 6)
1. First speech and its effect (38. 1 to 40. 5).
   (1) Job's ignorance of inanimate nature upon earth and in heaven (38. 1-38).
   (2) Job's ignorance of animal creation (38. 39 to 40. 2).
   (3) Job's recognition of the transcendent majesty of God (40. 3-5).
2. Second speech and its effect (40. 6 to 42. 6.)
   (1) God's challenge to Job: he is to assume the divine attributes and rule the world (40. 6-14).
   (2) Job's inability to control Behemoth and Leviathan (40. 15 to 41. 34).
   (3) Job's confession and penitence (42. 1-6).

V. THE EPILOGUE—THE END OF JOB'S TRIALS (42. 7-17)
1. Condemnation of Job's friends (42. 7-9).
2. Restoration of Job's prosperity (42. 10-17).

Literary Form of the Book. The literary excellence of the book of Job is universally acknowledged. "In

THE BOOK OF JOB

range of imagination, and sustained splendor of diction, the book not merely stands alone in the Old Testament, but takes a foremost place also among the masterpieces of the world's literature. Tennyson but expresses the common feeling of literary critics when he pronounces it 'the greatest poem whether of ancient or of modern times.' "[9] But there are differences of opinion as to its proper classification; whether it should be called an epic, or a dramatic, or a didactic poem; which simply shows that the book cannot easily be assigned to any one of the commonly recognized types of poetry. Peake is right when he says: "We cannot force this splendid piece of Hebrew wisdom into a Greek scheme, and it is really futile to discuss whether it is a drama or an epic. It is itself."[10]

It is an epic in the sense of a heroic poem, for it celebrates, in stately verse, the spiritual and intellectual accomplishments of its hero. In structure it resembles a drama; hence it may well be called a dramatic poem. As in a drama, the action it portrays, though it is far less certain and swift than in Greek tragedy, passes through the successive stages of entanglement, development, and solution.[11] Its designation as a dramatic poem is appropriate, even though it may never have been intended for the stage,[12] and though it may be admitted

---
[9] A. R. Gordon, *The Poets of the Old Testament*, p. 202.
[10] A. S. Peake, *Job*, in *New Century Bible*, p. 41.
[11] "The action is for the most part internal and mental, the successive scenes exhibiting 'the varying moods of a great soul struggling with the mysteries of fate rather than trying external situations'" (Driver, *Introduction to the Literature of the Old Testament*, p. 411). It may therefore be called a psychological or spiritual drama.
[12] Though it can be acted; it was performed at Smith College a number of years ago. See H. T. Fowler, *A History of the Literature of Ancient Israel*, p. 333.

that the characters "lack the strong, clear-cut profile of great dramatic heroes. One may distinguish the grave, courtly Eliphaz, with his awesome revelations of the Divine, from the more timid and shrinking Bildad, who can but rely upon the traditions of the fathers, and the rough, coarse-grained Zophar, seeking rather to browbeat than to argue with his friend. Yet all three are rather mere lay figures, to whom has been committed the defense of rusty maxims, and who repeat the same old saws, to the increasing embitterment of Job's racked and tortured soul, than the imposing personalities whose wills clash in deadly conflict on the Greek or Shakespearian stage."[13] It is also a didactic poem, for it is intended to teach the contemporaries of the author "a much-needed lesson on the mysterious discipline of life." There seems good reason, therefore, for following Dillmann in calling it "an epic-dramatic didactic poem."[14]

The Problem of the Book. That the central theme of the book of Job is human suffering, more especially the suffering of the righteous, is generally conceded, but there has been and still is wide divergence of opinion regarding the specific aspect of the question thought to be emphasized and the solution thought to be offered by the author. Some, basing their conclusion almost entirely upon the prologue, find the problem underlying the discussion in the question, "Doth Job fear God for nought?"[15] which is another way of saying, Is there such a thing as disinterested goodness or religion? According to this view the book was written for the purpose of proving that there is a disinterested service of God. Why,

---
[13] A. R. Gordon, *The Poets of the Old Testament*, p. 210.
[14] *Hiob*, p. xxiii.
[15] 1. 9.

THE BOOK OF JOB

then, did the righteous Job suffer? Affliction was sent to test his character;[16] and by remaining loyal to his God he proved his essential and disinterested goodness. No doubt the prologue teaches this lesson, but to make it the theme and purpose of the entire discussion fails to do justice to the book as a whole, and is, to say the least, a precarious proceeding in view of the uncertainty that exists regarding the relation of the prologue to the rest of the book.[17]

Others, seeing in the speeches of Elihu the author's own solution of the problem raised by the suffering of an apparently righteous man, understand the doctrine of the disciplinary or purifying value of suffering to be the principal theme of the book. Budde, for instance, points out that Job, though righteous before the visit of his friends, fell into sin while defending himself against their accusations; moreover, he claims, spiritual pride was latent in Job's nature from the beginning.[18] The object of the suffering was to bring this hidden sin to his consciousness, to lead him to confess it, and thus to purify his spiritual nature. Altogether aside from the critical questions raised by the speeches of Elihu, in view of the subordinate position of the doctrine of the disciplinary value of suffering in the book as a whole, this interpretation also cannot be accepted as offering a satisfactory definition of the theme and purpose of the book as a whole.

Still others consider the aim of the book to be purely negative, to clear the ground of the outworn theory that suffering is always punishment for sin; or, more broadly,

---

[16] A. B. Davidson, *Commentary on the Book of Job*, p. xxvi.
[17] See further on this point, below, pp. 139ff.
[18] *Das Buch Hiob*, pp. xxv, xxxff., etc.

to disprove the theory of retribution which insisted that every man receives exactly and immediately what he deserves: the good, prosperity, the bad, adversity.[19] This theory was advocated by the friends of Job; and there can be no doubt that the author meant to condemn their position, for he introduces Yahweh himself as saying to them: "Ye have not spoken of me the thing that is right";[20] but, like the views already discussed, the interpretation fails to do justice to the book as a whole.

The same criticism may be urged against those who, led astray by some of the rash and radical utterances of Job, can see nothing but skepticism and pessimism in the book. Only a partial and superficial study can account for the inclusion of Job among the skeptics of the Old Testament,[21] or for the designation of the book as "the Song of Songs of Skepticism,"[22] or for its characterization as atheistic, setting forth "the absolute unrighteousness of God as the solution of the problem."[23] Nor does Ewald's interpretation of the book[24] as the dramatic representation of a heroic soul's struggle toward light and peace furnish an entirely adequate explanation.

All these interpretations contain elements of truth, but no one of them expresses fully or adequately the central theme and purpose, in other words, the problem of the book of Job. A comprehensive study of the book as a whole, not of some particular portion, makes it clear that

---

[19] G. B. Gray, *A Critical Introduction to the Old Testament*, pp. 120, 123; Bennett and Adeney, *A Biblical Introduction*, p. 134; H. T. Fowler, *A History of the Literature of Ancient Israel*, p. 335.
[20] 42. 7.
[21] E. J. Dillon, *Sceptics of the Old Testament*.
[22] Friedrich Delitzsch, *Das Buch Hiob*, p. 15.
[23] E. Mueller, *Der echte Hiob*.
[24] *Dichter des Alten Bundes*, vol. iii, pp. 12, 13.

THE BOOK OF JOB

the entire discussion centers around the one question, *How can the suffering of a righteous man be harmonized with the belief that a holy and just God orders the affairs of this world?* The popular view, reflected in the greater part of the Old Testament, was that suffering always comes as punishment for sin, prosperity as reward for piety. This belief appeared to be the only one that could be brought into accord with the righteousness of Yahweh: a righteous God must reward the righteous and punish the wicked. No doubt exceptions to the rule were noted, but as long as the individual was swallowed up in the community, the apparent contradictions of the dogma did not constitute a serious problem. When, however, the individual came to receive proper recognition, an experience like that of Job was bound to create difficulties, for the suffering of a God-fearing man seemed to imply unfairness on the part of the God whom he served and who was thought to govern the world. That this perplexity was keenly felt in Israel may be learned from allusions in the prophetic books and other parts of the Old Testament.[25] At last the time came when a wise man, whose own experience and life may have prompted the effort, sought to solve the problem in the light of all the religious knowledge he possessed. As the basis of the discussion he used the experiences of Job, the tradition of which he may have found common property; but he treated this material with perfect poetic freedom, arranging it in the form of a drama, in which different speakers are introduced, each suggesting his own solution of the problem.

Solutions of the Problem. The solutions suggested in different parts of the book are as follows: 1. The solution of the prologue—Suffering is a test of character. 2.

---
[25] See above, pp. 89ff.

THE PSALMS AND OTHER SACRED WRITINGS

The solution of the three friends—Suffering is always punishment for sin, though at times it may serve also disciplinary ends. 3. The solution of Job—Job struggles long and persistently with the problem; once or twice he seems to have a glimpse of a possible straightening out of the present inequalities in an after life,[26] but it remains a glimpse; he always sinks back to a feeling of uncertainty and perplexity. His general attitude is that there must be something out of gear in the world, for the righteousness of God cannot be seen as things are going now. Even after listening to the speeches of Yahweh he can see no explanation; but now he is ready to place his confidence in God. 4. The solution of Elihu—Elihu agrees with the three friends that there is close connection between suffering and sin; but he emphasizes more than they the disciplinary purpose of suffering which, he points out, is the voice of God calling the sinner to repentance. 5. The solution of Yahweh—To the human mind the whole universe is an unfathomable mystery, in which the evil is no more perplexing than the good. In the presence of all these mysteries the proper attitude is one of faith and humble submission to God. 6. The solution of the epilogue—In a sense the epilogue grants the contention of the friends, for it teaches that righteousness will sooner or later receive its reward even in this world.

The author nowhere states which of these solutions he accepts as true; one thing alone is absolutely certain, namely, that he means to reject emphatically the traditional view of the friends, that suffering must always be regarded as punishment for sin. The failure of the author to commit himself is at least in part responsible for the wide divergence of opinion respecting the pur-

---
[26] Job 19. 23-27.

THE BOOK OF JOB

pose, and teaching of the book. It may well be that he was conscious of his inability to present an entirely satisfactory solution, and, therefore, offered in the epilogue a sort of compromise with the orthodox position of the times. However, it is not unnatural to look in the speeches of Yahweh for a more or less definite indication of the author's preference; and in this expectation the student is not disappointed. For, while these speeches offer no solution in the true sense of the word, they do show, on the one hand, that human intellect alone cannot solve the riddle, and on the other, that the only solution possible is a religious solution, a solution of faith. In the words of George A. Barton: "With a touch too artistic to permit him to descend to a homiletic attitude the poet has shown that his solution of life's problem is a religious one. He had portrayed with great power the inability of man's mind to comprehend the universe or to understand why man must suffer, but he makes Job, his hero, find in a vision of God the secret of life. Job's questions remain unanswered. He cannot solve life's riddle, but is content to trust God, of whose goodness he is convinced, and who, Job is sure, knows the answer. The poet has thus taught that it is in the realm of religion, and not in that of the intellect, that the solution of life's mysteries is found."[27]

It was not easy in the days of the author to exercise such sublime faith, for he had to solve the problem without reference to a future life. Though there may be in the book glimpses of a life after death, or at least cries for a temporary restoration to life, the tone of the book from beginning to end shows that the author neither holds a doctrine of immortality or resurrection, nor

[27] *The Book of Job*, p. 12.

offers it as a solution of the problem of suffering. For a firm faith in a life with God after death there is no acute problem, for it can find its compensations elsewhere; but the basis for this higher solution was established centuries after the composition of Job by Jesus, who brought "life and immortality" to light. His fuller revelation of the truth made it possible to exercise the more vital faith, with a sufficiently high conception of God as a loving Father, and a vision of life comprehensive enough to include eternity, in which the apparent inequalities of this present life may be equalized by a holy and just God.

Original Extent of the Book. According to the preceding paragraphs each division of the book has its own more or less clearly defined place in the development of the argument; nevertheless, questions have been raised concerning the originality of several of these divisions. While prologue and epilogue are accepted as parts of the book in its original form, it is thought by many that they are not the work of the author of the book of Job, but were taken by him from an earlier production; most modern scholars consider the speeches of Elihu a later addition; questions have also been raised concerning the speeches of Yahweh in whole or in part. To these more or less extensive divisions may be added as doubtful, besides a number of shorter passages, chapters 7, 12, 14, 17, 24, 26, 27 and 28; so that, according to many scholars, the book consisted originally only of the prologue, the dialogues between Job and his friends—not in their present but in a simpler form—and the epilogue; and of these the prologue and the epilogue are thought to have been borrowed bodily from an earlier writer. This would leave to the author of the book nothing but the dialogues,

THE BOOK OF JOB

found, with some interpolations, in chapters 3 to 26, or 3 to 31. The purpose of this original book is stated by G. B. Gray in these words: "The purpose of the book—consisting of the prologue, the speeches of the friends and of Job, and the epilogue—is to show the falseness of the prevalent judgment that a man in adversity was necessarily wicked and forsaken of God: the prologue and epilogue alike show the falseness of the judgment in the particular case of Job, and Job in the debate shows that it is widely inapplicable."[28] Are these views regarding the original form and extent of the book of Job justified?

1. *The Prologue and Epilogue.* As has been stated, many scholars deny the prologue and the epilogue to the author of the dialogues between Job and his friends. Especially since the exhaustive investigations and discussions of Budde it has become customary to consider these two sections the beginning and end, if not the main part, of an older prose folk-tale—*Volksbuch*—of Job's sufferings, which the author of the dialogues adopted, and perhaps adapted, as the framework of his own contribution.[29] In support of the view that prologue and epilogue are not from the same hand as the dialogues, attention is called to facts like these: (1) the prologue and epilogue are in prose, the rest of the book is in poetry; (2) in the prologue and epilogue the divine name is *Yahweh,* in the rest of the book it is *El,* or *Eloah,* or *Shaddai.*[30] (3) The Job of the prologue and epilogue

---

[28] *A Critical Introduction to the Old Testament,* p. 123.

[29] *Beitraege zur Kritik des Buches Hiob;* and *Das Buch Hiob,* in *Hand-Kommentar zum Alten Testament.*

[30] Except 12. 9, which many commentators consider an interpolation, and 38. 1, which is simply the introduction to the speeches of Yahweh.

does not seem to be the same as the central figure of the rest of the book: The Job of the prologue is patient, submissive, and resigned, and this is also the Job of the epilogue, for Yahweh commends him without qualification;[31] but the Job of the dialogues is impatient, bitter, and even defiant, and this is the Job whom Yahweh addresses in his speeches when he rebukes him for darkening counsel by words without knowledge, for finding fault and arguing with God.[32] (4) The whole center of interest seems to change as one passes from the prologue and epilogue to the dialogues:[33] In the prologue Job is on trial, and the epilogue testifies that he has stood the test to the divine satisfaction; in the rest of the book it is not the fidelity of Job but the justice of the divine administration of the world that is in question. In the words of Godet: "The Being who is brought to the bar of judgment is in reality not Job, it is Yahweh. The point in debate is not only the virtue of Job; it is at the same time, and in a still higher degree, the justice of God."[34] These facts may not establish diversity of authorship beyond the possibility of doubt;[35] nevertheless, they receive a more satisfactory explanation if it is assumed that prologue and epilogue do not come from the author of the dialogues.[36]

---

[31] 42. 7.
[32] 38. 2; 40. 2.
[33] A. R. Gordon, *The Poets of the Old Testament*, p. 204.
[34] *Old Testament Studies*, p. 186.
[35] J. E. McFadyen, *Old Testament Introduction*, pp. 275, 276; and K. Kautzsch, *Das sogenannte Volksbuch von Hiob, passim*.
[36] See also *Journal of Biblical Literature*, XIV, pp. 63-71, and *American Journal of Semitic Languages*, XIV, pp. 137-164. In order to save at least a part of the present prologue for the author of the dialogue it has been proposed to omit 1. 6-12 and 2. 1-7a as a later interpolation—see, for example, E. Koenig, *Einleitung in das Alte Testament*,

THE BOOK OF JOB

On one point, however, Budde and his followers have gone astray, namely, in making the *Volksbuch* a preexilic production. Karl Kautzsch has shown conclusively that the prologue in its present form cannot have originated in preexilic times.[37] It may, indeed, be that there was current in Israel before the exile a tradition of a righteous man Job who, in spite of extraordinary affliction, remained faithful to his God,[38] but this popular story probably lacked the didactic element so prominent in the present prologue. A postexilic writer used this tradition or folk-tale in producing what has been called "the first draft" of Job—the *Volksbuch* of Budde. The date and purpose of this *Volksbuch* can be determined only on the basis of internal evidence. The idea of the Satan, or adversary, for instance, appears to be somewhat in advance of that found in Zech. 3. 1ff.,[39] and the problem raised by the prosperity of the wicked and the affliction of the righteous seems to have been especially troublesome in the days of Malachi.[40] It may well be, therefore, that the prose story of Job, of which the prologue and epilogue of the present book of Job were a part, was written in the age of Malachi "to cheer the downcast hearts of the people of God in those troublous times that followed the restoration, when the righteous suffered and the wicked saw long and prosperous years

---

p. 415, and compare E. Sellin, *Einleitung in das Alte Testament*, p. 118—but if these sections are omitted, the rest of the prologue loses all significance.

[37] K. Kautzsch, *Das sogenannte Volksbuch von Hiob*, pp. 22ff. Compare also J. E. McFadyen, *Old Testament Introduction*, p. 276; N. Schmidt, *Messages of the Poets*, pp. 97ff.

[38] Compare Ezek. 14. 14, 20.

[39] B. C. 520.

[40] About B. C. 450; compare Mal 2. 17 to 4. 3, and see above, p. 91.

and devout souls were often sadly tempted to renounce their faith, for it seemed so profitless to serve God in sincerity. By the picture of Job, the upright, suffering the loss of all things, and even the extreme of personal agony, yet holding fast his faith in God, and even blessing the hand that smote, the writer encourages the suffering saints of his own day to bear their afflictions bravely; for these are not, as they imagine in their heaviness of heart, the outpouring of the divine wrath because of their sins, but the test by which God is even now revealing before angels and men the sterling purity of their faith and piety. Thus, if they hold fast their integrity, as Job did, they too will be witnesses for God in their generation; and soon he will arise in his glory to champion their cause, and will bless their latter end more than their beginning."[41]

The tone of the epilogue, which may have formed the close of the prose story, suggests that it was preceded by speeches of the friends in very much the same strain as the utterance of Job's wife,[42] and by replies of Job, not full of impatience and rebellion like his speeches in the present book, but full of faith and humble submission; hence the commendation of Job and the condemnation of the friends.[43] The author of the present book, taught perhaps by bitter experience, felt that the treatment of the problem in the prose story was inadequate; his own faith may have been severely tried, he may have been driven almost to despair by mysterious suffering, he may have had to endure the heartless consolation of friends who showed no real sympathy, and in spite of it all he

---

[41] A. R. Gordon, *The Poets of the Old Testament*, pp. 207, 208.
[42] 2. 9.
[43] 42. 7, 8.

THE BOOK OF JOB

may have gloriously triumphed in the end. Such may have been the experience òf the man who, while retaining the opening and closing sections of the *Volksbuch* as a suitable framework, introduced between the two his own more profound discussion of the problem, picturing in the speeches of Job the bitter agony and despair which he himself experienced until he found rest in patient submission to God.

2. *The Speeches of Elihu.* Driver calls the view that the Elihu speeches were not a part of the original book of Job "the general opinion of commentators and critics."[44] Important exceptions are Budde, Wildeboer, Cornill, and a few other scholars, who not only defend the authenticity of these speeches, but find in them the real solution of the problem of the book.[45] Against the originality of these chapters the following considerations are urged: (1) Elihu is not mentioned in the prologue nor, what is more significant, in the epilogue. The silence of the prologue might be explained by the fact that Elihu does not join in the principal debate, which is between Job and his friends, and that 32. 1-5 furnishes a suitable and adequate introduction. The silence of the epilogue, however, is not so easily explained, for Yahweh passes judgment on Job and his friends; and if Elihu had been one of the participants in the debate, would Yahweh have passed him over in silence? (2) Not only are the speeches of Elihu loosely connected with the poem as a

---

[44] *Introduction to the Literature of the Old Testament*, p. 428.

[45] See above, p. 133; hence Cornill calls the speeches of Elihu "the crown of the book of Job," *Einleitung in das Alte Testament*, p. 237; the most exhaustive discussion is that of Budde, found in *Beitraege zur Erklaerung des Buches Hiob*, his commentary on *Hiob*, in Nowack's *Hand-Kommentar* series and in his *Geschichte der althebraeischen Litteratur*.

whole, so that they might easily be omitted without affecting the argument, but, what is much more significant, they actually are a disturbing element in the discussion. They interrupt the connection between the dramatic appeal to Yahweh at the close of Job's defense[46] and Yahweh's appearance,[47] while the opening words of Yahweh[48] imply that he speaks in immediate reply to Job's challenge; moreover, Elihu anticipates, at least in part, the argument of Yahweh.[49] (3) The speeches of Elihu do not contribute anything essentially new to the argument. Following in the footsteps of the friends, he connects Job's sufferings with his sins.[50] True, he places greater emphasis than they upon suffering as an expression of the divine goodness, sent for disciplinary purposes;[51] but Eliphaz had already advanced the same argument[52] and Job had rejected it.[53] In language and style chapters 32 to 37 differ materially from the rest of the book. The style, says Driver, "is prolix, labored, and sometimes tautologous; the power and brilliancy which are so conspicuous in the poem generally are sensibly missing. The reader, as he passes from Job and his three friends to Elihu, is conscious at once that he has before him the work of a writer, not indeed devoid of literary skill, but certainly inferior in literary and poetical genius to the author of the rest of the book. The language is often involved and the thought strained; these

---

[46] 31. 35–37.
[47] 38. 1.
[48] 38. 2.
[49] Compare Chapters 36, 37.
[50] 34. 37.
[51] 33. 14–30; 36. 8–25.
[52] 5. 8ff., 17ff.
[53] 6. 24ff.

THE BOOK OF JOB

speeches are marked also by many peculiarities of expression, and by a deeper coloring of Aramaic than the poem generally."[54] Budde admits the presence of these differences, and goes so far as to say that the more he fixes his attention on the whole rather than on details, the stronger the impression becomes that there is a marked difference between the style of Elihu and that of the rest of the book; and that these differences would be sufficiently striking to establish diversity of authorship if they could not be explained as due to interpolation and corruption of the text. With the troublesome passages[55] removed, he thinks the reasons for denying the speeches to the author of the rest of the book disappear.

In the nature of the case, absolute certainty cannot be had, but the evidence against the authenticity of the Elihu speeches appears stronger than any consideration that may be urged in their favor. On the whole, it seems reasonable to conclude that they were added to the original book of Job by a serious thinker who felt that the preceding dialogues were defective in some points, which shortcoming he desired to correct: (1) In rebuke of Job's attitude, which he thought was lacking in reverence, he laid greater stress on the greatness, power, and love of God, which should inspire reverence in man. (2) In rebuke of the ineffective arguments of the friends he seeks to show that any arguments that will silence Job must be drawn from the character and attributes of God. (3) Feeling that insufficient weight has been given to

---

[54] *Introduction to the Literature of the Old Testament*, p. 429.

[55] 32. 2-5, 11, 12, 15-17; 33. 4, 15b, 33; 34. 9, 10a, 25-28, 29c; 35. 4; 36. 13, 14, 17, 25, 26, 29, 30; 37. 13, 15, 16. It is always precarious to omit passages simply because they refuse to support a theory. In this case there are no other reasons for these wholesale omissions.

the disciplinary value of suffering, he seeks to supply this lack.

3. *The Speeches of Yahweh.* Even some scholars who believe that Yahweh appeared as one of the speakers in the book from the beginning doubt the originality of the speeches placed in the mouth of Yahweh in their present form. Questions are raised, for instance, regarding the descriptions of Behemoth and Leviathan.[56] It is pointed out that "the heavy sensuous art of the descriptions . . . stands in broad contrast to the swift, imaginative beauty of the preceding pictures of natural life and order. Their effect is, further, to divert attention from the main issue of the poem." Emphasis is also placed on the difference in the use of the word "leviathan" in 41. 1 as compared with 3. 8,[57] on the fact that all the other animal pictures are drawn from the desert, and on the unnecessary postponement of the crisis between Yahweh and Job, for which the sympathetic reader is impatiently waiting. In reply to the objections it has been urged that the descriptions are needed to complete Yahweh's argument: whereas the preceding chapters were to convince Job of his ignorance, these are to convince him of his impotence. The arguments against the originality of the descriptions of Behemoth and Leviathan cannot be considered conclusive; and yet it must be admitted that the plea of Yahweh would gain in dignity and power if they were omitted and certain other changes were made that would inevitably follow the omission.

If the section indicated were eliminated, the second speech of Yahweh would lose its significance as an independent speech; which may suggest that originally there

---

[56] 40. 15 to 41. 34.
[57] In the latter passage the mythological element is very pronounced.

THE BOOK OF JOB

was only one utterance of Yahweh. Moreover, the words introducing the second speech[58] seem to be only a variant of 38. 1-3, and Job's reply in 40. 3-5 does not read smoothly after 40. 1, 2. These peculiarities have led many modern scholars to regard chapters 38 and 39 *plus* 40. 2, 8-14 as one speech of Yahweh, and 40. 3-5 *plus* 42. 2-6, exclusive of some clauses which seem to have been introduced from the speech of Yahweh, as one reply of the awestruck Job.

Others favor more radical measures: Disappointed because the words of Yahweh offer no direct solution of the problem, they deny to these chapters a place in the original book of Job. They consider them a later addition written for the purpose of exalting the greatness and glory of Yahweh, without any attempt to solve the problem beyond suggesting that it is a mystery which should be treated with reverence by man.[59] The objections urged against the speeches of Yahweh, or against one great, impressive speech are by no means conclusive: (1) The difference in the attitude of Yahweh toward Job, as compared with the attitude reflected in the prologue and epilogue—in the prologue and epilogue he defends and commends him, in the speech he accuses him of folly[60]— is easily explained, because (*a*) the prologue and epilogue were taken from an earlier work, and (*b*) the rebuke of Job was due to Job's impatience manifested in the dialogues with his friends. (2) The objection that this view implies that "what the Satan had been unable to achieve by depriving Job of riches, children, and health,

---
[58] 40. 6, 7.
[59] T. K. Cheyne, *Job and Solomon*, p. 69; N. Schmidt, *Messages of the Poets*, pp. 90, 91; Buchanan Blake, *The Book of Job and the Problem of Suffering*, pp. 185ff.
[60] 38. 2.

the friends by their persistent presentation of a banal orthodoxy that had no relation to the facts in Job's life did achieve" carries no weight against Yahweh's words; it could be used only against Job's own words uttered in the course of the debate. (3) The fact that Job recognized the divine power and wisdom before Yahweh's appearance[61] does not make the speeches of the latter superfluous. The vision and words of Yahweh gave him an appreciation of the divine transcendence such as he had not had before; for this is the meaning of Job's confession:

> I had heard of thee by the hearing of the ear;
> But now mine eye seeth thee.[62]

(4) The nearness of Job's self-condemnation in 42. 3 to Yahweh's commendation in 42. 7 constitutes no real difficulty. The self-condemnation proved to Yahweh that his purpose, to bring Job to his senses, had been successfully accomplished, and that the time for showing approval had arrived. And if this explanation seems unsatisfactory, all difficulty disappears on the twofold assumption for which there is abundant support, (a) that the original book of Job contained only one speech of Yahweh and one reply of Job; if so, 42. 3 may have been brought in at a later time from 38. 2; and (b) that the author of the rest of the book took the prologue and epilogue from an earlier prose work. While, thus, the arguments against the originality of the Yahweh speeches are inconclusive, their omission would take the very heart out of the discussion. It is quite safe, therefore, to conclude that the original book of Job contained at least one speech of Yahweh.

---

[61] 9. 4-10; 12. 12-25.
[62] 42. 5.

THE BOOK OF JOB

4. *The Soliloquy on Wisdom.* If chapters 38ff. reproduce correctly at least the substance of Yahweh's utterance, and if this address was in the book from the beginning, it becomes exceedingly difficult to accept the soliloquy on wisdom in chapter 28 as a part of the original discussion. According to chapter 28 Job expresses the conviction that wisdom, by which the author means "the intellectual apprehension of the principles by which the course of the physical world and the events of human life are regulated," belongs in its fullness only to God; as a substitute God has imposed upon man the duty of living a holy and righteous life. But if Job had attained to this submissive frame of mind at the close of the debate with his friends, why was it necessary for Yahweh to appear in order to bring him into this attitude? Moreover, if Job had come to this conviction at that point in the discussion, how is it that it exerted no influence whatever on his subsequent utterances? In the final summing up of his case,[63] sometimes called Job's *Apologia pro Vita Sua*, which immediately follows the soliloquy, he reveals the same bitterness, impatience, and rebellion which marked his earlier speeches. It has, indeed, been suggested that the author regarded Job's tranquil state of mind as temporary only; but this assumption would make the transition too abrupt, and the context gives no hint as to any cause for either the coming or the passing of such temporary tranquillity. Budde's explanation, that the chapter reflects a spirit, not of resignation, but of dissatisfaction and despair,[64] removes this difficulty, but it is without support in the text: chapter 28 reveals no trace of resentment and bitterness; on the contrary, it

---
[63] Chapters 29 to 31.
[64] *Das Buch Hiob*, pp. xxvii, 156.

makes the impression that the speaker finds entire satisfaction in the truth expressed. The soliloquy might possibly be saved for the author of the rest of the book by removing it from its present position and assigning it a more suitable place, perhaps after 42. 6; but on the whole it may be better to regard it as an independent fragment of choice wisdom poetry, similar to Prov. 8, which found a place in the book of Job at a later time. Both in literary and religious power the chapter ranks with the best parts of the book.

5. *Original Form of the Third Cycle.*[65] In the first two cycles the discussion proceeds smoothly and consistently, but the third cycle presents peculiarities as well as difficulties: (1) Zophar is absent; (2) the speech of Bildad is unusually brief; (3) though chapters 26 to 31 are all placed in the mouth of Job, there are three distinct introductions.[66] (4) Chapter 26. 5-14 seems unsuitable in the mouth of Job at this stage of the argument; on the other hand, it closely resembles chapter 25 and furnishes an appropriate continuation of Bildad's speech. (5) In 27. 7-23 Job appears to go back on the position defended by him previously and resumed in chapters 29 to 31, and to adopt the position of the friends. It is not easy to remove these difficulties without rearranging a part of the utterances in the cycle. The discussion progresses more smoothly if rearranged as follows: Eliphaz, chapter 22; Job, chapters 23, 24; Bildad, 25. 1-3; 26. 5-14; Job, 26. 1-4; 27. 2-6, 11, 12; Zophar, 27. 7-10, 13-23; Job, chapters 29 to 31.

There are various questions centering around passages in addition to those discussed in the preceding para-

---
[65] Chapters 22 to 31.
[66] 26. 1; 27. 1; 29. 1.

THE BOOK OF JOB

graphs, which have bearing on the original form and extent of the book of Job, but these can be discussed adequately only in connection with a detailed exegetical study. However, the facts and considerations already presented warrant the conclusion that the book of Job in its original form consisted of the prologue, taken probably from a somewhat earlier prose work, the dialogues between Job and his friends, one impressive utterance of Yahweh followed by a confession of Job, and the epilogue, coming from the same source as the prologue. Of extensive sections, therefore, chapter 28 and the speeches of Elihu would have to be considered additions by a later hand or by later hands.[67]

Date and Authorship of the Book. Jewish tradition preserved in the Talmud[68] makes Moses the author of the book of Job, and this view has had defenders among scholars until recent times. In support of this view attention has been called to the undoubtedly primitive aspect of the book: it has been claimed, for instance, that there are no references to Mosaic laws and observances, that there is complete silence regarding some of the most important events in Hebrew history, such as the exodus, the desert wanderings, the conquest, as well as events during later periods; that the commonly used divine

---

[67] E. Sellin, who admits that the book in its present form cannot have been written by one author at one and the same time, still insists that, with the exception of the prologue and epilogue, the book is the work of one single author, who wrestled with the problem during his entire life and produced different sections at different times to express different stages in his contemplation of the problem of suffering. *Einleitung in das Alte Testament*, p. 121.

[68] F. C. Eiselen, *The Books of the Pentateuch*, p. 86. Some writers, both ancient and modern, have assigned the book even to pre-Mosaic days.

THE PSALMS AND OTHER SACRED WRITINGS

names are the primitive *El* and *Eloah,* Yahweh being used very rarely in the body of the book, that the civilization reflected is that of patriarchal times, etc. But can facts like these, even if true, determine the date of the production? Does not the assignment of the book to an early date on the basis of such evidence involve a confusion between the period in which the hero is thought to have lived and that in which the record of his experiences assumed its present literary form? Are these primitive features beyond the power of a skillful writer of a later date to conceive and represent? On the other hand, closer examination has brought to light unmistakable indications of a later, post-Mosaic date. Among the more important of these the following may be mentioned: (1) References to laws and legal practices that had their origin subsequently to the age of Moses.[69] (2) The book presupposes an advanced state of society, and a considerable range and faculty of observation on the part of its author. (3) The book presupposes much reflection on the problems of life and society. (4) The great literary power of the poem, its finished form, and the ability which its author displays not merely of expounding a subject briefly, but of developing it under different aspects in a regularly progressing argument, implies that a mature stage of literary culture had been reached. (5) The theology and ethics of the book point to a date subsequent to the great eighth-century prophets. (6) The language reveals characteristics of a late date.[70] As a result of these considerations the Mosaic date and authorship have now been given up by practically all scholars; but no consensus of

---
[69] See further, below, p. 155.
[70] S. R. Driver, *Introduction to the Literature of the Old Testament,* p. 432.

THE BOOK OF JOB

opinion regarding the exact date of the book has been reached. Luther was the first to suggest that the book may have been written by one of the wise men who flourished during the reign of King Solomon, a view strongly advocated during the nineteenth century by Haevernick, Delitzsch, Zoeckler, and other adherents of the more conservative school.[71] The principal support for this theory was found in the similarities between Job and some psalms credited to David,[72] and between Job and Proverbs 1 to 9, believed by these scholars to be the work of Solomon. Unfortunately, the relevant psalms and the section in Proverbs which seems to have most in common with Job are now generally considered late and are assigned to the postexilic age. Moreover, though it is no easy task to determine priority in cases of literary parallels, in some cases the author of Job is clearly the borrower.[73] Further support has been found in the alleged dependence of Amos, Isaiah, and other preexilic writers upon Job;[74] but here again the dependence is more likely on the side of Job.

Internal evidence appears to favor a still later date: Several passages[75] read like reminiscences of a recent national disaster, perhaps the captivity of Israel in B. C. 722 or that of Judah in B. C. 586. Those who believe that the former furnished the background favor a date soon after the fall of Samaria. Thus the book has been

---

[71] It has even been ascribed to King Solomon himself.
[72] For example, Psalms 8, 39, 88, 107.
[73] For example, Job 7. 17 seems to be a parody on Psalm 8. 5.
[74] Compare Job 9. 8, 9 with Amos 4. 13 and 5. 8; 12. 15 with Amos, 9. 6; 18. 16 with Amos 2. 9; 30. 31 with Amos 8. 10; 14. 11 with Isa. 19. 5, etc.
[75] For example, 9. 24; 12. 6, 13-25; 24. 12.

THE PSALMS AND OTHER SACRED WRITINGS

credited to a contemporary of Isaiah,[76] or to some one living between Isaiah and Jeremiah, perhaps during the bloody reign of Manasseh, whose persecutions of the faithful Yahweh worshipers must have made the problem of the sufferings of the righteous an acute one,[77] or to a contemporary of the prophet Jeremiah.[78]

However, in the light of the internal evidence outlined below it seems impossible to assign the book to a preexilic date; on the other hand, there are strong reasons for bringing it down to the later postexilic age, probably not earlier than B. C. 400:[79] (1) The author must have lived subsequently to Jeremiah. (a) There seems to be some kind of literary connection between Job 3 and Jer. 20. 14-18; and a close examination of the two passages makes it clear that the priority is on the side of the prophet. "Jeremiah was in no mood for quotation, his words are brief and abrupt. The book of Job is a highly artistic poem, and it is much more probable that Job 3 is an elaboration of the passionate words of Jeremiah than that Jeremiah adapted in his sorrow the longer lament of Job."[80] (b) The rise of the problem discussed in Job presupposes the teaching of Jeremiah, and of his younger contemporary Ezekiel. It was the suffering of the righteous *individual* Job that created the troublesome problem, but no problem of this sort could be felt until after the religious value of the individual had come

---

[76] Noeldeke, Merx, Hitzig, Reuss, etc.
[77] Bleek, Ewald, Schrader, C. H. H. Wright, W. T. Davison, etc.
[78] Kleinert, Koenig, etc.
[79] This is the date favored by a majority of recent writers; some assign the book to an even later date; Cornill, *Einleitung in das Alte Testament*, p. 348, suggests a date after B. C. 250; compare also Stade, *Geschichte des Volkes Israel*, II, pp. 348ff.
[80] J. E. McFadyen, *Old Testament Introduction*, p. 279.

THE BOOK OF JOB

to be recognized, which resulted directly from the teaching of Jeremiah and Ezekiel.[81] (c) The author's familiarity with Deuteronomy points in the same direction.[82] Though definite references to laws are rare in the book of Job, as in all wisdom literature, in a few cases the author's familiarity with Hebrew legal requirements betrays itself, and in some of these instances the reference is to Deuteronomic laws.[83] (2) The nature of the discussion is in advance of Ezekiel. In emphasizing the doctrine of personal responsibility the latter proposes an extremely mechanical doctrine of retribution, which made no provision for the kind of exceptions represented by the experiences of Job. The central teaching of the book of Job is that Ezekiel's doctrine is untenable; evidently, that doctrine had been weighed and found wanting.[84] (3) The verses which are thought to reflect a serious national calamity[85] receive a perfectly natural meaning when they are interpreted as referring back to the fall of Jerusalem in B. C. 586. (4) The figure of Satan appears again in the Old Testament only in Zech.

---

[81] For example, Jer. 12. 1, 2; 31. 29, 30; Ezek. 18 and 33. The mere fact that the problem of suffering has occupied the human mind from earliest times throws no light on the question of the date of the book of Job. That must be determined from the thought development in Israel, not from the literature of Babylonia or Egypt.

[82] For the date of Deuteronomy, see F. C. Eiselen, *The Books of the Pentateuch*, Chapter XII.

[83] Compare, for example, Job 22. 6 and 24. 9 with Deut. 24. 17; 24. 2 with Deut. 19. 14; 31. 9-11, 26-28 with Deut. 4. 19; 17. 3-7; 22. 22.

[84] Some have inferred from the mention of Job in Ezek. 14. 14, 20 that Ezekiel knew the book of Job, but all that may legitimately be inferred from these verses is that the prophet knew *the tradition of Job*, which is something entirely different from knowing the book in its present literary form.

[85] 9. 24; 12. 6, 13-25; 24. 12.

THE PSALMS AND OTHER SACRED WRITINGS

3 and in 1 Chron. 21. 1. The Chronicles passage marks an advance over Job because there the term has become a proper name, "Satan," while here, as in Zech. 3, it is still an appellative, "*the* satan," or "the adversary", on the other hand, in Job the position of "the adversary" is more dignified and secure than in Zechariah; which may indicate that Job is later than Zechariah, who prophesied about B. C. 520. (5) Attention has been called[86] to the similarity between the temper of the book of Job and the temper of the pious in the days of Malachi,[87] and between the solution of the problem suggested in the prologue and that of Malachi. Because of these striking resemblances the age of Malachi, about B. C. 450, was suggested as a suitable date for the *Volksbuch* of Job. But the rest of the book, even in its original extent, implies further and more profound reflection upon the problem. Thus, internal evidence, as well as comparison with other Old Testament books, would seem to point to about B. C. 400 as the most probable date of the book of Job.[88]

This conclusion is corroborated by other, though in some instances less direct, evidence: (1) Language and style. "The syntax," says Driver, "is extremely idiomatic; but the vocabulary contains a very noticeable admixture of Aramaic words, and (in a minor degree) of words explicable only from the Arabic."[89] So also

---
[86] See above, p. 141.
[87] Especially Mal. 2. 17; 3. 14.
[88] Sellin objects to a date after Ezra-Nehemiah on the ground that, had the author lived at that time, his silence concerning the Law as an expression of the divine will would be inexplicable. It should be remembered, however, that the wisdom literature as a whole refers but rarely to the Law.
[89] *Introduction to the Literature of the Old Testament*, p. 434; he favors a date "either during or shortly after the Babylonian captivity."

THE BOOK OF JOB

G. B. Gray, "The prose might well belong to the same age as Ruth; it is altogether superior to that of Esther or Daniel, and contains neither Greek words, like Daniel, nor Persian words, like Esther, Daniel, and other late books. On the other hand, there is a considerable Aramaic tinge to the language of the book. The language could be well explained as that of a work written after, yet not too long after, the Exile."[90] (2) The angelology of the book[91] and its easy use of mythology.[92] The angelology is in advance of Zech. 1-8, but not as highly developed as in Daniel. Monotheism seems to have been so firmly established that the use of mythology was in no danger of being misunderstood. (3) The absence of a definite doctrine of immortality or of life after death. True, 19. 25-27 marks a step in the direction of such doctrine, but it falls short of the conviction expressed in Dan. 12. 2 or even in Isa. 26. 19.[93] (4) Familiarity with the Pentateuch in its present form. The events of the book are located in the patriarchal age; the author seems to have gathered his information regarding primitive conditions not from any one of the Pentateuchal sources, but from the completed work.[94] (5) The use of Psalm 8. 5 in Job 7. 17, 18. If Psalm 8 is based upon the P account of creation,[95] it must be a postexilic poem; a parody of it, such as Job 7. 17, 18 seems to be, cannot, then, be earlier than the time of Ezra. All these different

---

[90] *A Critical Introduction to the Old Testament*, p. 127; the date suggested is about B. C. 400.
[91] 5. 1.
[92] 3. 8; 26. 5.
[93] Isa. 24 to 27 may come from the fourth century B. C.
[94] F. C. Eiselen, *The Books of the Pentateuch*, pp. 247ff.; 308-312.
[95] Compare especially Gen. 1. 27-30.

THE PSALMS AND OTHER SACRED WRITINGS

lines of evidence seem to point conclusively to about B. C. 400 as the date of the book of Job.

Historical Character of the Book. The didactic value and permanent significance of the book of Job are entirely independent of the question of historicity; nevertheless, it is of interest to seek an answer to the question, Is the book to be understood as strictly historical, or is it entirely a work of the imagination, or is it partly one and partly the other? Among the Jews and among Christians up to, and to some extent even after, the period of the Reformation the book was for the most part viewed as veritable history of things said and done.[96] Only here and there doubts were expressed: The Talmud has preserved the opinion of one early rabbi that Job never existed and that the book was merely a parable; Theodore of Mopsuestia,[97] while believing in the historicity of the man Job, considered the book a work of fiction and a wicked slander on the character of the patriarch; the renowned Jewish teacher Maimonides also expressed doubts regarding the historical character of the book.

Luther admitted the presence of a historical basis, but denied that the book recorded exact history. This is the opinion of a majority of modern writers, who hold that "on a basis of historical fact the writer has built up an imaginative poem dealing with the question of the sufferings of the righteous and their justification under the government of a righteous God."[98] In support of the

---

[96] It was generally held that if this position were given up, the book could be considered nothing but a fraud.

[97] In the fifth century A. D.

[98] W. T. Davison, *The Wisdom Literature of the Old Testament*, p. 27. "It is hardly conceivable," says the same author—pp. 27, 28—"that the author intended the scenes in heaven of Chapters 1 and 2 to be interpreted literally, or meant it to be understood that the long ad-

THE BOOK OF JOB

historicity of Job attention is called to Ezek. 14. 14, 20, where Job is named, by the side of Noah and Daniel, as renowned because of his righteousness.[99] But since the book of Job is later than Ezekiel,[100] the prophet cannot have secured his information from the book; hence it becomes necessary to assume the existence among the Hebrews of a tradition, oral or written, of a pious and perfect man by the name of Job, who in the face of the severest trials and sufferings remained loyal to his God and was finally delivered from all his dangers and distress. How much of the material in the present book was a part of this early tradition cannot be determined. It may have included the main facts recorded in the prologue and epilogue; the piety and wealth of Job, the loss of his property and children, the affliction with a dreadful disease, and his fidelity and ultimate deliverance. Other elements in the prologue and the rest of the book were supplied by the author of the *Volksbuch* or by the author of the biblical book of Job.

If the names of the persons and places mentioned in the book were a part of the early tradition, as is more than likely, it becomes quite certain that the story

---

dresses of Chapters 38 to 41 came directly as a voice from the skies. The numbers used in the prologue and epilogue are evidently symbolical and ideal. It is unlikely that the calamities described in Chapter 1 should fall with the dramatic suddenness and regularity that is there described, precisely one survivor only in each case being left to tell the tale. Further, the character of the speeches of Job and his friends is tolerably conclusive. Never did sufferer *in extremis* compose such elaborate poetical deliverances, or a number of friends meet to condole with him express themselves extemporaneously in sentences and images suggestive of the greatest skill of constructive genius."

[99] It may be well to remember that such a literary allusion can in no wise establish the historicity of the person or event referred to; see F. C. Eiselen, *The Minor Prophets*, pp. 318, 319.

[100] See above, p. 155.

THE PSALMS AND OTHER SACRED WRITINGS

originated outside of Israel, which may account for the difficulty of finding a satisfactory Hebrew explanation of the name "Job."[101] But there is wide difference of opinion as to the home of the hero and his friends. Many authors favor a district in or near Edom, for they insist that wherever else in the Old Testament the names occur they belong to that general region.[102] On the other hand, there is evidence pointing to a district farther to the north as the location of Uz;[103] moreover, Wetzstein, Barton, and others have pointed out that the localities named in the book may all be identified with places eastward of the Sea of Galilee, in the district known as Hauran; and that the tradition placing the story in the Hauran is older than that locating it in or near Edom. Barton, therefore, argues very strongly in favor of the Hauran as the home of the story of Job.[104]

The discovery of a Babylonian poem which presents numerous parallels to the book of Job has raised the question whether the story of Job may not have had a

---

[101] See above, p. 125.

[102] Lamentations 4. 21 connects Uz with Edom; see also Jer. 25. 20, but compare Gen. 10. 23; 22. 21, which connect Uz with Aram; Eliphaz and Teman are connected with Edom in Gen. 36. 11, 42, and Teman in Jer. 49. 7; Shuhite may be connected with Shuah, one of the sons of Abraham by Keturah, Gen. 25. 2; if so, the name points to the southeast; if Naamah is connected with the name of the daughter of Lamech, Gen. 4. 22, the name would point to the territory of the Kenites, near Edom. It is also worthy of note that the apocryphal addition to Job in the Septuagint identifies Job with the Edomite king Jobab, Gen. 36. 33, and locates him on the borders of Arabia and Edom.

[103] For example, Gen. 10. 23 and 22. 21. The Black Obelisk inscription of Shalmaneser III, line 154, mentions an Uz in the far north. Josephus, *Antiquities*, I, VI, 4, says, "Of the four sons of Aram Uz founded Trachonitis and Damascus."

[104] G. A. Barton, "The Original Home of the Story of Job," in *Journal of Biblical Literature*, XXXI, pp. 63–68.

THE BOOK OF JOB

Babylonian origin.[105] It is by no means certain, however, that there exists any kind of literary connection between the two stories: the similarities may be due to similarity of theme rather than to conscious or even unconscious borrowing. But if the nature of the resemblances should convince anyone that the biblical story is dependent on the Babylonian tradition, he must still admit the justice of Barton's statement: "It is quite clear that, if the story traveled westward from Babylonia, it traveled orally in bare outline, shorn of all local features. The name of the sufferer, Job, is quite different from the name of Ṭâbi-utul-Bêl, and the localities mentioned in our biblical story, indefinite as they are, certainly have nothing to do with the neighborhood of Nippur."[106]

While it may be impossible to determine with absolute certainty the original home of the story of Job, on the whole a locality to the southeast or the northeast of Palestine, near the borders of the great desert, is the most probable. From there it had to travel but a short distance to the territory of the Hebrews. The imported traditional material, the historical character of which can be neither proved nor disproved, was worked over, first into a prose-story, then, with various modifications and expansions, into the present book of Job.

---

[105] Morris Jastrow, in *Journal of Biblical Literature*, XXV, pp. 135–191; *Die Religion Babyloniens und Assyriens*, II, pp. 120–133; *The Civilization of Babylonia and Assyria*, pp. 374–383.

[106] *Journal of Biblical Literature*, XXXI, p. 64.

CHAPTER VI

THE SONG OF SONGS

CHAPTER VI

THE SONG OF SONGS[1]

Name. The title of the book in Hebrew is "The Song of Songs,[2] which is Solomon's";[3] hence it is known also as "Song of Solomon." "Song of Songs" is equivalent to "the best" or "the noblest of songs,"[4] and means to suggest that this is the best of the songs for which Solomon was famous.[5] The ascription to Solomon[6] is probably an inference on the part of a later writer[7] from the fact that Solomon is the most important personage named in the book.

Interpretation. The Song of Songs has been called the

---

[1] In the Jewish canon the book of Job is followed by a group of five short books known as the five *Megilloth*, or Rolls, so called because each of the five was written on a separate roll. The five books are still read on certain sacred days in the synagogues. The Song of Songs is read on the feast of Passover, the book of Ruth on the day of Pentecost, the book of Lamentations on the ninth day of the month Ab, on which day the destruction of Jerusalem is commemorated, the book of Ecclesiastes on the feast of Tabernacles, and the book of Esther on the feast of Purim.

[2] Hebrew שִׁיר הַשִּׁירִים *Shir hashshirim*, Septuagint, ᾀσμα ᾀσμάτων, *Āsma āsmatōn*, Vulgate, *Canticum canticorum*.

[3] 1. 1.

[4] Compare "holy of holies," that is, the most holy place.

[5] Compare 1 Kings 4. 32.

[6] The translation "which is concerning Solomon," while possible, is not probable; the author of the title probably meant to indicate authorship; see above, on psalm titles, p. 47.

[7] That the title does not come from the author of the book is suggested by the use of a form of the relative pronoun that is never used in the body of the book.

enigma of the Old Testament. It is such not only because of the obscurity of certain details but also because of the uncertainty regarding the interpretation of the book as a whole.

1. *The Allegorical Interpretation.* The book owes its place in the canon of Sacred Scripture in large measure to what may be called the allegorical, or mystical, or spiritual interpretation, which has been applied to it from very early times.[8] Though minor variations may be traced, the general Jewish view was that the book portrayed the close and loving relationship between Yahweh and Israel, manifested through the whole of its history, or, according to the Targum, from the Exodus to the coming of the future Messiah. The allegorical interpretation was accepted, without question, by the early church fathers, but they looked upon Solomon as the representative of Jesus the Christ, and the Shulammite as representing his bride, the church or the individual soul. Thus, according to the allegorical interpretation among Christians, the Song of Songs furnishes a picture of the intimate spiritual fellowship between Jesus the Christ and

---

[8] Like the books of Ecclesiastes and Esther, the Song of Songs had to struggle long and hard to secure a permanent place in the canon. Even after the final decision in favor of its canonicity at the Council of Jamnia, about A. D. 90, there seem to have been many Jews who failed to show proper respect for it, for about A. D. 120 Rabbi Akiba found it necessary to utter these words of warning: "Whoever sings from the Song of Songs in the wine-houses, making it a common song, shall have no share in the world to come." A fear for the standing of the book may be responsible for the assertion of the same rabbi: "The whole world does not outweigh the day on which the Song of Songs was given to Israel; all the Writings are holy, but the Song is the holiest of all." It may also be due to a sense of insecurity as to its spiritual interpretation that the prohibition was laid down that no Jew must read the book until he had reached the mature age of thirty years.

THE SONG OF SONGS

the church or the individual soul. For centuries Christian commentators, almost without exception, adopted unhesitatingly this interpretation.[9] As a modern example of this type of interpretation W. T. Davison quotes these words of Bishop Wordsworth:[10] "All the ancient Christian expositors agree in the opinion that the Song of Solomon represents the pure love and mystical union and marriage of Christ and his church. They teach us to see in this divine book of Holy Scripture a prophetical representation of Christ's incarnation, of his preaching, of his passion, when he purchased his Bride with his own blood, of his glorious Resurrection and Ascension into heaven, of the sending of the Holy Ghost, of the propagation of the gospel, the call of the Gentiles, and the future conversion of the Jews. . . . We must accept this spiritual interpretation of the Canticles if we would not degrade it into an amatory ballad and voluptuous ditty, and distort it into a strange and chimerical portraiture of unnatural and portentous monstrosities, unworthy of the Divine Author of Holy Writ."[11]

This quotation furnishes an outline of the teaching of the book according to the allegorical interpretation, and at the same time suggests the reason why it was proposed in the first place, and why it has maintained its hold for so many centuries: it was feared that a literal interpretation would reduce the book to the level of a purely human production, not worthy of a place in the canon of Sacred

---

[9] Origen wrote a ten-volume commentary on the book in which he gives a detailed exposition of the allegorical view; Bernard of Clairvaux wrote eighty-six sermons on the first two chapters; and many other writers give evidence of the profound influence exerted upon their spiritual life by the Song of Songs allegorically interpreted.
[10] *The Wisdom Literature of the Old Testament*, pp. 277, 278.
[11] Compare the chapter headings in the Authorized Version.

THE PSALMS AND OTHER SACRED WRITINGS

Scripture. However, the first duty of the Bible student is to discover the primary, obvious, and natural meaning of the biblical books, whatever the consequences of such a search may be. And as soon as the Song of Songs is approached in a thoroughly historical and scientific spirit the failure of the allegorical view to do justice to the primary purpose of the book is revealed: there is no hint of an allegorical significance anywhere in the book, and it can be maintained only by doing violence to all legitimate principles of interpretation. It cannot appear strange, therefore, that the bald allegorical interpretation has no longer any defenders among serious students of the Bible.

For a time a modified allegorical interpretation found favor among some scholars. Bishop Lowth, for instance, desirous of doing away with the extravagances of the older view, suggested that the primary purpose of the book was to portray the union of Solomon with the daughter of the king of Egypt, but that it contained at the same time an allegorical portrayal of Christ espousing the church chosen from the Gentiles. Others have followed in the footsteps of Lowth and, though admitting that the subject of the book is human love, they have, nevertheless, insisted that this human love is typical of a higher divine love. Thus Keil regarded the human love typical of the love between Yahweh and his people, M. Stuart, between God and the human soul, and Delitzsch thought it foreshadowed the love between Christ and his church. In this modified form the allegorical view may be less objectionable, and support may be found for it in the utterances of Hosea, who likened the relation between Yahweh and Israel to the relation between husband and wife, and in the New Testament comparisons

THE SONG OF SONGS

of the love of the Christ for his church to the love of a bridegroom for his bride; but even this interpretation goes beyond the original purpose of the author. Whatever symbolical use may be made of some of the highly poetic and imaginative expressions in the book, there can be no doubt that the central theme is human love; and McFadyen is right when he says, "Any love poem would be equally capable of such [allegorical] interpretation."[12]

2. *The Dramatic Interpretation.* Modern scholars rightly insist that the Song of Songs, like any other book, should be interpreted literally; but as soon as an attempt is made to put this principle into practice, differences of opinion arise. While all are agreed that the subject of the poem is love, human love, there is decided disagreement regarding the manner in which the subject is treated. One group of scholars interprets the book as a drama, with a full equipment of *dramatis personæ,* such as the king, his beloved, the ladies of the harem, etc.[13] The dramatic view has been held in a variety of forms, but on the whole all the different dramatic interpretations may be regarded as modifications of two fundamentally distinct views: (1) According to one of these there are two principal characters—King Solomon, assuming at times the role of a shepherd, and the Shulammite maiden, of whom he is enamored. The poem describes how this maiden is taken from her humble home and raised to

---

[12] *Introduction to the Old Testament,* p. 283.

[13] The dramatic view was first suggested by Origen in his description of the book as *"carmen nuptiale in modum dramatis conscriptum"* (thus translated by Jerome). It is generally recognized that much of the poetry is in the nature of lyrical monologues, the dialogues are of the simplest form, the plot is rudimentary, and the action is without definite movement; hence some hesitate to call it a drama, even though they may admit a general dramatic arrangement.

THE PSALMS AND OTHER SACRED WRITINGS

honor by being made Solomon's queen in Jerusalem; and the dialogue consists substantially of mutual expressions of love and admiration on the part of the two principal characters. According to this interpretation the didactic element is very scant; it is implied only in the assumed redemption of Solomon from his impure loves by his affection for the simple, true-hearted Shulammite; consequently, the book is a portrayal of the triumph of true love over lust.

The scheme of the poem, according to Delitzsch, who may be considered the best exponent of this view, is as follows:

Act I. The Meeting of the Lovers (1. 2 to 2. 7).
Act II. Monologue of the Shulammite, relating two scenes from her past life (2. 8 to 3. 5).
   1. First meeting with Solomon (2. 8-17).
   2. A dream (3. 1-5).
Act III. The royal espousals (3. 6 to 5. 1).
Act IV. Love lost and found again (5. 2 to 6. 9).
Act V. The lovely, but modest queen (6. 10 to 8. 4).
Act VI. The bridal pair together in the Shulammite's home (8. 5-14).[14]

Each of the six acts is, according to Delitzsch, divided into two scenes. The rapid shifting of scenes is suggested in these words: "The first act is played both in the dining room and in the wine room appertaining to the women of the royal palace. In the second act Shulamith is again at home. In the third act, which represents the marriage,

---

[14] W. H. Bennett suggests the following outline, using more modern phraseology, *A Biblical Introduction*, pp. 168, 169:
   I. Courtship (1. 2 to 3. 5).
   II. Marriage (3. 6 to 5. 1).
   III. Domestic difficulties (5. 2 to 6. 9).
   IV. Mutual satisfaction (6. 10 to 7. 9).
   V. A visit to the bride's home (7. 10 to 8. 14).

THE SONG OF SONGS

the bride makes her entrance into Jerusalem from the wilderness, and what we further then hear occurs during the marriage festival. The locality of the fourth act is Jerusalem, without being more particularly defined. That of the fifth act is the park of Etam, and then Solomon's country house there. And in the sixth act we see the newly married pair first in the way to Shulem, and then in Shulamith's parental home."[15]

(2) By far the greater number of scholars favoring the dramatic interpretation are of the opinion that the view just outlined fails to do justice to the contents of the book; hence they give their adherence to a view first outlined in modern times by J. S. Jacobi,[16] and more fully developed by Ewald.[17] According to this interpretation there are three principal characters—King Solomon, the Shulammite, and her shepherd lover; and the book relates how the beautiful Shulammite was surprised by Solomon and his suite and was brought to the palace in Jerusalem, where the king sought to persuade her to become his queen. However, she had already pledged her heart to a young shepherd, and all the efforts of the king to make her forget him failed. In the end she was permitted to return to her home, where, at the close of the poem, the lovers appear arm in arm glorifying, in the most glowing terms, genuine, spontaneous affection and love.

According to this view the chief incidents described in the poem are as follows:

---

[15] Franz Delitzsch, *The Song of Songs* (English translation), p. 11.

[16] In *Das durch eine leichte und ungekuenstelte Erklaerung von seinen Vorwuerfen gerrettete Hohelied*, published in 1771. In the twelfth century the Jewish commentator Ibn Ezra had introduced the distinction between the lover and the king.

[17] *Dichter des Alten Bundes*, III, pp. 333ff.

THE PSALMS AND OTHER SACRED WRITINGS

Act I. The Shulammite and king Solomon (1. 2 to 2. 7).
  Scene 1. The Shulammite and the ladies of the court, who fail to understand her longing for the shepherd lover (1. 2-8).
  Scene 2. Solomon seeks to win the Shulammite's love, but fails; she protests against the cruel attempts to make her transfer her affection (1. 9 to 2. 7).
Act II. The Shulammite and her shepherd lover (2. 8 to 3. 5).
  Scene 1. The Shulammite's reminiscence of her lover's visit; she hopes that they may soon be reunited (2. 8-17).
  Scene 2. A dream, in which the Shulammite goes in search for her lover (3. 1-5).
Act III. Attempts to win the Shulammite's love (3. 6 to 5. 8).
  Scene 1. The royal pageant, intended to portray the glory and splendor awaiting the Shulammite if she yields to the king (3. 6-11).
  Scene 2. Solomon renews his plea (4. 1-7).
  Scene 3. Interview, ideal or real, between the Shulammite and her shepherd lover (4. 8 to 5. 1).
  Scene 4. A second dream, in which the Shulammite seeks her lover in vain throughout the city (5. 2-8).
Act IV. The Shulammite's unswerving love for her shepherd lover (5. 9 to 8. 4).
  Scene 1. Dialogue between the Shulammite and the court ladies regarding the shepherd lover (5. 9 to 6. 3).
  Scene 2. Renewed endeavors on the part of Solomon to win the Shulammite's affection (6. 4 to 7. 9).
  Scene 3. Reaffirmation of the Shulammite's love for her absent lover; her longing to be with him (7. 10 to 8. 4).
Act V. Reunion of the Shulammite and her shepherd lover (8. 5-14).

This interpretation also finds in the poem numerous expressions of admiration and love on the part of the principal characters, but, in addition, it sees running through the book a definite didactic aim, namely, to glorify true human love, more especially true betrothed love, which remains steadfast even in the most dangerous and seductive situations. Thus the story of the book illustrates the triumph of love over temptation.

The material for the drama was found by the author in

THE SONG OF SONGS

the biblical story of Abishag the Shunammite,[18] which was arranged and reconstructed by him in accord with a definite purpose and aim. In the words of Rothstein: "The author, as we may perhaps assume with certainty, found the material for his work in the story of Abishag of Shunem. She remained true to the beloved of her heart, she steadily repelled all the advances of Solomon, into whose harem she had been brought, and finally she triumphed, was conducted home, and restored to her lover perfectly pure. The poem makes two presuppositions—one being that the Shunammite's heart belonged to a youth in her own home, and the other, that meanwhile, against her will, she had been brought into the royal apartments. The dramatic exposition commences at the time when the first meeting of the king with the maiden is close at hand and actually takes place. The dialogue between the Shunammite and the daughters of Jerusalem—the wives and maidens belonging to the royal harem—in 1. 2-8, serves to pave the way, in true dramatic fashion, for that meeting, and at the same time to explain the real inward disposition of the Shunammite toward the approaching royal suitor, which the poet henceforth makes her retain without wavering. If, now, we would understand aright the further structure of the poem, it must be observed that the scheme chosen by the author for the poetical disposition of his material is based upon the different stages in the courtship and the marriage festivities down to the moment when alone the real victory of loyal love, the preservation of bridely honor in the face of all temptations and assaults, was evidenced

---

[18] 1 Kings 1. 3ff.; Shulammite is probably a variation of Shunammite, 1 Kings 1. 3ff.; 2 Kings 4. 8ff.; that is, a native of Shunem, a town in Issachar, Josh. 19. 18.

THE PSALMS AND OTHER SACRED WRITINGS

and could be evidenced, namely, the morning after the bridal night passed with the real lover."[19]

3. *The Lyric Interpretation.* A few years after the publication of Jacobi's interpretation, J. G. Herder proposed a new theory of the Song of Songs,[20] which from that time on has proved a rival of the dramatic interpretation, and in some one of its various forms has found acceptance with a majority of the more recent writers on the subject. Herder interpreted the book as a collection of forty-four independent love songs, held together "by no closer link than that of a number of pearls on one string." While this view found favor with several Old Testament scholars, among them DeWette, Magnus, and Bleek, it exerted only a limited influence until it was taken up and placed on a firmer basis by J. G. Wetzstein, and especially by Budde. Renan had already suggested, influenced by accounts of wedding festivities in the East, that the Song of Songs is an old Palestinian wedding play, arranged in acts intended for the successive days of the marriage feast;[21] but the credit of marking a turning point in the interpretation of the book must be given to an article on "Die Syrische Dreschtafel,"[22] by J. G. Wetzstein, for many years Prussian consul at Damascus, though even this article received scant notice until the subject was popularized by Budde.[23]

---

[19] Hastings, *Dictionary of the Bible*, article "Song of Songs"; for the test to which Rothstein refers, see Deut. 22. 13ff.

[20] *Solomons Lieder der Liebe, die aeltesten und schoensten aus dem Morgenlande*, published in 1778.

[21] *The Song of Songs* (English translation), pp. 62, 63.

[22] That is, "The Syrian Threshing Board." Published in *Zeitschrift fuer Ethnologie*, 1873, pp. 270ff.

[23] *The Song of Solomon*, in *The New World*, 1894, pp. 56–71; *Was is das Hohelied?* in *Preussische Jahrbuecher*, 1894, pp. 92–117; *Das Hohelied*, in *Kurzer Hand-Commentar*, pp. xvi–xxi.

THE SONG OF SONGS

According to these writers and others holding the same view the marriage customs of Syria and Palestine furnish the key to a proper understanding of the Song of Songs. In modern Syria the first seven days after a wedding are called "the king's week," during which the bride and groom play the part of queen and king and are treated as such by their friends. The majority of important village weddings are celebrated in March, the most delightful of the Syrian year, which makes it possible to have the festivities in the open, ordinarily on the threshing-floor. The threshing board is turned into a mock throne, on which the bride and groom are seated, while their friends sing and dance before them. Among the songs of this occasion the *waṣf,* that is, a poetic description of the bodily perfection of the newly-weds and their ornaments, holds a prominent place. The first of these *waṣfs* is sung on the evening of the wedding day: in the presence of the friends of the bride and groom, the former, with a sword in her right hand and a handkerchief in her left, dances the sword dance, which is accompanied or followed by a *waṣf* in praise of her personal beauty and charm. Other similar *waṣfs* follow on the succeeding days of the celebration. During the entire week bride and groom are attired in their wedding garments, they are not permitted to do any work, their sole occupation being to watch the games played before them. According to this view, then, the Song of Songs is a collection of *waṣfs* and other wedding songs covering the seven days of the "king's week," with no other link of connection than their common theme of love and wedded bliss. The king is not Solomon, but a peasant bridegroom who during this one week bears the name of this splendid and splendor-loving monarch, the three score mighty men are the companions of the bridegroom, and the bride is called Shulammite or Shunammite because that term is suggestive of superlative beauty.[24]

When Budde wrote his commentary no examples of the use of such royal play names were known; later researches, however, have brought to light cases in which the bridegroom is not only likened to a king but in which he actually receives the name of a king.[25]

In the absence of all indications regarding the beginning or end of the individual songs scholars naturally are not agreed as to the number or length of the songs. The following outline, however, may serve as an illustration of the theory: The opening verses are introductory; the bride praises the bridegroom, depreciates her own beauty, and asks where the bridegroom may be found.[26] In the rest of the book each sings the other's praises:[27]

1. The happiness of the bride (1. 9 to 2. 7).
2. A spring wooing (2. 8-17).
3. The bride's dream (3. 1-5).
4. The bridegroom's procession (3. 6-11).
5. The charms of the bride (4. 1 to 5. 1).
6. The beauty of the bridegroom (5. 2 to 6. 3).
7. Praise of the bride (6. 4-12).
8. Praise of the bride, as she dances the sword dance (7. 1-10).
9. The bride's longing (7. 11 to 8. 4).
10. The incomparable power of love (8. 5-7).
11. The bride's reply to her brothers (8. 8-10).
12. The two vineyards (8. 11, 12).
13. Conclusion (8. 13, 14).

---

[24] 1 Kings 1. 3; compare Song of Songs 1. 8; 5. 9; 6. 1.
[25] E. Littmann, *Neuarabische Volkspoesie*, Texte, A, IV, 52, 98, 100; B, I, 31.
[26] 1. 2–8.
[27] It is not necessary to assume that all the songs were sung by the newly wedded pair; some of them may have been sung by the men and women participating in the festivities, who placed them in the mouths of bride and bridegroom.

THE SONG OF SONGS

Which of these views offers the most satisfactory interpretation of the Song of Songs? The allegorical view must be rejected because it disregards the clear meaning of the text. Of the two dramatic interpretations the one recognizing the presence of three principal characters is to be preferred.[28] The other dramatic interpretation not only is peculiar in that it makes Solomon "appear in the garb and character of a shepherd (1. 7, 16, 17; 6. 2, 3), visiting a country girl in her home (2. 8ff.), proposing to make her his bride (3. 6ff.), and appearing with her in the closing scene, not in his own palace which, *ex hypothesi*, was to be her future abode, but in her native village (8. 5ff.)"; but there are also numerous other passages which have no natural explanation unless a third character is introduced.

A much more important question, however, is whether the book is to be interpreted as a drama at all or simply as a collection of ancient love or wedding songs.[29] The principal arguments advanced in favor of the dramatic view are: (1) It is claimed that the apparent unity of the book cannot be harmonized with the other view.[30] (2) It is asserted that the poem reveals dramatic movement and action, all leading gradually and steadily to a definite goal. (3) It is pointed out that the dramatic interpretation, at least the one unfolded by Ewald, furnishes an ethical justification for the admission of the Song of Songs into the canon, which it would lack with

---
[28] Koenig, *Einleitung in das Alte Testament*, p. 423, rightly calls the other view "impossible."
[29] A mythological significance is seen in the Song of Songs by Erbt—*Die Hebraeer*, pp. 196ff.—but even if some of the songs should have a mythological basis, in their present form they rise above it.
[30] H. T. Fowler, *A History of the Literature of Ancient Israel*, p. 363; S. R. Driver, *Introduction to the Literature of the Old Testament*, p. 437.

THE PSALMS AND OTHER SACRED WRITINGS

the other view. Regarding argument (3) it may be stated that though of all modern theories the theory of Ewald offers "the noblest interpretation of the book as a drama of pure love tried and proved in the furnace of temptation," it was not the dramatic but the allegorical interpretation that secured the admission of the book into the canon. Moreover, the dramatic movement and action (2) are by no means as clear and definite as the dramatic interpretation assumes. Even Driver, an ardent advocate of Ewald's view, admits that "the poem can hardly be said to exhibit a 'plot' in the modern sense of the term," and that "as read, the Song is so difficult of comprehension that it would seem to have been originally designed to be acted, the different parts being personated by different actors, though even the varied gesture and voice of a single reciter might perhaps be sufficient to enable a sympathetic circle of hearers to apprehend its purport."[31]

Again, does the poem really lead to a definite goal? One would expect this goal to be the consummation of love in marriage, and so it may seem to the superficial reader;[32] but in reality this consummation is already presupposed in the earlier chapters of the book.[33] Once more, while there is a certain unity in the book (1), strict *dramatic unity* cannot be traced; the unity exhibited is the *unity of motive and theme,* which is in no wise affected by the other interpretation. Thus, the arguments in favor of the dramatic interpretation are by no means conclusive; a good deal has to be read between the lines;

---

[31] S. R. Driver, *Introduction to the Literature of the Old Testament,* pp. 444, 447.
[32] 8. 5ff.
[33] Compare 1. 2ff.; 1. 12ff.; 2. 1ff.; 3. 1ff., etc.

THE SONG OF SONGS

hence there seems abundant justification for the statement of Gray: "The main question is whether the little drama . . . constructed by Ewald was constructed by him out of the text, or simply read by him into the text."[34]

The absence of all headings or stage directions presents another perplexity. True, Ewald has supplied these, but his scheme has not proved satisfactory in details; practically every commentator distributes the verses among the different persons according to a scheme of his own. It has, indeed, been suggested that originally there were such directions, and that they were removed when it was decided that the poem should be interpreted as an allegory; but is there anything to support this suggestion? The brevity of the Song may be regarded as another objection: Is it natural to interpret one hundred and sixteen verses as constituting five acts or thirteen scenes of a drama? It is also well to remember that there is no other example of a drama in the proper sense of the term in the literature of any Semitic people. It may further be asked whether an Oriental poet would be likely to represent King Solomon as taking a refusal from a peasant maid. This is hardly the way of Oriental monarchs.

One can hardly escape the conclusion that the dramatic interpretation was not the outgrowth of an independent study of the book, but had its origin in the allegorical view. The allegorical scheme recognized two characters —Yahweh and Israel, or Christ and the church; when a saner exegesis led to the conviction that the theme was human love rather than divine love, two principal characters were retained; later it was found necessary to add a third, while some scholars introduced additional

---
[34] *A Critical Introduction to the Old Testament*, p. 158.

THE PSALMS AND OTHER SACRED WRITINGS

characters to take care of passages for which they could find no explanation under the commonly accepted scheme. It is not without reason, therefore, that the dramatic theory has been accused of furnishing a modern Targum to the book "which as completely transforms and misrepresents an ancient piece of literature as Jewish Targums which turned it into a history of Israel, or Christian commentators that made it relate the history of the incarnation."

It seems much more scientific to interpret the little book in the light of the customs, practices, and songs of the land in which it had its birth. If this is done, the theory of Wetzstein and Budde, in some form, is seen to attain a high degree of probability. The presence of ancient wedding songs is recognized even by some defenders of the dramatic interpretation. J. W. Rothstein, for example, admits "the possibility of older wedding songs having been worked up in the Song of Songs. But this does not exclude the supposition that the Song in its present form is of a dramatic nature, and that its author, not a redactor, or reviser, introduced 'movement' or 'development' into the material of which it is composed."[35] But even in this modified form the dramatic view cannot easily be maintained. On the other hand, it may be necessary to modify in certain details the theory proposed by Budde. As has been stated, he held that the Song is a collection of *wedding* songs; but further study of the folk-poetry of Palestine has brought to light many *waṣfs* celebrating the beauty and charms not of brides alone but of loved ones in general.[36] From which the

---

[35] Hastings, *Dictionary of the Bible*, artic'e "Song of Songs"; compare also H. T. Fowler, *History of the Literature of Ancient Israel*, p. 363.
[36] Compare G. Dalman, *Palæstinischer Diwan*, pp. xii, 100ff.

THE SONG OF SONGS

inference may be drawn that the collection contains not only wedding songs but also effusions of young and ardent lovers who have not yet reached the state of wedded bliss. If this inference is correct, the Song of Songs may be regarded as an anthology of ancient Hebrew love and wedding songs.[37] But it is not a haphazard collection, for there are throughout the Song suggestions of a certain literary unity. Whatever the origin and original form of the individual songs may have been, they were probably worked over and put in their present form by one editor, whose aim was "to present a ritual to be used in the wedding ceremonies that would be both noble and chaste. . . . While they do not adequately present the sanctity and beauty inherent in our modern ideal of marriage—for that ideal was unknown to the East—they do extol nobly and exquisitely the sanctity and beauty of true love between man and woman. Nowhere in literature has this divine passion been more beautifully described than in the words which the bride addresses to her husband as she enters his home, thereby making complete the marriage relation:

> Love is as strong as death;
> Jealousy is as irresistible as Sheol;
> Its flames are flames of fire,
> A very flame of Jehovah.
> Many waters cannot quench love,
> Nor can floods drown it."[38]

---

[37] P. Haupt, *Biblische Liebeslieder*, pp. xiii, xiv; N. Schmidt, *Messages of the Poets*, pp. 225ff.; C. F. Kent, *The Songs, Hymns, and Prayers of the Old Testament*, pp. 26ff.; W. Robinson, *Encyclopædia Britannica*, eleventh edition, article "Song of Songs"; for an outline of the book according to this theory, see A. R. Gordon, *The Poets of the Old Testament*, pp. 317ff.

[38] C. F. Kent, *The Songs, Hymns, and Prayers of the Old Testament*, p. 28.

THE PSALMS AND OTHER SACRED WRITINGS

Authorship and Date. Whatever may have been the intended meaning of the words of the title translated "which is Solomon's,"[39] tradition has interpreted them as meaning that King Solomon is the author of the Song of Songs; and no doubt belief in Solomonic authorship accounts in part, though in part only,[40] for the admission of the book into the canon. But whatever interpretation of the book may be accepted, Solomonic authorship is out of the question.[41] The ascription to Solomon is a mistaken inference from the fact that Solomon is the most famous person named in the book,[42] coupled with the statement in 1 Kings 4. 32 that he was the author of one thousand and five songs.

To go beyond this negative conclusion is not easy. Historical allusions are rare,[43] and there is no definite religious or theological teaching; hence the linguistic characteristics offer about the only criterion for the determination of the date. That the language of the book exhibits several peculiarities is generally admitted, but the origin of these has been variously explained. Some scholars have sought to account for them by assuming that the book originated in the northern kingdom, whose language differed dialectically from the language spoken

---

[39] See above, p. 165.

[40] Another, at least equally important, reason was the allegorical interpretation, see above, p. 166.

[41] The mention of Tirzah, the ancient capital of the northern kingdom, 6. 4, as a parallel to Jerusalem would in itself be sufficient to prove that the poem originated later than Solomon's reign; compare 1 Kings 14. 17; 16. 23.

[42] 3. 7-11; 8. 11, 20.

[43] The fact that David's name is connected with a tower in Jerusalem and that Solomon appears as a type of royal luxury and splendor may suggest that the reigns of the two kings are in the distant past, but how far no one can tell from these allusions.

THE SONG OF SONGS

in Judah. Another evidence pointing to a northern origin is seen in the frequent mention of northern localities, such as Tirzah, Carmel, Sharon, Hermon, Lebanon, Gilead, etc. Origin in the northern kingdom would imply a date earlier than B. C. 722, and from the mention of Tirzah it has been inferred that the poem was written while Tirzah was the capital,[44] that is, between Jeroboam I and Omri; in other words, during the closing years of the tenth century or the opening years of the ninth century.

But these arguments are by no means conclusive. Tirzah seems to have remained a city of prominence for some time after it ceased to be the capital,[45] and there seems to be no good reason why it might not have been coupled with Jerusalem as late as the postexilic period. Moreover, its mention may not be due to political or commercial prominence, but to the suggestiveness of its name —Tirzah, meaning pleasantness, would naturally suggest beauty. Over against the mention of northern localities stands the naming of Jerusalem, Engedi, Kedar, and Heshbon in the south and southeast; and there is at least equal ground, especially in view of the frequent references to the daughters of Jerusalem, for believing that the Song originated in Jerusalem. All the northern localities named are such as might be known to a Judæan. That the language of Israel differed to some extent from that of Judah is probable, but regarding the significance of the linguistic argument in this particular case two things should be noted: (1) that the linguistic peculiarities of the Song of Songs are not found in the book of Hosea, the one Old Testament book that is known with certainty to have originated in the northern kingdom;

---

[44] 1 Kings 14. 17; 16. 23.
[45] Compare 2 Kings 15. 14, 16.

THE PSALMS AND OTHER SACRED WRITINGS

and (2) that there is nothing to support the assumption, involved in the theory of a northern origin, that the characteristics peculiar to the language of the northern kingdom coincided with the characteristics found in the Hebrew of the late postexilic period.

The linguistic characteristics are more easily explained by assuming a postexilic date for the book in its present form. For instance, the relative pronoun *she,* used throughout the book to the exclusion of the usual form *asher,* is used elsewhere, with the exception of a few cases in Judges and in 2 Kings 6. 11, only in exilic and postexilic writings, with frequency only in the late book of Ecclesiastes, while in the Mishna it is the regular form of the relative pronoun. The occurrence of the Persian word *pardēs* in 4. 13 seems to point, at the earliest, to the Persian period; it is used elsewhere only in late postexilic books.[46] The word *appiriōn* in 3. 9 looks like a Hebraized form of the Greek φορεῖον; if so, it would favor a rather late date. In addition, there are many words and phrases which occur never or rarely in other biblical books, but are common in Aramaic.[47] On the whole, therefore, what evidence there is seems to favor a date during the late Persian or early Greek period; perhaps somewhere between B. C. 400 and 300. This applies to the work of the editor who gave to the Song its present form; he, however, "drew his material from the love and wedding songs that had long been current among the people of Palestine. Some of these may well come from the days preceding the exile, when the memory of the glories of Solomon's kingdom and the

---
[46] Neh. 2. 8; Eccl. 2. 5.
[47] These expressions are enumerated in S. R. Driver, *Introduction to the Literature of the Old Testament,* p. 448.

THE SONG OF SONGS

story of Abishag the Shulammite, the fairest maiden of Israel, were still fresh in the minds of the people."[48] But it is not possible to determine the dates of the individual songs within more closely defined limits.

[48] C. F. Kent, *The Songs, Hymns, and Prayers of the Old Testament* p. 28.

CHAPTER VII

THE BOOK OF RUTH

CHAPTER VII

THE BOOK OF RUTH

Name. The book of Ruth receives its name, Hebrew רוּת,[1] from its heroine, Ruth, the Moabitess. In the Jewish canon it is one of the Writings and one of the five *Megilloth,* or Rolls;[2] in the English Bible[3] it is placed after the book of Judges, because the incidents related in it belong to the period of the Judges.[4]

Contents and Outline. The book of Ruth narrates how Elimelech of Bethlehem, his wife, Naomi, and his two sons, Mahlon and Chilion, went to live in a town of Moab. After the death of the father the sons married Moabitish wives, Orpah and Ruth. Before long both Mahlon and Chilion died, which left Naomi alone with her two daughters-in-law. On Naomi's decision to return to Bethlehem Ruth insisted on accompanying her. In Bethlehem Ruth made the acquaintance of her kinsman Boaz, who in the end married her. A son was born to them, Obed, the father of Jesse, who became the father of David. The following is a brief outline:

---

[1] From the fuller form רְעִי, meaning "friendship."

[2] See above, p. 165; Ruth is read on the day of Pentecost.

[3] Following the Vulgate, which, in turn, is dependent on the Septuagint.

[4] Bertheau, Ewald, and others, depending largely on the order of the books in the Septuagint, have advocated the view that originally Ruth was a kind of appendix to the book of Judges; but there is no good reason for such assumption.

THE PSALMS AND OTHER SACRED WRITINGS

1. Elimelech and his family in Moab (1. 1-5).
2. Return of Naomi and Ruth to Judah (1. 6-22).
    (1) Naomi's desire to return (1. 6-14).
    (2) Ruth's choice (1. 15-22).
3. Ruth in the field of Boaz (2. 1-23).
    (1) Ruth's gleaning (2. 1-7).
    (2) Kindness of Boaz (2. 8-23).
4. Ruth's request of Boaz (3. 1-18).
5. Ruth's marriage to Boaz (4. 1-12).
6. Ancestry of David (4. 13-22).

Aim of the Book. The literary beauty of the little book can be appreciated even without a knowledge of its aim or purpose. "Whatever be its didactic purpose," says McFadyen, "it is, at any rate, a wonderful prose poem, sweet, artless, and persuasive, touched with the quaintness of an older world and fresh with the scent of the harvest fields. The love—stronger than country—of Ruth for Naomi, the gracious figure of Boaz as he moves about the fields with a word of blessing for the reapers, the innocent scheming of Naomi to secure him as a husband for Ruth—these and a score of similar touches establish the book forever in the heart of all who love nobility and romance."[5]

Nevertheless, it is of interest to inquire why this beautiful story was written. The more important answers suggested are three: 1. The book was written out of interest in the family history of David. The books of Samuel have nothing to say regarding the ancestry of David, giving only the names of his father and of his brothers;[6] this lack the book of Ruth is intended to supply. The information furnished here would be of special interest because Ruth was not a native of Judah but a member of a hostile people, Moab. 2. The story was told to com-

---

[5] *Introduction to the Old Testament*, p. 290.
[6] 1 Sam. 16. 1-13.

THE BOOK OF RUTH

mend the so-called levirate marriage.[7] 3. The book was written and circulated as a protest against the prohibition of mixed marriages in the days of Ezra-Nehemiah.[8]

The first answer undoubtedly explains the rise of the story in its original form. That it rests upon an historical basis may be inferred from 1 Sam. 22. 3, 4, where it is stated that David committed his father and mother to the care of the king of Moab. Moreover, it would be exceedingly difficult, in the face of Hebrew exclusiveness and bigotry, to explain the *invention* of a Moabitish ancestress for the great national hero, David.[9] But the acceptance of the story as substantially historical does not exclude the possibility of the book in its present form having been written or published at a certain time for a specific didactic purpose, as is suggested in answers 2 and 3. However, it is very doubtful that the aim was to commend the levirate marriage. In the first place, the marriage of Ruth and Boaz was not a levirate marriage at all, for neither Boaz nor the other kinsman was Ruth's brother-in-law. And though this may not be an insuperable objection—for the marriage of Ruth to Boaz might be considered a legitimate extension of the principle of the levirate marriage, which was established for the purpose of perpetuating the dead man's name—when the story is taken as a whole it becomes evident that the marriage, though it occupies considerable space in the narrative, is, after all, only a subordinate incident. Moreover,

---

[7] That is, the marriage of a widow to the deceased husband's brother, to perpetuate the name of the deceased, Gen. 38. 8; Deut. 25. 5, 6. Since Boaz was not the brother-in-law of Ruth, it has been suggested that in this case it is only the marriage of a widow to the next-of-kin that is encouraged.

[8] Ezra, Chapters 9 and 10; Neh. 13. 23–29.

[9] H. L. Strack, *Einleitung in das Alte Testament*, p. 142.

there is no indication that the first born was recognized as the son of Ruth's first husband, as would have been required by the levirate law.

On the other hand, if the book could be dated in connection with the reform movement under Ezra-Nehemiah, it might well be interpreted as a protest against the narrow exclusiveness advocated by these reformers; the book would then be of the greatest significance in the religious history of Israel, for it would take its stand by the side of the book of Jonah as teaching the universality of the divine interest and love. The significance which this interpretation gives to the book is admirably set forth by McFadyen in these words: "It was in all probability the dignified answer of a man of prophetic instincts to the vigorous measures of Ezra, who demanded the divorce of all foreign women; for it can hardly be doubted that there is a delicate polemic in the repeated designation of Ruth as *the Moabitess,* 1. 22; 2. 2, 6, 21; 4. 5, 10—she even calls herself 'the stranger' in 2. 10. It would be pleasant to think that the writer had himself married one of these foreign women. In any case he champions their cause not only with generosity but with insight; for he knows that some of them have faith enough to adopt Israel's God as their God, 1. 16, and that even a Moabitess may be an Israelite indeed. Ezra's severe legislation was inspired by the worthy desire to preserve Israel's religion from the peril of contagion: the author of Ruth gently teaches that the foreign woman is not an inevitable peril; she may be loyal to Israel and faithful to Israel's God. The writer dares to represent the Moabitess as eating with the Jews, 2. 14—winning by her ability, resource, and affection, the regard of all, and counted by God worthy to be the mother of Israel's greatest king. The

THE BOOK OF RUTH

generous type of religion represented by the book of Ruth is a much needed and very attractive complement to the stern legislation of Ezra."[10]

Date and Authorship. Jewish tradition credits Samuel with the authorship of the book of Ruth;[11] but this is nothing but a guess. The book itself contains no definite indication regarding its date or the sources from which its information was derived; and the few more or less indefinite data are ambiguous, if not conflicting. Clearly, the book in its present form cannot be earlier than the age of David;[12] and the general impression made is that it was written long after his time. There is no reference to his brothers; evidently, the heroic king had completely overshadowed them in popular thought. The period of the Judges seems to be in the distant past, for the point of view reflected in 1. 1 is that of the Deuteronomic reviser of the narratives, who represents the Judges as exercising authority over the whole of Israel.[13] The custom of throwing away the shoe, connected with the levirate marriage,[14] is spoken of as obsolete in the writer's day;[15] moreover, it differs from the practice described in Deuteronomy. There are also a few linguistic characteristics pointing to a late date, but these are confined to a few passages which for other reasons are considered additions to the original story.[16] The fact that the book

---

[10] J. E. McFadyen, *Introduction to the Old Testament*, p. 293.
[11] F. C. Eiselen, *The Books of the Pentateuch*, p. 86.
[12] Compare 4. 17-22.
[13] See Volume II in this series of Introductions, soon to be published, chapter on "Book of Judges."
[14] Deut. 25. 9, 10.
[15] Ruth 4. 7.
[16] See S. R. Driver, *Introduction to the Literature of the Old Testament*, p. 455.

THE PSALMS AND OTHER SACRED WRITINGS

belongs to the third division of the Jewish canon instead of the second, with the book of Judges, is also thought by some to favor a postexilic date. However, this argument has little weight, for the book of Judges, like Ruth, did not receive its final form until after the exile; and there is no evidence to show that date of origin was a determining factor in assigning books to the second or third division of the Jewish canon.[17] All these arguments are inconclusive; and over against the few late linguistic characteristics stands the undeniable fact that the general style of the story has all the characteristics of pure classical Hebrew as found in the early portions of the books of Samuel and Kings.

In the presence of this conflicting evidence it is not strange that the book should have been dated in preexilic, exilic, and postexilic times. The view which on the whole furnishes the most satisfactory explanation of all the facts in the case is that the present book was preceded by a preexilic narrative of Ruth and her marriage to Boaz, which embodied traditions that had been handed down orally for many generations. In the days of Ezra-Nehemiah, and under the influence of their reform efforts, a prophetic writer, with a clear vision of the all-inclusive love of God, saw the didactic possibilities of this early narrative; in order to make it even more suitable for his purpose he may have revised it, idealized some of the characters and scenes, and added the verses which do not seem to have been a part of the original story;[18] then

---

[17] Except in cases where the books were not written until after the completion of the second canon; but the second canon was not formed until long after the days of Ezra-Nehemiah, to which the book of Ruth is assigned.

[18] 1. 1; 4. 7, 18-22. These are the portions which contain the most pronounced late characteristics.

THE BOOK OF RUTH

he sent forth the story of Ruth in its present form as a protest against the narrow, exclusive tendencies of the age.[19] This view as to the origin of the book preserves substantially the historical character of the narrative, explains the presence of the preexilic and postexilic elements, and furnishes a satisfactory interpretation of the object and aim of what Goethe has characterized as the loveliest little idyl that tradition has transmitted to the present age.

---

[19] The view of Budde, *Zeitschrift fuer Alttestamentliche Wissenschaft*, 1892, pp. 37ff., that the book of Ruth was at one time a part of the "commentary (Midrash) of the book of kings," mentioned in 2 Chron. 24. 27, while possible, cannot be substantiated.

CHAPTER VIII

THE BOOK OF LAMENTATIONS

CHAPTER VIII

THE BOOK OF LAMENTATIONS

Name. The usual Hebrew name is simply *Ēkhāh*, which means "How," from the opening word of the book; but, influenced by the contents, the Talmud gives it also the name *Ḳīnōth*, which may be translated "Lamentations," or "Dirges." From this is derived the Septuagint designation θρῆνοι, *Thrēnoi*, a word having the same meaning, to which is sometimes added "of Jeremiah." The Greek name is reproduced in the Vulgate as *Threni*, and translated into English as "Lamentations" or the fuller "Lamentations of Jeremiah." The term *Ḳīnōth* is commonly applied to dirges over deceased individuals;[1] but it is also used with reference to the overthrow of cities or nations.[2] The latter usage is common in the book of Lamentations, especially in chapters 1, 2, and 4, which consist largely of dirges over the downfall of Judah and Jerusalem.

Contents and Outline. The book of Lamentations consists of five independent poems, all centering, though in different ways, around one common theme: the calamities that befell the people of Judah, and especially of Jerusalem, during the siege and subsequent capture of the holy city. Chapters 1, 2, and 4 are in the nature

---
[1] 2 Sam. 1. 17–27; 3. 11.
[2] Amos 5. 2; Ezek. 26. 17, 18.

THE PSALMS AND OTHER SACRED WRITINGS

of dirges over the death of the city and nation in B. C. 586, while chapter 3 describes the sufferings endured by the poet and his compatriots in the course of this calamity. These sufferings are traced to the anger of Yahweh, aroused by the sins of the people, but the knowledge of Yahweh's loving-kindness inspires a hope that the sufferings will not continue forever. Chapter 5 is a prayer: after lamenting the sorrows and sufferings of the people, due to their own sins as well as to the sins of their fathers, the author, representing the community, prays for speedy deliverance.

I. MISERY AND DESOLATION OF JERUSALEM (1. 1-22)
1. Solitariness and desertion of Jerusalem (1. 1-11).
2. Severity and justice of the affliction (1. 12-19).
3. Prayer for retribution upon her enemies (1. 20-22).

II. THE ANGER OF YAHWEH THE CAUSE OF JERUSALEM'S RUIN (2. 1-22)
1. Suffering and affliction a divine judgment (2. 1-10).
2. Depth of distress and despair (2. 11-17).
3. Prayer for deliverance (2. 18-22).

III. HOPE OF RELIEF THROUGH DIVINE LOVING-KINDNESS (3. 1-66)
1. Lament of the people (3. 1-20).
2. Yahweh's loving-kindness the basis of hope (3. 21-39).
3. Prayer of confession and penitence (3. 40-54).
4. Prayer for vengeance (3. 55-66).

IV. SORROWS AND HORRORS OF THE SIEGE (4. 1-22).
1. Distress of the people (4. 1-11).
2. Faithlessness of the religious leaders (4. 12-16).
3. Utter hopelessness of the situation (4. 17-20).
4. Doom of the Edomites (4. 21, 22).

V. PRAYER FOR MERCY AND DELIVERANCE (5. 1-22)
1. Miseries of the exiles (5. 1-18).
2. Prayer for speedy deliverance (5. 19-22).

THE BOOK OF LAMENTATIONS

Literary Form. The first four poems are arranged as alphabetic acrostics.[3] In chapters 1 and 2 each stanza consists of three long lines, the characteristic letter marking the beginning of each successive stanza. In chapter 3 each of three successive lines begins with the same letter.[4] The stanzas in chapter 4 consist of two lines each, the characteristic letter marking the beginning of each couplet. Chapter 5 agrees with chapter 4 in having two-line stanzas. The order of the letters in chapter 1 differs in one respect from that in the three succeeding chapters: in the former ע precedes פ, as is the case in the modern arrangement of the Hebrew alphabet; in the others פ precedes ע.[5]

Chapters 1-4 are in the *Kînāh* meter;[6] indeed, it was the study of Lamentations that led to the discovery of the *Kînāh* verse. The consistent use of this particular meter and the alphabetic arrangement of the verses make it clear that the poems were "constructed with conscious art: they are not the unstudied effusions of natural emotion, they are carefully elaborated poems, in which every trait which might stir a chord of sorrow or regret is

---

[3] Chapter 5 is not arranged alphabetically; it is noteworthy, however, that it consists of twenty-two stanzas, the number of letters in the Hebrew alphabet. Perhaps the author, or compiler, of the book meant to form another acrostic, but after composing or compiling the right number of stanzas he was prevented by death or otherwise from carrying out his original purpose.

[4] So far as the thought is concerned, the alphabetic arrangement of Chapter 3 is altogether arbitrary. Sometimes the break in thought occurs within a group of verses beginning with the same letter of the Hebrew alphabet.

[5] Does this difference point to diversity of authorship? It is not quite clear whether there was a time when פ regularly preceded ע, or whether there was a time when the order was not definitely fixed.

[6] See above, pp. 22, 23.

brought together, for the purpose of completing the picture of woe."[7]

Date and Authorship. In the English Bible the book of Lamentations, entitled "The Lamentations of Jeremiah," follows the book of Jeremiah, in harmony with the common Jewish and Christian tradition that the prophet Jeremiah is the author of the book.[8] This tradition is very early. The full title, "Lamentations of Jeremiah," is found in the Sinaitic MS. of the Septuagint,[9] and in the Syriac[10] and Latin versions. The tradition may be traced even to pre-Christian times, for it is found not only in the Jewish Fathers and the Talmud, but also in the Targums[11] and in the Septuagint translation of the book. The latter has at the head of the first chapter this statement: "And it came to pass after Israel had been led captive and Jerusalem made desolate, that Jeremiah sat down weeping and lamented *this lamentation* over Jerusalem, and said." While it is uncertain whether the singular "this lamentation" should be interpreted as referring to the whole book or only to the poem in chapter 1, the translators evidently meant to connect the prophet Jeremiah with at least some of the contents of the book. In the same direction points the Septuagint grouping of Lamentations with other books connected with Jeremiah;

---

[7] S. R. Driver, *Introduction to the Literature of the Old Testament*, p. 459.

[8] The conception of Jeremiah as the weeping prophet is based largely on the assumption that he is the author of Lamentations.

[9] Written in the fourth century A. D.; the Vatican MS., also of the fourth century, and numerous other MSS. of the Septuagint, have the shorter title.

[10] Probably to be dated in the second century A. D.

[11] Aramaic translations or paraphrases of the Old Testament. Though these did not reach their final form until some centuries after the opening of the Christian era, they embody pre-Christian material.

THE BOOK OF LAMENTATIONS

but the date of this arrangement cannot be definitely fixed.[12]

What are the facts in the case? The Hebrew text of Lamentations contains no statement regarding the authorship of the book, nor does the Hebrew text of the rest of the Old Testament furnish direct information on the subject. Moreover, the Hebrew Bible, unlike the Greek, or Latin, or English, does not place the book after the prophecies of Jeremiah, but in the third division of the canon, called the Writings, where it forms one of the five *Megilloth*, or Rolls,[13] Lamentations being read on the ninth day of Ab, the day on which the destruction of Jerusalem was commemorated. In the absence of all early external evidence the tradition must be tested by the internal evidence presented in the book. Now, while there have been those who believed that the internal evidence favored tradition, it is not without significance that depending almost exclusively on this internal evidence, modern scholarship, with practical unanimity, has declared against the traditional view that

---

[12] The statement in 2 Chron. 35. 25 to the effect that "Jeremiah lamented for Josiah" and that lamentations for Josiah were embodied in "the lamentations" is interpreted by some as implying a belief on the part of the Chronicler that Jeremiah wrote at least some of the dirges in the canonical book. If this interpretation could be accepted it would mean that the tradition concerning Jeremiah's authorship of Lamentations was current at least as early as B. C. 300; that is, less than three centuries after the close of Jeremiah's activity. However, this interpretation of the Chronicles passage is exceedingly doubtful. In the first place, no lamentation in the canonical book has for its subject King Josiah; moreover, the verse itself, interpreted naturally, does not imply that the lamentation uttered by Jeremiah was included in "the lamentations"; nor is it clear that the latter expression refers to the canonical book. Hence the passage in Chronicles throws no light on the authorship of the book of Lamentations.

[13] See above, p. 165.

THE PSALMS AND OTHER SACRED WRITINGS

Jeremiah is the author of Lamentations in whole or in part.[14]

The principal arguments drawn from internal evidence both for and against the traditional view may be grouped as follows:[15]

1. *Evidence Thought to Favor Jeremiah as the Author.* (1) Lamentations reveals the same sensitive temper as is reflected in the book of Jeremiah; its author is profoundly sympathetic in national sorrow and is ready to pour forth his emotions without restraint.[16] (2) In the two books national calamities are traced to the same causes, such as national sin,[17] the faithlessness of prophets and priests,[18] and misplaced confidence in weak and treacherous allies.[19] (3) The two books contain similar figures, ideas, and expressions. For instance, both books speak of the virgin daughter of Zion as broken with an incurable breach;[20] the speaker's eyes are said to be flowing down with water;[21] terrors are said to be on every side;[22] there is the same appeal for vengeance to the righteous judge[23]

---

[14] A generation or more ago K. F. Keil, always conservative, labored valiantly to maintain the traditional view, while Thenius sought to save at least Chapters 2 and 4 for Jeremiah; but they have few, if any, adherents among careful Old Testament students to-day.

[15] Compare also S. R. Driver, *Introduction to the Literature of the Old Testament*, pp. 461-464.

[16] Compare with Lamentations especially Jer. 14 and 15.

[17] Compare Lam. 1. 5, 8, 14, 18; 3. 42; 4. 6, 22; 5. 7, 16 with Jer. 14. 7; 16. 10-12; 17. 1-3, etc.

[18] Compare, for example, Lam. 2. 14; 4. 13-15 with Jer. 2. 7, 8; 5. 31; 14. 13; 23. 11-40, etc.

[19] Compare, for example, Lam. 1. 2, 19; 4. 17 with Jer. 2. 18, 36; 30. 14; 37. 5-10.

[20] Compare, for example, Lam. 1. 15; 2. 12 with Jer. 8. 21, 22; 14. 17.

[21] Lam. 1. 16; 2. 11, 18; 3. 4, 8, 49 and Jer. 9. 1, 18; 13. 17; 14. 17.

[22] Lam. 2. 22 and Jer. 6. 25; 20. 10.

[23] Lam. 3. 64-66 and Jer. 11. 20.

and expectation of desolation for the nations that rejoiced in the destruction of Jerusalem.[24] (4) Attention is further called to numerous other expressions found in both books. Among these the more striking are: "Among all her lovers she hath none to comfort her" and "All thy lovers have forgotten thee";[25] the detailed description of Jerusalem's awful condition;[26] the references to women eating their own children;[27] the author's description of himself as a derision or laughingstock;[28] the use of the terms "bitterness," "wormwood," "gall";[29] of "fear," "pit," "snare;" [30] of "chase" and "hunt";[31] the figures of the cup of judgment,[32] and of the falling down of the crown.[33]

2. *Evidence Thought to Militate Against Authorship of Jeremiah.* (1) The variation in the alphabetic order, which may indicate that the poems do not all come from one and the same author.[34] (2) The two books reveal such striking differences in point of view that it is difficult to believe that one and the same author is responsible for both. For instance, (*a*) The complaints and prayers for retribution in Lamentations[35] do not read as if they came from the prophet who considered the Chaldeans instru-

---

[24] Lam. 4. 21 and Jer. 49. 12.
[25] Lam. 1. 2 and Jer. 30. 14.
[26] Lam. 1. 8, 9 and Jer. 13. 22, 26.
[27] Lam. 2. 20; 4. 10 and Jer. 19. 9.
[28] Lam. 3. 14 and Jer. 20. 7.
[29] Lam. 3. 15, 19 and Jer. 9. 15; 23. 15.
[30] Lam. 3. 47 and Jer. 48. 43.
[31] Lam. 3. 52 and Jer. 16. 16.
[32] Lam. 4. 21 and Jer. 25. 15; 49. 12.
[33] Lam. 5. 16 and Jer. 13. 18.
[34] The order in Chapter 1 differs from that in Chapters 2, 3, and 4; see above, p. 201.
[35] Lam. 1. 20-22; 3. 59-66.

THE PSALMS AND OTHER SACRED WRITINGS

ments in the hands of Yahweh.[36] (*b*) The author's lament over the fate of king, princes, and prophets is hardly consistent with utterances regarding the same classes in the book of Jeremiah.[37] (*c*) The author of Lamentations looked to the last for outside help, while Jeremiah had no thought that any outside nation would save Jerusalem.[38] (*d*) Is it probable that the two estimates of king Zedekiah[39] came from the same person? (*e*) It is, to say the least, doubtful that Jeremiah would admit that the sufferings of his contemporaries were due to the sins of their fathers.[40] (3) There are significant differences in vocabulary. It cannot be mere accident, for instance, that the unusual relative *she,* never used by Jeremiah, is used several times in the short book of Lamentations;[41] or that the term *Adōnai,* "Lord," is used fourteen times in Lam. 1-3, while Jeremiah never uses it by itself, but only in combination with Yahweh.[42] (4) The allusions in Lam. 5. 18-20 seem to imply that these verses were written a considerable time after the destruction of Jerusalem in B. C. 586; in other words, the contents point to a period later than that of Jeremiah. (5) Though it is impossible to prove that the author is dependent on Ezekiel, passages like Lam. 2. 14 and 4. 20 may

---

[36] For example, Jer. 25. 1-11. Would Jeremiah be so overcome by the thought that Yahweh had turned against his people? Compare Lam. 2. 1ff.
[37] Compare Lam. 2. 6-14 with Jer. 23. 9-40 and 24. 8-10.
[38] Compare Lam. 4. 17 with Jer. 37. 6-10.
[39] Lam. 4. 20 and Jer. 24. 8-10.
[40] Compare Lam. 5. 7 with Jer. 31. 29, 30.
[41] For example, Lam. 2. 15, 16; 4. 9; 5. 18.
[42] *Zeitschrift fuer Alttestamentliche Wissenschaft,* 1894, pp. 31ff.; compare also S. R. Driver, *Introduction to the Literature of the Old Testament,* p. 463.

THE BOOK OF LAMENTATIONS

imply familiarity with the writings of that prophet.[43] (6) Another objection is expressed by McFadyen in these words: "It is very unlikely that one who was so sorely smitten as Jeremiah by the unconsolable sorrow of Jerusalem would have expressed his grief in alphabetic elegies: men do not write acrostics when their hearts are breaking."[44]

It can easily be seen that the evidence outlined in the preceding paragraphs is far from being conclusive; nevertheless, on the whole, the evidence against the authorship of Jeremiah is stronger than that favoring his authorship. At any rate, it would be easier to explain the resemblances on the assumption that the elegies were written by a person or persons other than Jeremiah than to explain the marked differences on the assumption that the book of Lamentations was written by the author of the book of Jeremiah.

Modern scholarship not only denies that Jeremiah is the author of Lamentations; it goes even farther and is almost unanimous in denying the unity of the book. W. R. Smith was, perhaps, the last to argue strongly in favor of one author;[45] Driver, who in the earlier editions of his Introduction wrote, "The opinion that the author is throughout the same has, perhaps, on the whole, probability in its favor; but the criteria at our disposal do not authorize us to pronounce dogmatically upon either side,"[46] is quite ready to admit, in the latest edition, that

---

[43] Compare Ezek. 19. 2ff.; 22. 28; see also C. H. Cornill, *Einleitung in das Alte Testament*, p. 247. Some have claimed that they have discovered also evidence of familiarity with Isa. 40ff., but this is less clear.

[44] J. E. McFadyen, *An Introduction to the Old Testament*, p. 296.

[45] Article "Lamentations" in *Encyclopædia Britannica*, ninth ed.

[46] *Introduction to the Literature of the Old Testament*, p. 465.

THE PSALMS AND OTHER SACRED WRITINGS

the poems may not come from one and the same author.[47] Again, the evidence may not be absolutely conclusive; at the same time the book presents some phenomena which find a more natural interpretation on the assumption that the book consists of poems coming from different authors: (1) The difference in the order of the letters of the Hebrew alphabet;[48] (2) the difference in the length of the stanzas, and in the placing of the characteristic letter of the alphabet;[49] (3) the description in chapters 2 and 4 is much more vivid than in chapters 1, 3, and 5, which may indicate an earlier date or earlier dates for the poems in chapters 2 and 4.

If there is diversity of authorship, the dates of the individual poems are not easily determined.[50] In view of the vivid descriptions in chapters 2 and 4 these two poems might be assigned to about B. C. 570; they are probably the work of one, or perhaps, two men who passed through the distressing experiences of the siege and capture of Jerusalem, or, at least, who lived near enough to the calamity to feel its full weight. Chapter 3, on account of its highly artificial structure and its pronounced didactic tone, is generally considered the latest of the five poems, to be dated about B. C. 325, or even later.[51] Opinions differ widely regarding the date of chapter 1;[52] on the whole, however, a date shortly before

---

[47] Revised Edition, same page.
[48] See above, pp. 201.
[49] See above, p. 201.
[50] Almost every independent investigator reaches conclusions which differ from those of his predecessors.
[51] Compare C. Steuernagel, *Einleitung in das Alte Testament*, p. 761.
[52] For example, Loehr, about 530, Budde, not earlier than 430, Driver, soon after 586. Chapter 1 is probably dependent upon Chapter 2, but there is no need for making it very much later.

THE BOOK OF LAMENTATIONS

the return under Cyrus seems to satisfy best the internal evidence.[53] To the same general period must be assigned chapter 5. While considerable evidence may be adduced in support of the dates here suggested, still it may be wise to admit the justice of Selbie's statement: "On this subject criticism has not yet spoken the last word."[54]

Nothing is known regarding the time when the individual poems were brought together to form the present book. It has been suggested that at first, about the time of Nehemiah, a collection was formed consisting of Chapters 1, 2, and 4; and that subsequently, about B. C. 300, Chapters 3 and 5 were added by the author of the poem in Chapter 3; but no certainty can be had on this point.

Significance. The book of Lamentations is of interest and value because it furnishes a vivid and, in some cases at least, a contemporaneous picture of the thoughts and emotions aroused by the fall of Jerusalem in the survivors of that catastrophe. No doubt the faith of some was shattered; but there were many others who remained loyal to their God and who were convinced that, in spite of all appearances to the contrary, Yahweh's compassion and loving-kindness would never cease. However, these faithful ones were also persuaded that heartfelt repentance must precede the return of the divine favor. This conviction inspired the confessions of guilt, exhortations to repentance and prayers for mercy, which constitute such an important element in the book.

---

[53] Especially, verses 3 and 4.
[54] Article "Lamentations," in Hastings, *Dictionary of the Bible.*

CHAPTER IX

THE BOOK OF ECCLESIASTES

CHAPTER IX

THE BOOK OF ECCLESIASTES

Name. The Hebrew name of the book called Ecclesiastes in English[1] is קֹהֶלֶת, *Kōheleth*, in form a feminine participle of the verb *ḳāhal*, which is a derivative from the noun *ḳāhāl*, which may be translated "an assembly"; the verb, therefore, refers to some activity in connection with the holding of an assembly. The feminine is that of official status; that is, it is a designation not only of an office, but also of the holder of an office, a usage not uncommon in Hebrew.[2] The exact meaning of *Kōheleth* is uncertain; among the translations proposed are "caller of assemblies," "preacher," "debater," "great orator," "ideal teacher," "collector of wise sayings." W. T. Davison suggests that a combination of "debater" and "ideal teacher" is needed, and since he cannot find a single word expressing the full meaning, he proposes the following definition of the term: one officially discharging the duties of a teacher in the schools, conducting a discussion concerning grave questions of faith and conduct which he desires to bring to satisfactory issue.[3] That the word contains a didactic element is without question, for the contents of the book clearly show that the author aims to impress upon the listeners and readers the conclusions

---

[1] The English word is a transliteration of the Greek Ἐκκλησιαστής, which is retained in the Vulgate.
[2] Gesenius-Kautzsch, *Hebrew Grammar*, 122r.
[3] *The Wisdom Literature of the Old Testament*, p. 215.

which he has reached on the basis of experience and observation.

Contents and Outline. The book of Ecclesiastes, like the book of Job, represents speculative wisdom;[4] but while the latter deals with a single problem, namely the problem of suffering,[5] Ecclesiastes reflects upon life as a whole, the author emphasizing from beginning to end the emptiness of the whole of human life. The author evidently had passed through many disappointments; as a result his spirit had grown pessimistic and even skeptical, and he had reached the conclusion, stated both at the beginning[6] and near the close,[7] that all is vanity. He seeks to establish this conclusion by appeal to various fields of human interest and endeavor: labor, riches, pleasure, honor, and even search for wisdom and righteousness fail to bring satisfaction; and since he has no clear vision of a life after death he can find no consolation in the hope of immortality. Over against these disappointing experiences stands the faith of his fathers, that the affairs of this world are ordered by a holy and righteous God. The book *in its present form* seems to portray the struggle between this faith and the actual experiences of life, a struggle which ends in the triumph of faith.

For reasons that will be set forth in the next section it is difficult to make an analysis of the book; nevertheless, at least a general outline may be attempted. The book consists of a prologue, an epilogue, and, between the two, the main discussion in four parts. The prologue states

---

[4] See above, p. 92.
[5] See above, pp. 132.
[6] 1. 2.
[7] 12. 8.

the author's contention, the epilogue his conclusion, while the main discussion is intended to furnish the proof of the contention, each part giving the result of an experiment, or of a group of efforts, to satisfy the yearnings of the human heart.

I. THE PROLOGUE—THE AUTHOR'S CONTENTION (1. 1-11).

On the assumption that there is no life after death, and that, consequently man's deepest longings must be satisfied in this life, the author declares all human efforts to find satisfaction and happiness to be in vain.

II. PROOF OF THE CONTENTION (1. 12 to 12. 8)

1. Vanity of wisdom, pleasure, and riches (1. 12 to 2. 26).
2. Vanity of labor and industry (3. 1 to 5. 20).
    Everything is foreordained; death is preferable to a life spent in vain struggle with the foreordained order of things. Nothing is left, therefore, but to make the best of the few fleeting years of life and to enjoy them.
3. Vanity of wealth, prudence, and righteousness (6. 1 to 8. 15).
    Wealth cannot overrule providence; common sense is staggered when it beholds the inequalities of life. There is no solution of the mystery; hence eat, drink, and be merry.
4. Recapitulation of arguments and summing up of the findings (8. 16 to 12. 8).
    The author sees no prospect of ever finding satisfaction in this life, for man's life ends as it begins, in vanity. Therefore let the young man rejoice in his youth, yet not so as to forget his responsibility to his Creator.

III. THE EPILOGUE—CONCLUDING OBSERVATIONS (12. 9-14)

1. Aim of the author—to teach words of truth (12. 9, 10).
2. Sufficiency of the book (12. 11, 12).
3. Supreme duty of man—Fear God and keep his commandments (12. 13, 14).

Is the Book of Ecclesiastes a Unity? The imperfections in the literary form of the book of Ecclesiastes have long been recognized; and Cheyne expresses the consensus of modern scholarship when he calls the book "disjointed" and "rough."[8] There are frequent breaks in the thought and not a few apparent inconsistencies. The general outlook of the discussion is dark and gloomy, and is accurately reflected in the often repeated, "Vanity of vanities, all is vanity." The more important elements in this pessimistic picture are well summarized by McFadyen: The world is clearly out of gear and there is no chance for improvement, for everything is unalterably fixed.[9] Life is a weary round of contradictions,[10] and by reason of the fixity of these contradictions all human effort is in vain.[11] This is true not only of the labor for food and drink or riches, but also of the search for knowledge and wisdom; not only of the physical world but of the moral world as well. There is no goal in nature;[12] history runs on and runs nowhere; all effort is swallowed up by death. Man is no better than the beast;[13] beyond the grave there is nothing. Everywhere is disillusionment, and woman is the bitterest of all.[14] The moral order is clearly turned upside down; wrong seems to be on the throne; Providence, if there be such a thing, seems to be on the side of cruelty, and there is no one to comfort the oppressed.[15] The just perish and the wicked live long;[16] and, in general, it happens to the righteous man according to the work of the wicked and to the wicked according to the work of the righteous.[17]

---

[8] *Job and Solomon*, p. 204.
[9] 1. 15; 7. 13.
[10] 3. 1–8.
[11] 3. 9.
[12] 1. 2-11.
[13] 3. 19.
[14] 7. 26.
[15] 4. 1.
[16] 7. 15.
[17] 8. 14; 9. 2.

THE BOOK OF ECCLESIASTES

Surely, to be dead is better than to live in such a world;[18] yea, it is better not to have been born at all.[19]

But this is by no means the attitude toward life in all parts of the book. Intermingled with expressions of hopelessness are some of brighter hue: "Truly the light is sweet, and a pleasant thing it is for the eyes to behold the sun."[20] In some cases the differences amount to actual contradictions. Over against the thought that there is nothing better than to eat, drink, and have a joyous time in general,[21] stands the assertion that it is better to go to the house of mourning than to the house of feasting,[22] or the summing up of the whole discussion in the words: "Fear God, and keep his commandments."[23] According to 3. 9 human labor is useless, because all things are unalterably fixed; in other words, the fixity is deplored; but in 3. 11 it is called "beautiful." While several passages imply a belief that the moral order is turned upside down, there are others which recognize the reality of a righteous administration of the world: the fate of the righteous is not the same as that of the wicked, for it is well with him who fears God and ill with the man who fears him not;[24] moreover, a judgment is sure to come, both to the righteous and to the wicked.[25] It may be better to be dead than to be alive,[26] but the definite assertion is also made that it is far better to be alive

---
[18] 4. 2.
[19] 6. 3.
[20] 11. 7.
[21] 2. 24.
[22] 7. 2.
[23] 12. 13; compare verse 1.
[24] 8. 12, 13.
[25] 3. 17; 11. 9; 12. 14.
[26] 4. 2, 3.

than to be dead.[27] The search for wisdom, like the search for madness and folly, is striving after wind;[28] on the other hand, "wisdom excelleth folly, as far as light excelleth darkness."[29] Labor is a burden and vanity, for it leads nowhere;[30] on the other hand, there is nothing better than that a man should rejoice in his works.[31] In addition to these more or less pronounced contradictions the disconnectedness of entire sections[32] and the frequency of abrupt transitions[33] tend to break up the continuity and unity of the book.

How are these phenomena to be explained? (1) In the first place, it has been suggested that the book has had its "disjointed" form from the beginning, and that the disconnectedness and the apparent contradictions are to be explained on the assumption that the book records either the varying moods of one and the same man,[34] or the opinions of two or more disputants. In the latter case, the book might perhaps be regarded as the report of a discussion held in a religious academy.[35] A still different explanation would be that the more skeptical passages are the sayings of an infidel objector, quoted by the author for the purpose of refuting them. The common element in these views is the assertion that the book has undergone no essential alterations since it was

[27] 9. 4, 5.
[28] 1. 17, 18.
[29] 2. 13.
[30] 2. 22.
[31] 3. 22.
[32] For instance, Chapter 10 looks very much like an independent collection of proverbs, not an integral part of the general discussion.
[33] Compare, for example, 7. 19, 20.
[34] Compare Tennyson's *Two Voices*.
[35] The closing verses, 12. 13, 14, might then be regarded as the final word or conclusion of the whole discussion.

THE BOOK OF ECCLESIASTES

first written.[36] (2) Other scholars believe that the breaks are too abrupt and the contradictions too pronounced to be accounted for on the theory that they were in the original work, whatever its purpose may have been; hence they have searched for other explanations. Thus Bickel has sought to account for them by assuming that the leaves of the book, in manuscript form, had become disarranged, through some accident, and that subsequently, in the attempt to construct a coherent whole out of the disarranged leaves, editorial additions and changes were made, which only increased the confusion.[37] Similarly, Cheyne has suggested that Chapters 3-12 were compiled from loose notes after the author's death. (3) Still other scholars are dissatisfied with all of these explanations. They favor the view that the confusion has arisen from changes and interpolations introduced into the original work by one or more editors, in a desire to correct the skeptical tone of the original work.[38]

In the absence of all external evidence there is naturally wide difference of opinion regarding the number and extent of these interpolations. Even some otherwise very conservative scholars question the originality of the epilogue,[39] or at least of the closing verses.[40]

---

[36] This is essentially the view of Nowack, Plumptre, Wildeboer, Tyler, von Baudissin, Driver, and others.

[37] Compare G. Bickell, *Kohelets Untersuchung ueber den Werth des Daseins*.

[38] The theory of C. Siegfried may serve as an illustration of the interpolation theory in its more extreme form. He holds that there were at least four distinct revisions: at first, the original essentially pessimistic work was interpolated and changed by an Epicurean Sadducee, then by a "wisdom" glossator, then by a "pious" glossator, and finally by other glossators, whose work cannot be individualized (*Prediger und Hoheslied*, pp. 6ff.).

[39] 12. 9-14.

[40] Verses 13, 14.

THE PSALMS AND OTHER SACRED WRITINGS

Among the reasons for this view are the following: (1) The speaker, who speaks throughout the rest of the book in the first person, is here spoken of in the third; (2) the introduction of the command in verse 13 is rather abrupt; (3) nowhere else is the reader addressed as "my son";[41] (4) and most important of all, verse 13, like verse 1a, emphasizes *godliness* in a manner foreign to the general spirit of the book, "whose *summum bonum* is the discreet and temperate *enjoyment of life*." Moreover, while the thought of the closing verses is not necessarily incompatible with the rest of the book, it certainly cannot be considered a summing up either of the book as a whole, or of the "preacher's" own feelings. In the words of Driver: "Chapter 12. 13 lays stress upon a thought *implicit* in the teaching of the book but disregards that which is explicit." Thus, there seems to be good reason for the same writer's conclusion: "The truth is, 12. 13, 14 can be vindicated for the author only at the cost of an inconsistency."[42]

Ideas not in accord with what seems to be the general thought of the book are expressed also in 2. 26; 3. 17; 7. 18b, 26b, 29; 8. 2b, 3a, 5, 6a, 11-13; 11. 9c; 12. 1a.

---

[41] Verse 12.

[42] *Introduction to the Literature of the Old Testament*, p. 478. It may well be that the sentiment of the epilogue was at least in part responsible for the admission of the book into the canon; but there is insufficient reason for the assumption that the verses were added as late as the Council of Jamnia, about A. D. 90—which finally determined the extent of the Jewish canon—for the purpose of adapting Ecclesiastes for reception into the canon and furnishing a suitable close for the third division of the canon. No doubt verse 12a might be rendered so as to give support to this view: "As for more than these—that is, the canonical books—beware, my son"; but the reference is rather to books other than Ecclesiastes.

THE BOOK OF ECCLESIASTES

In addition, in various parts of the book proverbs are found which seem to interrupt the continuity of the main argument.[43] Many modern scholars consider these passages, as well as the epilogue, later interpolations, and there is a growing tendency to trace them to at least two hands, one representing orthodox wisdom, the other, orthodox religion.[44]

In the nature of the case, one cannot speak dogmatically on a question of this kind; yet on the whole the presence of interpolations can hardly be doubted; at any rate, the elimination of some or all of the passages enumerated removes inconsistencies which are quite serious and leaves a connected argument that can readily be understood as the production of a single mind. This does not mean, however, that the more radical interpolation theories should or can be accepted as furnishing the correct solution of the problem. On the contrary, "there is no necessity of supposing that more than two hands have made additions to Ecclesiastes since it left the hands of Koheleth. One was an editor deeply interested in the wisdom literature, and the other who came after him, was deeply imbued with the spirit of the Pharisees. The first edited the book because it formed an important addition to the wisdom literature, and possibly, too, because he thought it a work of Solomon. The second, finding such a work attributed, as he supposed, to Solomon, added his glosses, because he thought it wrong that the great name of Solomon should not support the orthodox doctrines of the time. The material added by these

---

[43] For example, 4. 5, 9-12; 7. 4-6, 7-12, 19; 10. 1-3, 8-14, etc.
[44] See further, J. E. McFadyen, *Introduction to the Old Testament*, p. 308; G. B. Gray, *A Critical Introduction to the Old Testament*, pp. 151, 152. George A. Barton, *Ecclesiastes*, pp. 43ff.

THE PSALMS AND OTHER SACRED WRITINGS

glossators is, however, but a small part of the material in the book."[45]

Date and Authorship. From the days of the Midrashim and the Targums to long after the period of the Reformation the title in I. 1, "The words of the Preacher, the son of David, king in Jerusalem," were almost universally interpreted, both among Jews and Christians, as implying Solomonic authorship.[46] True, Luther threw out a suggestion that Solomon was not the author,[47] but it was more than a century before he found any followers.[48] However, beginning with the latter part of the eighteenth century, the number of scholars denying the Solomonic authorship of Ecclesiastes steadily increased, and at present it is universally admitted that both language and contents make it impossible to believe that Solomon wrote the book.

Modern scholars base their view principally upon the following considerations: (1) The expression in I. 12, "I *was* king," seems to imply that the author's reign was ended when he wrote; Solomon continued as king to the day of his death. (2) The author contrasts himself with all who were before him in Jerusalem, the context show-

---

[45] George A. Barton, *Ecclesiastes*, p. 46.

[46] Solomon is not named, but the son of David who was king in Jerusalem can be no other than Solomon, who was renowned for his extraordinary wisdom.

[47] He says in his *Table Talk:* "Solomon himself did not write the book of Ecclesiastes, but it was produced by Sirach at the time of the Maccabees.... It is a sort of Talmud, compiled from many books, probably from the library of King Ptolemy Euergetes of Egypt."

[48] Grotius wrote in his Commentary, published in 1644: "I believe that the book is not the production of Solomon, but was written in the name of this king, as being led by repentance to do it. For it contains many words which cannot be found except in Ezra, Daniel, and the Chaldee paraphrases."

THE BOOK OF ECCLESIASTES

ing that he means all kings;[49] this would seem to imply that he was preceded by a line of kings, but there had been but two kings of Israel prior to Solomon, only one of whom had lived in Jerusalem, namely, his father David.[50] (3) Some of the utterances are inappropriate on the lips of Solomon. For example, would he condemn so bitterly the maladministration of justice, for which he as king would have been responsible?[51] The references to kings read as if they came from one who suffered from their misrule rather than from an author who was one of them. (4) In the light of present-day knowledge regarding the history of Hebrew literature the complaint against the making of many books[52] seems inappropriate in the days of Solomon. (5) The very existence of the problem that troubled the author, especially in its individual aspect which is emphasized throughout, presupposes a much later stage in the thought development of the Hebrews.[53] (6) The language cannot be harmonized with the early date. The argument from language is rarely conclusive, but in this case it clearly and definitely militates against an early date. "If the book of Koheleth is of old Solomonic origin," says the cautious and conservative Franz Delitzsch, "then there is no history of the Hebrew language." Indeed, the evidence against the traditional view is so strong that more than thirty years ago Dean Plumptre could write, "No one now dreams of

---

[49] 1. 16; 2. 7–9.
[50] It is not natural to interpret the phrase as referring to a line of unknown Canaanite kings who reigned in Jerusalem before David captured the city.
[51] 3. 16; 4. 1; 5. 8, etc.
[52] 12. 12.
[53] See above, p. 91.

THE PSALMS AND OTHER SACRED WRITINGS

ascribing it to Solomon." [54] The use of Solomon's name, therefore, is a literary device, commonly used during the later postexilic period, which finds another illustration in the apocryphal "wisdom of Solomon," written during the first century B. C. What would or could be more natural than to ascribe these observations and reflections to the wise King Solomon? He with his limitless wealth, splendor, magnificence, and harem had enjoyed every opportunity of tasting and testing life; moreover on account of his extraordinary wisdom, sayings coming from him would have more than ordinary significance and weight.

All available evidence combines to prove, not only that Ecclesiastes could not have been written in the tenth century, but also that it is one of the latest books in the entire Old Testament: (1) While the historical references and allusions are all more or less indefinite, the general historical background is clearly that of the late postexilic period. Evidently, the author lived in an age of social and political disorder and upheaval; folly was set in great dignity, while the wise occupied the low places; servants rode upon horses, and princes had to walk like servants;[55] the rulers were young, inexperienced, and tyrannical, and their representatives in the provinces were cruel and rapacious; justice was perverted and the land was full of spies seeking to ruin the upright.[56] This is a truthful picture of conditions during the late Persian period, when the empire founded by Cyrus had become the "happy hunting-ground of political exploiters and adventurers." But the description would fit equally well the years im-

---
[54] *Ecclesiastes*, p. 21.
[55] 10. 6, 7.
[56] 3. 16ff.; 4. 1; 5. 8, 9; 10. 8ff.

THE BOOK OF ECCLESIASTES

mediately preceding the Maccabean uprising: the woe upon the land whose king is a child[57] might be interpreted as a reference to Ptolemy V,[58] who was less than five years of age when he came to the throne; the succeeding verses might then be applied to Antiochus, who in B. C. 198 wrested Palestine from Egypt and made it a province of Syria.[59] Thus interpreted, the historical allusions would be in perfect accord with a date early in the second century B. C., but before the Maccabean uprising, which caused a decided change in the situation; moreover, the depressed tone of the book would not suit the stirring age of the Maccabees.

The theology of the book, if its teaching can be called theology, points to the same late period. The author was a serious thinker: he was perplexed by his experiences and observations, he sought to solve life's problems and mysteries, but was baffled in his attempts; hence he rebelled against the limitations of knowledge and wisdom. The discussion is more abstract than that of Job, the speculation is more advanced, and the pessimism more developed and deliberate than anywhere else in the Old Testament. There is no trace of the religious enthusiasm of the prophets, or even of the early legalists; the book reflects, rather, the later spirit of indifference as found, for example, among the Sadducees.

The presence of numerous parallels with Greek thought has led some scholars to believe that the author was influenced more or less directly by Greek philosophy. Thus, the warning against extremes[60] is thought to be

---
[57] 10. 16.
[58] B. C. 205–181.
[59] Compare also 4, 13–16,
[60] 7. 16–18.

related to Aristotle's doctrine of the mean; the influence of Heraclitus has been seen in 3. 1-8, while 2. 1-11 is placed alongside of the Stoic doctrine of recurring cycles, and Chapter 3 is compared with the doctrine of determinism held by the same school. The influence of Epicurus has been traced in the numerous statements which imply that the only attainable happiness lies in the rational enjoyment of the good things of this present life. The theory of direct dependence, though advocated by earlier scholars, was first fully developed by Tyler in 1874, and has since been adopted by many more recent writers, among them Pfleiderer, Plumptre, Wildeboer, Siegfried, and Cornill. Others have insisted with equal emphasis that the entire discussion is an independent development of Jewish thought. Cheyne, for example, writes: "I do not see that we *must* admit even a vague Greek influence";[61] and with him agree both McNeile and Barton, who have made a careful and extensive study of the whole question. The latter reaches the conclusion that "the book of Ecclesiastes represents an original development of Hebrew thought, thoroughly Semitic in its point of view, and quite independent of Greek influences."[62] The truth lies, perhaps, between these two extreme views. In the words of A. R. Gordon: "While agreeing with these[63] and other scholars that the Preacher is at heart a Jew, the tone of the book, its frank materialism, and its almost cynical commendation of the 'golden mean' as the only course of wisdom, with its thought of the endless flux of nature reducing life to mere 'vanity,' seem to the present writer clearly to suggest that he was

---

[61] *Job and Solomon*, p. 271.
[62] *Ecclesiastes*, p. 49.
[63] McNeile and Barton.

THE BOOK OF ECCLESIASTES

influenced by the general currents of Greek culture that were then sweeping over the Eastern world."[64] If the author was under the influence of Greek thought, he must have lived subsequently to the time of Alexander the Great, for it was he who opened the way for the influx of Hellenism into Syria and Palestine. But whether the reality of Greek influence is admitted or not, the general thought of the book points to a time later than the fourth century B. C.

In the case of Ecclesiastes the argument from language is not without weight. Clearly, it represents the very latest stage in biblical Hebrew: Many words occur again only in late books like Chronicles, Ezra, Nehemiah, Esther; there are some Aramaic words, and some words and idioms found otherwise only in the post-biblical Hebrew of the Mishna.[65] In the light of these facts Gray is undoubtedly right when he says, "On the ground of language alone it must be held that the book was written at the earliest in the fourth century B. C., and more probably at least a century or two later."[66]

But while all the evidence points to the later postexilic period, the precise date of Ecclesiastes cannot be determined. Some scholars have advocated a date during the later Persian age, in the fifth or fourth century,[67] while

---

[64] *The Poets of the Old Testament*, p. 333; J. E. McFadyen, *An Introduction to the Old Testament*, p. 301; S. R. Driver, *Introduction to the Literature of the Old Testament*, p. 477, etc.

[65] Some have discovered in the language even traces of Greek influence (for example, Graetz, Tyler, Wildeboer), but this is less certain (T. K. Cheyne, *Job and Solomon*, p. 260; A. H. McNeile, *Introduction to Ecclesiastes*, p. 43).

[66] *A Critical Introduction to the Old Testament*, p. 153.

[67] Ewald, Delitzsch, Keil, and others.

THE PSALMS AND OTHER SACRED WRITINGS

a few have dated it as late as the first century B. C.,[68] but scholars are coming to be more and more agreed in placing the origin of the book at about B. C. 200. If the conquest of Palestine by Antiochus is presupposed, the date cannot be earlier than B. C. 198. If, on the other hand, the author of Ecclesiasticus knew Ecclesiastes,[69] it cannot be later than B. C. 180. Probably at some time between these two dates the original book of Ecclesiastes was written. Nothing is known of the writer. It would seem, however, that he was a man of wealth, culture, and social position, who had drunk deeply of life's enjoyments, but had found nothing but disappointment of spirit.[70]

Teaching and Significance. The book of Ecclesiastes did not secure a permanent position in the canon until the Council of Jamnia, about A. D. 90. Though it had acquired some degree of sanctity before that time, it was objected to by some Jewish teachers, chiefly on three grounds: (1) It contradicted itself;[71] (2) it made the assertion that the creatures of God are vain, and placed greater value upon worldly pleasures than upon higher and more spiritual things: (3) its pronounced skepticism

---

[68] Tyler and Koenig during the reign of Alexander Jannaeus, B. C. 104-78; Graetz, during the reign of Herod, B. C. 39-4.

[69] It has been questioned whether such familiarity exists, but the evidence seems to be conclusive that the author of the one book knew the other; and if so, the priority of Ecclesiastes is beyond doubt (Plumptre, *Ecclesiastes*, pp. 56ff.; A. H. McNeile, *Introduction to Ecclesiastes*, pp. 34ff.; G. A. Barton, *Ecclesiastes*, pp. 53ff.). The last named reaches the conclusion that the author of Ecclesiasticus used the words of Ecclesiastes, "as a modern writer might weave into his work the words of Browning or Tennyson or any other well known author."

[70] Dean Plumptre has written a suggestive, if fanciful, ideal biography of the author; *Ecclesiastes*, pp. 35ff.

[71] See above, pp. 216-218.

THE BOOK OF ECCLESIASTES

was said to tend toward infidelity and atheism. The defenders of the book also depended chiefly upon three arguments: (1) It was the production of the great and wise Solomon; (2) it was early recognized as sacred scripture; (3) it begins with the law and ends with the law.[72] No doubt it was the alleged Solomonic authorship of the book and the religious emphasis in the closing verses that finally decided the controversy in favor of the book's retention among the sacred writings.

If modern scholars are right in assuming that back of the present Ecclesiastes lies a book permeated from beginning to end by a spirit of pessimism and skepticism, the aim of this original work would have been simply to expose the emptiness and vanity of human life.[73] In the words of E. J. Dillon: "He [that is, the author of the original Ecclesiastes] is an uncompromising pessimist, who sees the world as it is. Everything that seems pleasant or profitable is vanity and a grasping of wind; there is nothing positive but pain, nothing real but the eternal Will, which is certainly unknowable and probably unconscious. . . . When all has been said and done, the highest worldly wisdom is but a less harmful species of folly. Existence is an evil, and the sole effective remedy renunciation."[74] This very skepticism has proved an attraction

---

[72] The statement is true of the close, 12. 13, but as to the beginning it finds its only support in an artificial, rabbinical interpretation of 1. 3.

[73] Connecting Ecclesiastes with Job, it has been suggested that the former "deals the last fatal blow to the popular doctrine of retribution." If prosperity, wealth, power, wisdom, long life, etc., are all vanity, how can they be regarded as signs of God's favor? Or, how can the opposite be regarded as evidence of the divine wrath? (Bennett and Adeney, *A Biblical Introduction*, p. 166). Though these inferences may be drawn from the discussion, it is doubtful that the author desired to throw any light on the doctrine.

[74] *Sceptics of the Old Testament*, p. 113.

THE PSALMS AND OTHER SACRED WRITINGS

to many modern minds. Renan considered Ecclesiastes "the most charming book" in the Old Testament; he preferred the attitude of its author to that of the prophets who, he thought, lived in the clouds; he admired the Preacher because "he is content to shrug his shoulders over abuses and say to the would-be reformer, 'No use!' " Even some philosophers have made its vanity of vanities the keynote of their own systems.[75]

Whatever else, however, the author may have been—Renan considers him to have been a man of the world, a skeptic, a materialist, a fatalist, and a pessimist—he certainly was not an atheist. In spite of his pessimism he retained a belief in God, and vague though it may have been, it proved sufficient to keep him "clean in heart and true to the compass of honest duty." "Koheleth's moral principles," says A. R. Gordon, "read like undiluted Epicureanism. But when touched by the fear of God, his Epicureanism becomes, not, indeed, the heroic virtue of the prophet and saint, but at all events *decent moderate morality*."[76]

In the present book of Ecclesiastes, whether it represents the work in its original form or as it left the hands of later revisers, the more cheerful note of faith occupies a larger place. In this form it may well be called a "cry for light." The light does not yet shine clearly, though here and there glimpses appear. An element of doubt and perplexity remains, because the horizon of the author, and even of the latest editor, is bounded by the grave. He can find no hope in this life, and the book shows conclusively the utter insufficiency of this present life to solve its own mysteries. This forces him to look with

---
[75] Compare, for instance, Schopenhauer, *The World as Will and Idea*.
[76] *The Poets of the Old Testament*, pp. 341, 342.

THE BOOK OF ECCLESIASTES

longing for a possible solution of the mysteries of the present in an after life; but it remains a hope and a cry; it never becomes a conviction.[77] In the presence of this uncertainty the retention of faith in God assumes even greater significance. The author is conscious of a moral order in the universe; though its operation is often frustrated, in many cases the God-fearing man is seen to have an advantage over the wicked. Hence, with all his doubts and questionings, he maintains that it is his duty, as it is the duty of all men, to fear God and keep his commandments; God somehow will take care of the perplexities and mysteries of life. The manifestation of this faith causes Cornill to write: "The piety of the Old Testament has never celebrated a greater triumph than in the book of Koheleth";[78] and it is the preservation of this faith in the midst of confusion and perplexity that gives to the book its unique value and significance in the present age of intellectual unrest.

---

[77] In this Ecclesiastes resembles Job. The very emphasis placed on the emptiness of the present life would in the end point the way to a belief in resurrection and immortality.

[78] *Einleitung in das Alte Testament*, p. 251.

CHAPTER X
THE BOOK OF ESTHER

CHAPTER X

THE BOOK OF ESTHER

Name and Extent. The book is named Esther after the heroine of the story,[1] a Jewish maiden who is said to have lived in the days of Xerxes.[2] It belongs to the third division of the Jewish Canon, and is one of the five *Megilloth,* or Rolls,[3] appointed to be read on the feast of Purim. The Septuagint translators treated the Hebrew text with considerable freedom. Not only did they modify in many places the text before them, but in addition they made more or less extensive interpolations in several parts of the book. In the Vulgate the most important of these are separated from their contexts and placed together at the end of the canonical book. In the English Apocrypha they are arranged, following the order of the Vulgate, as a separate book, bearing the title "The Rest of the Book of Esther."[4]

Canonicity. The tone of the book compares unfavorably with the spirit of almost every other Old Testament

---

[1] Hebrew, אֶסְתֵּר, *Estēr;* Septuagint, 'Εσθήρ, *Esthēr;* Vulgate, *Esther.*
[2] B. C. 485–465.
[3] See above, p. 165.
[4] The more extensive additions are:
   1. The Dream of Mordecai.
   2. The Exposition of Mordecai's Dream.
   3. The Decree for the Destruction of the Jews, drawn by Haman.
   4. The Prayer of Mordecai.
   5. The Prayer of Esther.
   6. The Interview of Esther with the King.
   7. The Edict in Favor of the Jews.

THE PSALMS AND OTHER SACRED WRITINGS

book. The absence of the divine name, God, or Yahweh, while noteworthy, is perhaps of little significance. It may easily be explained on the assumption that the writer considered it more appropriate not to use the divine name in a book intended for use on a festival celebrated with much feasting and revelry. Moreover, the presence and activity of God as the protector and preserver of Israel is assumed throughout.[5] Of much greater significance is the absence, from beginning to end, of a truly religious atmosphere. Its conception of the character of God is low, and its religion lacks a truly ethical note.[6] On account of the pronounced secular character of the contents the canonicity of Esther continued to be questioned even after the Council of Jamnia, which decided in favor of its retention in the canon. It is omitted from the list of canonical books ascribed to Melito, Bishop of Sardis; and even some of the Jewish rabbis sought to exclude it. The exaggeration of its value by others[7] suggests uneasiness regarding its standing. Again and again voices of protest were raised among Christians. As late as the fourth century Athanasius and Gregory Nazianzen refused to include it among the canonical books, and in the east, where the conception of canonicity was more rigid, opposition continued to manifest itself throughout the Middle Ages.[8] The action of the Council of Carthage, in A. D.

---

[5] See, for instance, 4. 14.

[6] It may be that the interpolations of the Septuagint are due to a desire to remedy this defect. At any rate, the terms "God" and "Lord" occur frequently in these additions, and both Mordecai and Esther are made to offer prayer.

[7] Maimonides, A. D. 1135–1204, for example, declares that the Law and Esther will survive all the rest of the Old Testament.

[8] In the fourteenth century it was rejected by the Ecclesiastical Historian Nicephorus Callistus.

THE BOOK OF ESTHER

397, gave the book a securer position in the Western church, but Luther spoke very slightingly of it and said that he wished it did not exist.

Contents and Outline. The book of Esther contains the story of Esther, a Jewish maiden in the Persian capital Susa, who rose to be queen of Xerxes, and as such rescued her countrymen from the evil plottings of Haman, a favorite of the king. The story is well told: At a royal banquet Xerxes, the king, ordered Vashti his queen to appear before the assembled guests; when she refused to come he put her away. After a diligent search, extending over several years, the queen's crown was placed upon the head of Esther, the cousin and adopted daughter of Mordecai, a man of the tribe of Benjamin, living in Susa. Soon afterward Mordecai saved the king's life by revealing a plot to assassinate him. A short time later the king promoted a certain Haman above all the other nobles at court and ordered his servants to do obeisance to him. Mordecai refused, whereupon Haman, out of hatred, procured from the king a decree for the destruction of the Jews.

Esther, acting on the suggestion of Mordecai, succeeded in frustrating the cruel scheme, Haman suffered disgrace, and was hung on the very gallows he had prepared for Mordecai, while the latter was exalted to the position formerly occupied by Haman. Since Persian law did not permit the revocation of the decree secured by Haman, the king, to offset it, granted permission to the Jews to defend themselves against their foes on the day appointed in the earlier decree for their own destruction. Thus it happened that on the thirteenth and fourteenth days of the month Adar[9] the Jews slew, through-

---
[9] Equivalent to latter part of February and early part of March.

out the Persian empire, more than seventy-five thousand of their enemies. In commemoration of the deliverance the fourteenth and fifteenth days of Adar were set apart each year as "days of feasting and gladness, and of sending portions one to another, and gifts to the poor." To this festival was given the name Purim, that is "Lots," with allusion to the casting of the lot by Haman, for the purpose of fixing the date of the massacre.[10] The book closes with an account of the greatness and power of Mordecai.

I. Exaltation of Esther (1. 1 to 2. 18).

1. Feast of Xerxes (1. 1-8).
2. Disobedience and rejection of Vashti, the queen (1. 9-22).
3. Choice and exaltation of Esther (2. 1-18).

II. Haman's Plot Against the Jews (2. 19 to 3. 15)

1. Mordecai's discovery of the plot against the king (2. 19-23).
2. Haman's promotion; Mordecai's refusal to do obeisance (3. 1-6).
3. Plot for the destruction of the Jews (3. 7-15).

III. Frustration of Haman's Plot (4. 1 to 8. 2)

1. Esther's decision to intercede for her countrymen (4. 1-17).
2. Esther's banquet for the king and Haman (5. 1-8).
3. Erection of gallows by Haman for Mordecai (5. 9-14).
4. Exaltation of Mordecai (6. 1-11; 8. 1, 2).
5. Disgrace and execution of Haman (6. 12 to 7. 10).

IV. Deliverance of the Jews; Institution of Purim (8. 3 to 10. 3)

1. Authorization of the Jews to defend themselves (8. 3-17).
2. Slaughter of the enemies (9. 1-16).
3. Institution of the feast of Purim (9. 17-32).
4. Power and greatness of Mordecai (10. 1-3).

Historical Character of the Narrative. The purpose of the book of Esther is twofold: (1) to explain the origin of the feast of Purim, (2) to glorify the Jewish

---

[10] 3. 7.

THE BOOK OF ESTHER

people.[11] But many students of the book have been led to ask the question: Did the feast of Purim actually originate as narrated in the book? This immediately raises a question as to the historical character of the narrative, which has been differently estimated by different writers. Generally speaking, three attitudes toward the narrative may be distinguished:

1. In the first place, there are those who accept the narrative as credible and reliable history from beginning to end; and they support their contention by arguments like these: (1) It is impossible to suppose that a national feast like that of Purim should have originated, in historical times, without some adequate cause such as that described in the book. (2) Internal evidence clearly shows that the author intended to write history; for instance, he gives the names of even unimportant persons,[12] he refers several times to the chronicles of the Persians,[13] he notes frequently the year, month, and even day on which an event occurred.[14] (3) The feast of Purim, called in 2 Maccabees 15. 36 "Mordecai's Day," and celebrated since the days of Josephus[15] by Jews throughout the world, constitutes to the present day a witness to the historicity of the events narrated in the book. (4) Archæology has shown the statements of the author regarding Persian manners and customs, espe-

---

[11] The contents make it clear that (2) is at least a secondary purpose: Esther, the Jewess, is favored above all other virgins; Mordecai, the Jew, refuses to make obeisance to Haman, and Providence justifies his refusal; Mordecai is exalted to a place beside the king, while Haman is hanged; the Jews are destined to rule, while all who oppose or oppress them are doomed to destruction.

[12] For example, 1. 10, 14; 2. 8, 14, 21, etc.

[13] For example, 2. 23; 6. 1; 10. 2.

[14] For example, 1. 3; 2. 16; 3. 7, 13, etc.

[15] *Antiquities*, XI, vi, 13.

cially regarding court practices, to be strikingly accurate. (5) The description of the general character and conduct of King Ahasuerus is in agreement with the information regarding the character of Xerxes derived from other sources. (6) Vashti was deposed in the third year of Xerxes,[16] Esther was made queen in the seventh.[17] The long interval between the two events is easily accounted for by the fact, reported by Herodotus, that the intervening years were devoted to the Grecian war. The feast described in Chapter 1 may have been connected with the great council of war the king is said to have held before his departure. (7) The proper names in the book are, without exception, such as might be used in the days of Xerxes and Darius.

2. A moment's consideration must show that no one can expect to prove, by arguments like these, that the narrative of Esther is throughout credible and reliable history; at the most they may justify the inference that the author was well informed concerning the character of Xerxes as well as concerning Persian customs and practices; and that he made skillful use of his knowledge in the development of the narrative, which may or may not be history. In view of the inconclusive character of this line of evidence, it is hardly strange that others, on the basis of alleged historical improbabilities and impossibilities, should have reached the conclusion that the book is throughout a work of the imagination, developed, perhaps, from mythological material, and written for the purpose of making the feast of Purim popular among the Jews.

Scholars favoring this view support their position by facts like these: (1) The length of the feast provided

---

[16] 1. 3.
[17] 2. 6.

THE BOOK OF ESTHER

by Xerxes: It is pointed out that a feast lasting one hundred and eighty days,[18] that is, nearly six months, would involve in the case of some of the officials an absence from their posts of almost a full year. (2) The contents of the decree suggested by the royal counselors:[19] In view of the position occupied by women in the ancient Oriental household, it is doubted that a Persian ruler would issue a royal decree to the effect that "every man should bear rule in his own house." (3) The representation of Esther as queen of Xerxes after the seventh year of his reign:[20] According to Herodotus,[21] the queen of Xerxes between his seventh and twelfth years was Amestris, whose character was such that she cannot be identified with Esther; nor is there room for the latter beside her. Esther might, indeed, have been one of the women of the harem, but this is not the thought of the biblical narrative, which represents her always as chief queen, if not as sole queen.[22] (4) The manner in which the successor of Vashti is said to have been selected is contrary to the law of Persia, according to which the Persian king was limited to seven noble families of Persia in the choice of his queen.[23] (5) The promulgation of the decree for the destruction of the Jews *eleven months* before it was to be executed. True, it has been suggested that Haman's object in announcing his plan so long in advance was to induce the Jews to leave the empire; but the narrative itself gives no intimation of such object; on the contrary,

---

[18] 1. 4.
[19] 1. 19–22.
[20] 2. 16, 17.
[21] VII, 114; IX, 112.
[22] 2. 17.
[23] Herodotus, III, 84.

THE PSALMS AND OTHER SACRED WRITINGS

it makes the definite impression that Haman, from the very beginning, was bent on the actual destruction of the Jews.[24] (6) The ignorance of Haman regarding the nationality of Esther, though she constantly communicated with Mordecai, who was well known as a Jew.[25] Ahasuerus seems to have shared this ignorance; or, if the statement in 7. 5 does not imply ignorance regarding Esther's nationality, it involves ignorance as to the existence of the decree which, according to 3. 8-11, he himself had authorized. (7) The slaughter of more than seventy-five thousand Persians by the Jews, apparently without any opposition on the part of officials and people, and the ready granting of a second day of vengeance in Susa. (8) The events narrated in the book took place during the reign of Xerxes, who ascended the throne in B. C. 485; Mordecai was not exalted until the twelfth year of the king,[26] that is in B. C. 473 or 472; he continued in power for some years afterward,[27] and there is no suggestion that at the time he was a feeble old man; and yet, according to 2. 6, he was one of the exiles carried away in B. C. 597; which means, that at the time of his exaltation he was at least one hundred and twenty-five years old. (9) It is further pointed out that the narrative as a whole reads like a romance rather than strict history: At each stage the incidents seem to be laid so as to prepare the way for the next, and they follow one another without hitch or interruption—the explanation of the delay between the third and the seventh years of Xerxes, as due to the preparations necessary properly

---

[24] 3. 9; 4. 1-3, 13, 14.
[25] 3. 4, 6.
[26] 3. 7ff.
[27] Compare 10. 1-3.

THE BOOK OF ESTHER

to introduce all the maidens to the king; the discovery of the plot against the life of the king by Mordecai, who, however, received no suitable reward; the offense taken by Haman, who, however, postponed the punishment; the two banquets of Esther, giving opportunity in the interval to picture, first Haman's exultation, then his vexation, in preparation for the disaster which followed; the erection of the gallows by Haman, only to suffer death on it himself; the wakeful night of the king, which becomes the turning point in the life of Haman and of Mordecai; the two edicts and the circumstances of their promulgation—these and other similar features seem to "authorize the inference that whatever materials the narrator may have had at his disposal, he has elaborated them with the conscious design of exhibiting vividly the dramatic contrasts which they suggested to him."[28] (10) Moreover, certain mythological elements have been discovered in the story. Esther is so similar to the name of the Babylonian goddess Ishtar, and Mordecai to that of the Babylonian god Marduk that the existence of some connection between these names can hardly be doubted. Haman suggests the name of the Elamite deity Humman, and Vashti may be the same Mashti,[29] the name of an Elamite goddess. Thus two Babylonian deities would be arrayed against two Elamite deities, the two former gaining the victory. It has been suggested, therefore, that the story in its original form portrayed the conflict between Babylonia and Elam, which was, according to

---

[28] S. R. Driver, *Introduction to the Literature of the Old Testament*, p. 483.
[29] A similar change from *m* to *v* in the reproduction of a foreign name in Hebrew is seen in 2 Kings 25. 27; Evil-merodach is the Babylonian Amel-Marduk.

ancient ways of thinking, a conflict between the gods of Babylonia and the gods of Elam. Another form of the mythological theory sees in the deposing of Vashti followed by the crowning of Esther, and in the passing of Haman followed by the exaltation of Mordecai, a representation of the passing of winter and the coming of spring. The persons named would then be personifications of the powers of nature that had a part in the annual struggle. It is pointed out that the celebration of this change in nature by a feast held in the spring or during the last month of the year, that is, around the first of March, would be very appropriate.

That the Purim festival, with its non-Jewish name, was of foreign origin is not improbable; moreover, the book may be correct in tracing it to Persia, though no Persian word *Pur* meaning "lot" has as yet been found. Nor is it impossible that there exists some connection between the feast of Purim and a Persian spring festival called *Farwardigan,* observed in commemoration of the dead. It is also to be noted that the Babylonian New Year's festival, on which the gods, under the leadership of Marduk, were thought to draw lots for the purpose of determining destinies during the new year,[30] was celebrated in the spring, in the month Nisan, which followed Adar. May it not be that there is some connection between the feast of Purim and the *Farwardigan* festival, and between the casting of the lots in the book of Esther and the determining of destinies on the Babylonian New Year's Day? In other words, the Jews may have adopted a Persian festival, which in turn was derived from a Babylonian original. With the festival may have come

---

[30] E. Schrader, *Die Keilinschriften und das Alte Testament* (Dritte Auflage), pp. 515-520.

THE BOOK OF ESTHER

the myths explaining its origin; and these mythical elements, transformed under the influence of the higher Jewish religion, may still be traced in the story of Esther.

3. A third view takes a position between the two extremes discussed thus far. Scholars holding this view admit that the internal evidence, as outlined in the preceding paragraphs, makes it impossible to accept the narrative as literal history; on the other hand, they insist that there is insufficient reason for denying a historical basis to the story. They suggest that, even admitting that no other literature contains any reference or allusion to persons or events mentioned in the book of Esther,[31] it is not difficult to imagine that a Jewish maiden became the favorite concubine, if not the chief wife, of a Persian ruler[32] and that, as such, she frustrated a plot against her countrymen and delivered them from imminent disaster. This mediating view of the historical significance of Esther is well expressed by the late Professor Driver in these words: "The conclusion to which, on the whole, the facts point . . . is that though the narrative cannot reasonably be doubted to have a substantial historical basis, it includes items that are not strictly historical: the elements of the narrative were supplied to the author by tradition, and, aided by his knowledge of Persian life and customs, he combined them into a consistent picture; in some cases the details were colored already by tradition before they came to the author's hand; in

---

[31] Persian history knows no queens or concubines of Xerxes named Vashti or Esther, no prime ministers named Haman or Mordecai, no decrees for the destruction of the Jews.

[32] The similarity of the name "Esther" to "Amestris," the name of the queen of Xerxes, may be responsible for assigning the events to the reign of Xerxes.

THE PSALMS AND OTHER SACRED WRITINGS

other cases they owe their present form to the author's love of dramatic effect."[33]

Now, the mere possibility that the story of Esther rests upon some kind of historical basis may readily be admitted; but in the absence of all external evidence any attempt to determine the nature of the historical nucleus is bound to end in disappointment. Moreover, internal evidence shows not only that the author gave free play to the imagination in the disposition of all material which he may have derived from tradition, but also that he was quite willing to use mythological material for the purpose of making his story more impressive and beautiful. On the whole, the present writer is inclined to agree with L. B. Paton when he says, "The conclusions seem inevitable that the book of Esther is not historical, and that it is doubtful whether even a historical kernel underlies its narrative."[34]

Date. In the absence of all specific information the date of the book of Esther must be determined entirely on the basis of the language and such indirect internal evidence as may be available: (1) The feast of Purim seems to have been considered an old established institution when the book was written.[35] (2) The references to the reign of Xerxes in 1. 1 and to the capital Susa in 1. 2 read as if the author regarded the Persian empire a thing of the past. (3) The fact that the author found it necessary to explain Persian customs[36] may imply that they were no longer familiar to the people for whom he intended the story. (4) The difficulty raised by

---

[33] *Introduction to the Literature of the Old Testament*, p. 483.
[34] *The Book of Esther*, p. 75.
[35] Compare 9. 19.
[36] For example, 1. 13, 19; 4. 11; 8. 8.

THE BOOK OF ESTHER

the extraordinary age of Mordecai[37] suggests that the past had come to assume an aspect of vagueness with the writer. (5) The whole spirit of the book is late. The narrow nationalism, with its fierce hatred of foreigners, developed gradually from the time of Ezra-Nehemiah onward—first, a narrow exclusiveness, then a sense of oppression and wrong, followed by a spirit of revenge. Though one cannot speak dogmatically, there is much to be said in favor of the view that "its intensely national pride, its cruel and fanatical exclusiveness, can be best explained as the result of a fierce persecution followed by a brilliant triumph; and this condition is exactly met by the period which succeeded the Maccabean wars (B. C. 135 or later). The book with its strong Persian setting may, indeed, have been written earlier in Persia, but it more probably represents a phase of the fierce Palestinian Judaism of the last half of the second century B. C."[38] (6) Ecclesiasticus, written about B. C. 180, does not seem to know the book. Had he known it, the absence of Esther and Mordecai, so prominently identified with the Purim festival, from his roll of honor would be difficult to explain. (7) Language and style favor a late date. True, there is an attempt to imitate classic Hebrew, but, generally speaking, the linguistic affinities of Esther are with Daniel, Chronicles, and the postbiblical Hebrew. It may be safe, therefore, to date the book after 200, perhaps about B. C. 150.

The place of its composition cannot be determined. Some have drawn the inference from the absence of all

---

[37] See above, p. 242.
[38] J. E. McFadyen, *An Introduction to the Old Testament*, p. 313. It has been suggested that Haman is modeled after Antiochus Epiphanes; compare Esther 3. 9 with 1 Mac. 1. 41; 3. 34-36.

reference to Jerusalem and to the postexilic community, and from the intimate knowledge of Persian customs, that the book was written in Persia; but the evidence is not conclusive. Since the author lived some time after the age of Xerxes, he could not in any case speak from personal observation, but had to depend upon other sources of information, which might have been available in Palestine, as well as elsewhere. The silence concerning Palestine is easily explained by the fact that the whole scene is laid in Susa. McFadyen's suggestion is as good as any, namely, that the book is the outgrowth of fierce *Palestinian* Judaism.

CHAPTER XI

THE BOOK OF DANIEL

CHAPTER XI

THE BOOK OF DANIEL

Name and Place in Canon. The name under which the book appears in the Hebrew Bible[1] is the name of the hero of the book,[2] who, according to tradition, was also its author.[3] In the English Old Testament it occupies last place among the so-called Major Prophets; in the Hebrew Bible it is one of the Writings. In other words, in the Jewish canon it belongs to the third division rather than to the second, in which all the other prophetic books of the English Bible are found.[4]

Various explanations have been suggested to account for the separation of Daniel from the other prophetic books. If the book was written subsequently to B. C. 170,[5] as is now generally thought, this fact in itself would be sufficient to explain its position among the Writings, for the prophetic canon was completed about B. C. 200. Of the writers who believe that the book originated during the exile, some hold that it owes its position among the Writings to an error on the part of the early Jews; others, that its apocalyptic character prevented it from taking rank among the prophets; still others believe that at one time it was in the second division, but that subse-

---

[1] דָּנִיֵּאל, Septuagint, Δανιήλ.
[2] Compare the titles of the books of Ruth, Esther, Job, etc.
[3] See further, below, pp. 256, 257.
[4] Except Lamentations.
[5] See further, below, pp. 263–273.

THE PSALMS AND OTHER SACRED WRITINGS

quently to the opening of the Christian era the rabbis, prompted in part by their hostile attitude toward Jesus, "degraded Daniel from the prophetic rank and put his book into the Hagiographa."[6]

The Greek translations of Daniel[7] contain several passages not found in Hebrew.[8] The longer and more important of these additions are found among the Apocrypha of the English Bible: (1) The prayer of Azariah and the song of the Three Holy Children, inserted in the Greek after 3. 23 of the Aramaic Text; (2) the history of Susanna, which in the Septuagint and in translations influenced by it follows at the end, as Chapter 13, while it is found at the beginning in MSS. containing the translation of Theodotion; (3) the account of the destruction of Bel and the Dragon, forming Chapter 14, following the history of Susanna. Of the three additions only the first one can in any sense be regarded as a supplement or expansion of a narrative in the canonical book: its object is to teach, more emphatically than is done in the canonical text, that piety and faith have their reward.[9] The other two stories are independent of the biblical narrative and probably originated independently. The

---

[6] K. F. Keil, *Introduction to Old Testament*, II, pp. 21, 22; H. M. Harman, *Introduction to the Study of the Holy Scriptures*, pp. 401, 402.

[7] Both the Septuagint and the translation of Theodotion; also other translations influenced by the Septuagint. The Septuagint text of Daniel has been preserved in a single MS., the *Codex Chisianus*, perhaps of the eleventh century, which was not published until 1772. Very early the Septuagint text was displaced by the translation of Theodotion; perhaps the former's treatment of the Hebrew text was considered too arbitrary.

[8] See, for similar additions to the book of Esther, above, p. 235.

[9] Both the prayer and the song use such general terms that it is not improbable that they originated independently as liturgical psalms and were subsequently inserted in Daniel.

THE BOOK OF DANIEL

story of Susanna is meant to show that God watches over the innocent and will not permit them to become the prey of the wicked. The stories dealing with the destruction of Bel and the Dragon are intended to teach the folly of idolatry.

Contents and Outline. The book of Daniel falls naturally into two parts: Chapters 1 to 6 narrate six experiences of Daniel and his three companions: (1) The loyalty of the four Hebrew young men at the court of Nebuchadnezzar, and their reward; (2) the dream of Nebuchadnezzar and its interpretation; (3) the episode of the golden image, the faithfulness of Daniel's companions and their deliverance; (4) Nebuchadnezzar's second dream and its interpretation by Daniel; (5) the feast of Belshazzar and the interpretation of the handwriting on the wall; (6) Daniel's courageous loyalty and his deliverance from the lions' den. Chapters 7 to 12 relate four visions of Daniel and their interpretations: (1) the four beasts; (2) the ram and the he-goat; (3) Daniel's prayer and the appearance of the angel Gabriel; (4) the ultimate triumph of the kingdom of God.[10]

I. EXPERIENCES OF DANIEL AND OF HIS COMPANIONS (1. 1 to 6. 28)
1. Daniel's youth and education (1. 1-21).
    (1) A captive at the court of Babylon (1. 1-3).
    (2) Education and fidelity of Daniel and of his companions (1. 4-17).
    (3) Their proficiency and renown (1. 18-21).
2. The dream of the image and its significance (2. 1-49)
    (1) The troublesome dream (2. 1).
    (2) Failure of the wise men and their condemnation (2. 2-13).
    (3) Daniel's intercession (2. 14-16).
    (4) Daniel's vision of the dream (2. 17-24).

---

[10] A fuller statement of the contents may be found in F. C. Eiselen, *Prophecy and the Prophets*, pp. 302–308.

THE PSALMS AND OTHER SACRED WRITINGS

(5) The dream and its interpretation (2. 25-45).
The image seen by the king represents successive world powers, beginning with Nebuchadnezzar; the stone represents the kingdom of God, which will destroy the world powers and, embracing the whole earth in its sway, will abide forever.
(6) Exaltation of Daniel and his companions (2. 46-49).

3. Faithfulness of Daniel's companions and their deliverance (3. 1-30).
   (1) Nebuchadnezzar's golden image and his decree (3. 1-7).
   (2) Refusal of Daniel's companions to worship the image (3. 8-12).
   (3) Deliverance from the fiery furnace (3. 13-27).
   (4) Nebuchadnezzar's change of mind and exaltation of Daniel's companions (3. 28-30).

4. Nebuchadnezzar's tree-dream and its fulfillment (4. 1-37).
   (Related in the form of a decree.)
   (1) Introduction to the decree (4. 1-3).
   (2) Failure of the wise men to interpret the king's dream (4. 4-7).
   (3) The dream related to Daniel (4. 8-18).
   (4) The dream interpreted by Daniel (4. 19-27).
       The tree represents the king in his greatness, but Yahweh has decreed to bring him low. His reason will leave him for seven years, which time he will spend among the beasts of the field, until he has learned to acknowledge the sway of the God of Israel. Afterward he will be restored.
   (5) Fulfillment of the dream and Nebuchadnezzar's gratitude (4. 28-37).

5. The feast of Belshazzar and the handwriting on the wall (5. 1-31).
   (1) The feast of Belshazzar (5. 1-4).
   (2) The handwriting on the wall (5. 5-9).
   (3) Reading and interpretation of the writing (5. 10-28).
       Daniel reads the words: "Mene, Mene, Tekel, Upharsin," and interprets them as meaning that the kingdom of Belshazzar is about to be given to the Medes and Persians.
   (4) Fulfillment of the threat (5. 29-31).

6. Daniel's deliverance from the lions' den (6. 1-28).
   (1) Exaltation of Daniel by Darius (6. 1-3).
   (2) Jealousy and plot of the nobles (6. 4-8).
   (3) Daniel's loyalty and condemnation (6. 9-17).

THE BOOK OF DANIEL

(4) Daniel's deliverance from the lions' den (6. 18-24).
(5) Darius's recognition of Yahweh's power (6. 25-28).

II. VISIONS OF DANIEL (7. 1 to 12. 13)

1. Vision of the four beasts and its interpretation (7. 1-28).
   (1) Vision of the four beasts (7. 1-8).
   (2) Vision of the heavenly judgment scene (7. 9-14).
   (3) Interpretation of the vision (7. 15-28).
   > The four beasts signify four kingdoms, all of which are doomed. After the destruction of the fourth "the saints of the Most High shall receive the kingdom, and possess the kingdom forever and ever."
2. Vision of the ram and the he-goat (8. 1-27).
   (1) The ram and the he-goat (8. 1-14).
   (2) Interpretation of the vision by Gabriel (8. 15-27).
   > The ram represents the Medo-Persian empire, the he-goat the kingdom of Greece, and the great horn between its eyes the first king. The four horns represent four kingdoms into which the kingdom of Greece is divided; the little horn is a king of fierce countenance, who will exalt himself even against the "prince of princes"; but in the end he will be brought low.
3. Daniel's prayer and the divine answer (9. 1-27).
   (1) Prayer for the restoration of the divine favor (9. 1-19).
   (2) The answer, transmitted through Gabriel (9. 20-27).
   > Gabriel explains that the seventy years of desolation foretold by Jeremiah must be interpreted as seventy weeks of years, which must pass before the kingdom of God will triumph. The seventy weeks are divided into three smaller periods, seven weeks from the going forth of the command to rebuild Jerusalem to "the anointed one, the prince"; then sixty-two weeks during which the holy city will exist. At the end of this period the anointed one will be cut off, and "the people of the prince that shall come" will destroy the city and the sanctuary. During one half of the remaining week sacrifice and oblation will cease, but after that the power of the desolation will be broken.
4. The ultimate triumph of the kingdom of God (10. 1 to 12. 13).
   (1) Appearance of the heavenly messenger (10. 1-12).
   (2) Struggles between the "prince" of the Jews and the "princes" of Persia and Greece (10. 13 to 11. 1).

THE PSALMS AND OTHER SACRED WRITINGS

(3) Defeat of Persia by Greece (11. 2-4).
(4) Struggles between north and south (11. 5-20).
(5) Rule of the "contemptible person" (11. 21-45).
(6) Resurrection and exaltation of the faithful (12. 1-3).
(7) Consummation of the kingdom (12. 4-13)

Authorship and Date. Though perhaps no book in the Old Testament contains more definite indications of its date than does the book of Daniel, there has been about as much controversy regarding its date and authorship as there has been with reference to any biblical book. On the one hand are those who insist that the book was written by the prophet Daniel, one of the captives carried away from Jerusalem during the reign of Jehoiakim, who attained a position of prominence at the court of Nebuchadnezzar and of his successors on the throne of Babylon.

I. *The following arguments are advanced to prove that Daniel is the author of the book bearing his name:*

1. The fact of its admission into the canon. This argument assumes that the Old Testament canon was closed in the days of Artaxerxes, which assumption is based on the following statement of Josephus: "From the death of Moses to the reign of Artaxerxes, king of Persia, who reigned after Xerxes, the prophets who were after Moses wrote what was done in their times in thirteen books. . . . It is true, our history has been written since Artaxerxes very particularly, but has not been esteemed of like authority with the former by our forefathers, because there has not been an exact succession of prophets since that time."[11] The argument continues: If the book of Daniel had not been written until about B. C. 165, that is, nearly three centuries after the age of Artaxerxes, how could it have found its way into the

---
[11] *Contra Apionem*, I, 8.

THE BOOK OF DANIEL

canon, when other books, written earlier in the same century,[12] failed to secure such recognition? Moreover, there is not the slightest hint anywhere that any question regarding the canonicity of Daniel was ever raised among the Jewish rabbis.

2. The testimony of tradition. It is pointed out that from the time of Josephus until long after the Reformation it was the common belief among Jews and Christians that the book was written by the Daniel of the exile.[13] As indicated in the discussion of the Pentateuch,[14] Christian tradition has little independent value, because it was taken over bodily from Judaism; consequently, here, as in the case of the Pentateuch, emphasis is rightly placed on Jewish tradition. The earliest statement on the subject is found in Josephus: "Our nation suffered these things under Antiochus Epiphanes, according to Daniel's vision, and what he wrote many years before they came to pass. In the very same manner Daniel also wrote concerning the Roman government, and that our country should be made desolate by them. This man left in writing all these things, as God had showed them to him; insomuch that such as read his prophecies, and see how they have been fulfilled, would wonder at the honor wherewith God honored Daniel, and may thence discover how the Epicureans are in error who cast providence out of human life."[15] This passage shows that Josephus believed—and there is no reason to doubt that his con-

---

[12] For example, Ecclesiasticus, written about B. C. 180.
[13] The Neo-Platonist Porphyry, about A. D. 300, denied the authorship of Daniel and assigned the book to the Maccabean age, but several of the church fathers answered his arguments; the question was not raised again until the seventeenth century by Spinoza.
[14] F. C. Eiselen, *The Books of the Pentateuch*, p. 85.
[15] *Antiquities*, X, x, 4.

temporaries shared the view—that Daniel was the author of the book.[16]

3. The language of the book is said to reflect exactly the age and position of Daniel. About two fifths of the book are in Hebrew, the remaining three fifths in Aramaic. The Hebrew, it is claimed, is as pure as that of books known to have been written during the period of the exile or during the years immediately following; there are no indications of decay such as might be expected had the book been written during the Maccabean age. Moreover, the Aramaic of Daniel is as pure as that of Ezra, "a striking proof that the Aramaic of Daniel must belong to the same age with that of Ezra, and consequently that the author of Daniel must have lived somewhere near Babylon during the captivity, or, at least, not long after it." Further support for this conclusion is derived from a comparison of the Aramaic of Daniel with that of the Targums coming from near the beginning of the Christian era, which is said to differ greatly from that of Daniel. The whole matter is summed up by Harman in this fashion: (1) The purity of the Hebrew of Daniel shows that the language cannot belong to an age posterior to the exile; (2) the correspondence of the Aramaic of Daniel with that of Ezra indicates its proximity to the age of the exile.[17]

4. The exact historical knowledge of the author.

---

[16] That the book belongs to the earlier period is inferred also from the statements that the book was shown to Alexander the Great; *Antiquities*, X, xi, 7; XI, viii, 3–5.

[17] *Introduction to the Study of the Holy Scriptures*, p. 417. Conclusion (2) should have been worded: The correspondence of the Aramaic of Daniel with that of Ezra indicates its proximity to *the date of the book of Ezra*. This would mean a date certainly not much earlier than B. C. 300.

THE BOOK OF DANIEL

Appeal is made to a carefully selected list of passages to prove that the author had such an exact knowledge of history and such an intimate acquaintance with Persian manners and customs that it is impossible to believe that he lived far from the events he relates. This argument is thought to assume even greater force in the presence of numerous historical inaccuracies and absurdities in the noncanonical books written during the second and first centuries B. C.

5. The testimony of the New Testament. Attention is directed to the fact that Jesus calls Daniel "the prophet" and refers to his prophecy concerning "the abomination of desolation";[18] that the phrase "Son of man" seems to be taken from Daniel 7. 13; that the imagery of the book of Revelation is in part borrowed from Daniel; that Paul's description of the man of sin[19] is derived from it, and that the Epistle to the Hebrews refers both to the Hebrew children in the fiery furnace and to Daniel in the lions' den.[20]

6. The use of the pronoun of the first person in expressions like "I Daniel,"[21] or "me Daniel."[22]

7. Various additional considerations are urged, though perhaps less weight is attached to them: (1) It is pointed out that the symbolism of the visions is such as might be looked for in the writings of a prophet living in a Babylonian environment. (2) The character of Daniel's prophecies is said to be in perfect agreement with his exalted position at the court of the greatest nation of his

---

[18] Matt. 25. 15.
[19] 2 Thessalonians 2. 1–12.
[20] Heb. 11. 33, 34.
[21] For example, 9. 2; 10. 2.
[22] For example, 7. 15; 8. 1.

THE PSALMS AND OTHER SACRED WRITINGS

age. (3) It is claimed that the lofty and pious Messianic conceptions are inconsistent with the assumption that the book is a fraud. (4) The references in 1 Maccabees 2. 49-60 are thought to imply the existence of the book of Daniel near the beginning of the Maccabean crisis. (5) The inclusion of Daniel in the Septuagint translation is said to prove that it was a well-known book before the middle of the second century B. C. (6) The absence of prayers in the midst of the narrative sections is said to differentiate Daniel from the apocryphal books of the first and second centuries. (7) It is claimed that if Daniel was not written near the time of the exile, no authentic history of the period has been preserved. And yet, in view of the importance of the period in Jewish history there is every reason for believing that such a history was produced.

Are these arguments conclusive? 1. If it could be shown that the Old Testament canon was actually closed in the days of Artaxerxes, the argument would have considerable weight; if, on the other hand, the canon of the Writings was not fixed until near the opening of the Christian era,[23] the admission of Daniel into the canon can throw no light on the question of its date. There is no reason why a book written in B. C. 165 should not have been admitted into the canon, provided it dealt with events during the prophetic period, especially if the book was one of intense spirituality and faith and could be connected with one of the heroes of the past.[24]

---

[23] The formation of the Old Testament canon will be discussed in detail in Volume IV of this Biblical Introduction Series.

[24] The words of Josephus quoted above may imply that only such books were admitted into the canon as were thought to have been

THE BOOK OF DANIEL

2. The persistency of Jewish and Christian tradition to ascribe the book to the prophet Daniel cannot be denied; but it must not be forgotten that the earliest "official" tradition does not ascribe the book to Daniel, but to the men of the Great Synagogue.[25] Moreover, Jewish tradition has been found unreliable in so many cases that it can serve only as a starting point in investigation, and must be set aside whenever the facts in the case fail to support tradition.[26]

3. The linguistic peculiarities point in the very opposite direction. Instead of favoring a date near the exile, they suggest a date several centuries later.[27]

4. When the author's "exact knowledge of history" is subjected to any kind of fair test so many imperfections reveal themselves that it becomes practically impossible to accept the book as the work of an eyewitness.[28]

5. The New Testament references do not raise or consider the question of date and authorship, hence they have no bearing on the subject under discussion.

6. The pronoun of the first person is used whenever Daniel is introduced as the speaker; in the narrative sections and in the verses introducing Daniel as the

---

written during the prophetic period, that is, according to the common Jewish notion, the period ending with Malachi. In harmony with this principle Job was admitted because, according to general belief, it was a book of venerable antiquity, Ruth as a narrative of an incident in the period of the Judges, Ecclesiastes as coming from Solomon, and Daniel because it was thought to have been written by the prophet bearing that name, etc. In no case does the admission of a book into the canon settle the question of date or authorship.

[25] The relevant passage from the Talmud is quoted in F. C. Eiselen, *The Books of the Pentateuch*, p. 86.
[26] See above, p. 46.
[27] See further, below, pp. 269–271.
[28] See further, below, pp. 265–269.

THE PSALMS AND OTHER SACRED WRITINGS

speaker the third person is used. This is just what might be expected if some one other than Daniel were the author.

7. (1) The argument based upon the character of the symbolism might be used to prove that other apocalyptic books, including the New Testament book of Revelation, were written in Babylon during the period of the exile. (2) The agreement between Daniel's prophecies and his exalted position proves nothing more than that the author, whoever he may have been and whenever he may have lived, was careful to avoid inconsistencies. (3) To assign the book to another author or to another date does not introduce an element of fraud. The literary method which secures dramatic effect by speaking in the name of some well-known person was known and used in Israel even before the exile;[29] its use became more common during the later postexilic period,[30] especially in the writings of an apocalyptic nature.[31] (4) The references in I Maccabees imply nothing more than that the book of Daniel was in existence at the time the former was written, that is, about B. C. 100; they throw no light on the date of the book. (5) The translation of the Septuagint was not completed until near the opening of the Christian era; hence books written even later than the Maccabean crisis might have been included in that translation, and, indeed, were included, as is shown by the presence of the apocryphal writings. The consideration urged under (6) possesses little weight. True, Daniel differs from the so-called apocryphal books, which is only what might be expected, because it is in the nature of an apocalypse;

---
[29] Deuteronomy is a good illustration.
[30] For example, Ecclesiastes.
[31] See further, below, p. 275.

but how the presence or absence of long prayers[32] in the midst of the historical sections can determine the date of the book is not easily seen. (7) It would be easy to turn this into an argument in favor of a late date. The people living near the time of the exile did not need a history of that age. On the other hand, such need might be felt a few centuries later; then the book of Daniel was written to supply the need.[33]

Evidently, the arguments commonly used to establish the claim that Daniel wrote the book are in no sense conclusive. No doubt, in the absence of all evidence to the contrary, the inference might be drawn from *some* of the facts presented in the book that it is essentially an autobiography; but no conclusion that has not due regard for *all* the facts in the case can be regarded as satisfactory. Hence, before the question of authorship and date can be decided it is necessary to consider the evidence which, in the opinion of a great majority of modern scholars, makes it impossible to believe any longer that Daniel is the author of the book bearing his name, or, that it was written during or soon after the period of the exile.[34]

II. *Arguments to prove that the book of Daniel is a product of the Maccabean crisis:*

---

[32] There are frequent references to prayer in the historical sections, and Chapter 9, in the apocalyptic section, contains a prayer.

[33] Regarding the purpose of the book, see further, below, pp. 274–278.

[34] It is by no means clear that the author, whoever he may have been or whenever he may have lived, ever intended the book to be received as the work of Daniel himself. In the narrative sections and in the verses introducing the visions Daniel is referred to in the third person; the first person is used only when Daniel appears as the speaker; which difference receives a natural explanation only if it is assumed that the author is some one other than the hero of the book.

THE PSALMS AND OTHER SACRED WRITINGS

1. **External evidence:** (1) The position of the book in the Hebrew Bible. As already stated, the book of Daniel belongs to the third division of the Jewish canon, the Writings. Now, it must be admitted that the proper place for the book is among the prophetic books, where it is found in the English Bible. Consequently, the only natural explanation of its omission from the prophetic canon is offered by the view that the book was not yet in existence when that canon was closed, about B. C. 200. The same inference may be drawn from 9. 2, where reference is made to "the books," which are said to have contained the prophecies of Jeremiah. The statement clearly implies that Jeremiah was one of a collection of books, perhaps the prophetic canon, when the book of Daniel was written.[35] (2) The silence of Jesus ben Sirach,[36] about B. C. 180. This writer mentions, in his list of Hebrew worthies,[37] Isaiah, Jeremiah, Ezekiel, and, collectively, the Minor Prophets, but is silent concerning Daniel. Now, while the argument from silence is hardly conclusive, the question may well be asked whether the author, had he been familiar with the book of Daniel, would have omitted the name of a prominent person like its hero, and made the assertion that there had been no man in Israel like Joseph.[38] (3) The earliest literary

---

[35] Other explanations, see above, p. 251, assume that radical changes were made in the classification of Old Testament books; for which assumption there is no evidence. True, there are indications of variations in the order of books within the limits of the second and third divisions of the canon; but there is no evidence that the Palestinian Jews ever transferred a book from one division to another.

[36] The author of Ecclesiasticus.

[37] Ecclesiasticus, Chapters 44-50.

[38] Ecclesiasticus, 49. 15.

THE BOOK OF DANIEL

references or allusions to the book of Daniel come from B. C. 140 and later.[39]

2. The author's knowledge of history. There can be no question that the author's knowledge of events that took place during the period of the exile or soon after was more or less hazy: (1) The assertion in 1. 1, 2, that in the third year of Jehoiakim, Nebuchadnezzar besieged Jerusalem, captured the king, and carried away some of the sacred vessels and a number of captives, is contradicted by Jeremiah, who certainly was a contemporary of the events recorded.[40] (2) Belshazzar is represented as the last king of the Babylonian empire and the son of Nebuchadnezzar.[41] He was neither: the last king of Babylon was Nabu-na'id,[42] a usurper, who was neither a son nor a descendant of Nebuchadnezzar. Belshazzar, in Babylonian, *Bel-shar-uṣur*, was the son of Nabonidus; his name occurs on several contract tablets, where he is always called "the son of the king";[43] Nabonidus calls him "the chief son";[44] nowhere in the native records is it stated or implied that he was king, or even coregent

---

[39] The Sibylline Oracles, Book III, 388-400 (about B. C. 140), contain a reference to Dan. 7. 20, 24; in the Testaments of the Twelve Patriarchs, written near the close of the second century, are several references to Daniel (R. H. Charles, *The Testaments of the Twelve Patriarchs*, p. 238, enumerates 11 such references); 1 Maccabees 2. 59, 60 (about B. C. 100) makes reference to the deliverance of Daniel and of his three companions.

[40] In referring to the *fourth* year of Jehoiakim (Jer. 25. 1, 9ff.), and again, to the *fifth* year (36. 9, 29), the prophet uses language which implies that up to the fifth year of Jehoiakim the Babylonian armies had not appeared in Judah.

[41] Dan. 5. 1ff.; 7. 1; 8. 1.

[42] Commonly given as Nabonidus, the Greek form with a Latin ending.

[43] Perhaps equivalent to "crown-prince."

[44] Perhaps equivalent to "first-born."

with his father. Moreover, the whole description in Chapter 5 is inconsistent with conditions in Babylon immediately preceding the death of Belshazzar, as they are known from the inscriptions. Thus all available evidence outside of the book of Daniel makes it impossible to accept the representation of the latter as correct.[45] (3) According to Daniel the last Babylonian king was succeeded by Darius the Mede,[46] and Darius the Mede was succeeded by Cyrus the Persian.[47] This is not in accord with the facts in the case, for Cyrus followed immediately upon Nabonidus; there is no room for Darius the Mede before Cyrus.[48] (4) Closely bound up

---

[45] Professor R. D. Wilson, in his *Studies on the Book of Daniel*, vol. I, Chapter VI, has attempted to show that the statements in Daniel with reference to Belshazzar are correct. How successful (?) the attempt has been is, perhaps, best seen from his own summary of the conclusions: "It is shown that Belshazzar, the son of Nabunaid, *may*, according to the usage of those times, have been also the son of Nebuchadnezzar; that there is *good reason to suppose* that he was king of the Chaldeans before he became king of Babylon; that he *may* have been king of Babylon long enough to justify the writer of Daniel in speaking of his first year as king of that city [8. 1 would have to be interpreted as the third year since he became king of the Chaldeans]; that the fact that he is not called king elsewhere by his contemporaries is simply an argument from silence, paralleled in other instances, and that the other biblical sources do not say that some other man was last king of Babylon" (*The Princeton Seminary Bulletin*, November, 1916, p. 26). One might grant almost everything that Professor Wilson here claims, and the difficulties would remain.

[46] Dan. 5. 1; 9. 1; compare also Chapter 6 and 11. 1.

[47] 6. 28; 10. 1; 11. 2.

[48] To identify Darius the Mede with Gubaru (Ugbaru) or Gobryas, the general of Cyrus, who might have acted for a time as viceroy for Cyrus, is not possible. Darius is represented, not as a vassal, but as an independent ruler: as sole ruler he divides the country into satrapies; as absolute despot he sentences the satraps to death by a single decree; when he dies he is succeeded by Cyrus the Persian. It may be that Darius the Mede is really "a reflection into the past" of Darius Hys-

THE BOOK OF DANIEL

with the statement that Nabonidus was followed by Darius the Mede is the view of the author that the Persian empire was preceded by a Median empire,[49] which, again, is not in accord with history, in the sense implied in the book of Daniel. (5) The use of the term "Chaldeans," not in an ethnic sense,[50] but as denoting a class of wise men, which is not consistent with an exilic or early postexilic date of the book.[51] (6) If "Aramaic" in 2. 4 is a part of the original text,[52] it implies that the author considered Aramaic to have been the court language in Babylon during the sixth century B. C., which

---

taspis, the father, not the son, of Xerxes, who organized the Persian empire into satrapies, though probably fewer than one hundred and twenty. All attempts to remove the difficulty are based upon the assumption that the identification with Gobryas is possible; if the identification cannot be made, the case collapses.

[49] This is the only natural interpretation of 6. 28; compare also the passages given in notes 46 and 47. The view reflected in the book finds no support anywhere else in the Old Testament, nor in any classical author, nor in the Babylonian or Persian inscriptions. On the other hand, it is easy to see how a later writer might be led astray: (1) There had been a Median empire long before the Persians established their supremacy; and (2) Old Testament prophecy had foretold that the Medes would bring about the downfall of Babylon (for example, Isa. 13. 17; Jer. 51. 11, 28).

[50] It is used in an ethnic sense in 5. 30; 9. 1.

[51] It is used as a designation of a class of wise men in 1. 4; 2. 2, 4, 5, 10; 4. 7; 5. 7, 11, and, perhaps, in 3. 8. Of this meaning there is no trace in the inscriptions; it appears first in Herodotus, I, 181, 183, that is, in the fifth century B. C. Professor Sayce, always cautious and conservative, is willing to say: "In the eyes of the Assyriologist the use of the word 'Kasdim' in the book of Daniel would alone be sufficient to indicate the date of the work with unerring certainty" (*Higher Criticism and the Monuments* p. 535).

[52] It is not impossible, however, that the word was not a part of the original text. It may have been placed in the margin by a reader of the book to indicate that the Aramaic section begins at this point. Subsequently it may have been transferred by accident to the text proper.

THE PSALMS AND OTHER SACRED WRITINGS

was not the case. No one living at the Babylonian court at the time could have made such statement, for he would have known that the court language was Babylonian.[53]

The author's knowledge with reference to the Persian period, that is, the centuries from the fall of Babylon to the conquests of Alexander the Great,[54] is still somewhat vague.[55] He becomes more specific when he speaks of Alexander,[56] and seems to be most familiar with events following B. C. 200, especially with the events in Jewish history in which Antiochus Epiphanes[57] played a prominent role.[58] The author seems to be thoroughly familiar with the character of Antiochus, his Egyptian campaign, his treatment of the Jews, the desecration of the altar of burnt offering,[59] the Maccabean revolt and its early successes.[60] The situation with reference to the historical knowledge of the author is admirably summed up by J. E. McFadyen in these words: "A book supposed to come from the exile, and to announce beforehand the persecutions and ultimate triumph of the Jewish people

---

[53] A few other matters, sometimes mentioned as favoring a later date, are less significant as parts of the argument, such as the spelling of the Babylonian king's name, Nebuchad*n*ezzar for Nebuchad*r*ezzar, the insanity of Nebuchadnezzar as described in Chapter 4, and the attitude Nebuchadnezzar and Darius are said to have assumed toward the God of Israel.

[54] About B. C. 538–332.

[55] For example, he seems to know of only four Persian kings, 11. 2.

[56] Dan. 11. 3 is a reference to Alexander the Great; 11. 4 to the division of his empire; verses 5–20 to the troubles between the Ptolemies of Egypt and the Seleucidæ of Syria.

[57] B. C. 175–164.

[58] Dan. 11. 25–39; R. Smend calls it for this period a "historical source of first rank"; *Zeitschrift fuer Alttestamentliche Wissenschaft*, V, p. 241.

[59] Dec., B. C. 168.

[60] Dan. 11. 34.

THE BOOK OF DANIEL

in the second century B. C., is occasionally inaccurate in dealing with the exilic and early postexilic period, but minute and reliable as soon as it touches the later period. Only one conclusion is possible—that the book was written in the later period, not in the earlier. It is a product of the period which it so minutely reflects."[61]

3. *The argument from language.* The facts are these: the book of Daniel is written, partly in Hebrew and partly in Aramaic;[62] there are also several Persian and a few Greek words. Do these facts throw any light on the question of date? (1) Driver enumerates fifteen words of *Persian* origin.[63] Whether this number is too large or too small, there can be no doubt as to the presence of some loan words from the Persian. Such words might be expected to appear in books written during or after the Persian age;[64] but one would hardly expect to find them in a book written before Persian influence could make itself felt, and in the description of Babylonian institutions.[65] There is much more reason for expecting Babylonian words, and yet the number of words of Babylonian origin is exceedingly small.[66] (2) The presence of at least three *Greek* words, names of musical instruments, has long been recognized even by those who

---

[61] *An Introduction to the Old Testament,* pp. 321, 322.

[62] The bilingual character of the book is discussed at some length in an appendix at the close of this chapter. The presence of the two languages has no special bearing on the question of date.

[63] *Introduction to the Literature of the Old Testament,* p. 501.

[64] It is only natural that Persian influence should reveal itself in Chronicles, Ezra-Nehemiah, and Esther.

[65] The inscriptions coming from the age of Nebuchadnezzar and his successors reveal no trace of such influence. Is it probable that Hebrew would yield more readily? Compare A. H. Sayce, *The Higher Criticism and the Monuments,* pp. 493, 494.

[66] A. A. Bevan, *The Book of Daniel,* p. 40.

THE PSALMS AND OTHER SACRED WRITINGS

defend the traditional date of Daniel.[67] Though it has been asserted that these words might easily have reached Babylonia five or six centuries before the opening of the Christian era, there is no evidence to support the assumption; while their use is readily accounted for on the supposition that the book was written after the dissemination of Greek influence as a result of the conquests of Alexander the Great.[68] (3) The *Aramaic* of Daniel is the Western Aramaic, that is, the Aramaic spoken, not in Mesopotamia, but in Palestine and the surrounding districts.[69] It represents a somewhat earlier type than the language of the Targums of Onkelos and Jonathan;[70] it is closely related to the Aramaic of the Palmyrene and Nabatean inscriptions,[71] and is practically identical with the Aramaic of the book of Ezra.[72] The Aramaic sections, therefore, might have been written any time between about B. C. 400 and the opening of the Christian era. (4) In considering the character of the *Hebrew* of Daniel it is well to remember that "the presence of late phrases is always an argument in favor of a late

---

[67] They are all found in Dan. 3. 5, *kaitherōs* = κίθαρις. *psantērin* = ψαλτήριον, *sūmpōnyāh* = συμφωνία.

[68] That is, after B. C. 332. The change from *l* to *n*, *psalterion* to *psanterin*, is thought to show the influence of the Macedonian dialect, which, again, would favor the later date.

[69] It has numerous resemblances with the Aramaic of the Elephantine Papyri, but the differences are at least equally numerous and, perhaps, more striking. See S. R. Driver, *Introduction*, Revised Edition, pp. 514, 515.

[70] Though these Targums embody earlier material, they did not reach their final form until the fourth or fifth century A. D.

[71] From the third century B. C. to the second century A. D.

[72] Certainly not earlier than B. C. 450, and in all probability much later. Bevan considers the Aramaic of Ezra to have been, in the main, "the dialect spoken by the Jews of Palestine in the third century B. C."

THE BOOK OF DANIEL

date," while "the absence of such phrases is no proof whatsoever of antiquity."[73] In other words, a late production, the work of a skillful imitator, may preserve numerous early characteristics; but an early writer is not able to use expressions or constructions originating in a much later age. Now, there can be no question that linguistically and stylistically Daniel differs materially from the writings of the exilic and early postexilic period. In its main features it agrees with the latest historical prose of the Old Testament, and in certain details it approaches the "new" Hebrew of the Mishna and other parts of the Talmud.[74] Driver is undoubtedly right when he says that the Hebrew of Daniel resembles in all essential features, "not the Hebrew of Ezekiel, or even of Haggai and Zechariah, but that of the age subsequent to Nehemiah."

The same writer sums up the argument based upon the linguistic characteristics of the book in these words: "The *Persian* words presuppose a period after the Persian empire had been well established; the Greek words *demand,* the Hebrew *supports,* and the Aramaic *permits,* a date *after the conquest of Palestine* by Alexander the Great (B. C. 332). With our present knowledge this is as much as the language authorizes us definitely to affirm; though συμφωνία, as the name of an instrument (considering the history of the term in Greek), would seem to point to a date somewhat advanced in the Greek period."[75]

4. The theological ideas of the book. The teaching of

---

[73] A. A. Bevan, *The Book of Daniel,* p. 28.

[74] The linguistic peculiarities of Daniel are considered at some length in S. R. Driver, *Introduction to the Literature of the Old Testament,* pp. 504-508; A. A. Bevan, *The Book of Daniel,* pp. 28-33.

[75] *Introduction to the Literature of the Old Testament,* p. 508; *The Book of Daniel,* p. lxiii.

THE PSALMS AND OTHER SACRED WRITINGS

the book of Daniel is discussed more fully later on;[76] here it may be sufficient to call attention to the more important theological ideas and conceptions peculiar to Daniel, which have a bearing on the question of date. Generally speaking, the theology of Daniel is very late; in several matters it reflects a more advanced stage of development than is seen anywhere else in the Old Testament. The transcendence of God is constantly emphasized.[77] As God is exalted, angels become more necessary as mediators between God and man; hence angels constitute a striking feature of the book. Nowhere else in the Old Testament appear patron angels determining the destiny of nations, or distinction in rank among angels, or angels bearing proper names. The views of life after death, resurrection, reward and punishment, are also in advance of other Old Testament teaching. In the words of E. L. Curtis: "While the determination of the date of an Old Testament writing from its religious doctrines is always a delicate procedure, yet, as far as doctrinal development can be found in the Old Testament, the book of Daniel comes after all the other Old Testament writings, and approximates most closely to the Jewish literature of the first century B. C."[78]

Summing up the evidence presented thus far, it would seem that all of it, without a single exception, points to a date not earlier than B. C. 300, while most of it points strongly to a date after B. C. 200, during the reign of

---

[76] See below, pp. 279–281.
[77] He is frequently called "the God of heaven," 2. 18, 19; and once "heaven" is used almost as a synonym of God, 4. 26; compare Luke 15. 18.
[78] Hastings, *Dictionary of the Bible*, article "Daniel, Book of." A more elaborate discussion of this subject may be found in S. R. Driver, *The Book of Daniel*, pp. lxiii–lxv.

THE BOOK OF DANIEL

Antiochus Epiphanes. The exact date during that reign can, perhaps, not be determined, but there are some indications which fix it within narrow limits. As has been pointed out, the author betrays familiarity with the Maccabean revolt and with the early Maccabean triumphs; on the other hand, the cleansing of the temple, which took place in December 165, was still in the future,[79] as also the death of Antiochus.[80] Consequently, a date between B. C. 167 and 165 would satisfy most completely all the evidence in the case.

The significance of the appearance of Daniel in the midst of the Maccabean struggles is well brought out by R. H. Charles: "At last the anguish of the faithful Jews became unendurable, and an insurrection burst forth at Modein, under the leadership of Mattathias and his five stalwart sons. All that were zealous for the Law and the Covenant speedily joined them, and amongst these notably the Hasidim, or the league of the pious ones. This small body of Jews met with many marvelous successes. Notwithstanding, in the face of the vast forces of Syria, the Jews could repose no hope in their own powers. If they were to succeed it could not be in reliance on the arm of flesh. Now, it was just at this crisis, this hour of mingled hope and despair, that the book of Daniel appeared with its sword-edge utterance, its piercing exhortation to endure in the face of the despot, and its promise, full of divine joy, of near and full salvation. No dew of heaven could fall with more refreshing coolness on the parched ground, no spark from above alight with a more kindling power on the surface so long heated with a hidden glow. With winged brevity the book gives

---

[79] Dan. 8. 14.
[80] Dan. 11. 45.

THE PSALMS AND OTHER SACRED WRITINGS

a complete survey of the history of the kingdom of God upon earth, showing the relations which it had hitherto sustained in Israel to the successive great heathen empires of the Chaldeans, Medo-Persians, and Greeks—in a word, toward the heathenism which ruled the world; and with the finest perception it describes the nature and individual career of Antiochus Epiphanes and his immediate predecessors, so far as was possible in view of the great events which had just occurred. Rarely does it happen that a book appears as this did, in the very crisis of the times, and in a form most suited to such an age, artificially reserved, close and severe, and yet shedding so clear a light through obscurity, and so marvelously captivating. It was natural that it should soon achieve a success entirely corresponding with its inner truth and glory. And so, for the last time in the literature of the Old Testament, we have in this book an example of a work which, having sprung from the deepest necessities of the noblest impulses of the age, can render to that age the purest service; and which, by the development of events immediately after, receives with such power the stamp of divine witness that it subsequently attains imperishable sanctity."[81]

Design and Purpose. The book of Daniel belongs to the apocalyptic literature. Apocalyptic elements are found also in other Old Testament writings,[82] but Daniel is the principal representative of this kind of literature in the Old Testament, and as such has exerted a marked influence on many subsequent writings both Jewish and Christian. The apocalyptic literature may be regarded

---

[81] *The Book of Daniel,* pp. x, xi, quoted in part from Ewald.
[82] Notably Isa. 24–27; Zech. 9–14; Joel, Chapter 3; Ezek, 38ff., etc.

THE BOOK OF DANIEL

as the latest form of prophetic writing among the Jews. Like the prophet, the apocalyptic writer sought to set forth the character, will, and purpose of God, as also the nature and laws of his kingdom; but there is a fundamental difference between the two in their attitude toward their own day and generation. Says R. H. Charles: "Prophecy still believes that this world is God's world, and that in this world his goodness and truth will yet be justified. Hence the prophet addresses himself chiefly to the present and its concerns, and when he addresses himself to the future, his prophecy springs naturally from the present, and the future which he predicts is regarded as in organic connection with it. The apocalyptic writer, on the other hand, almost wholly despairs of the present; his main interests are supramundane."[83] As a result the apocalyptic literature dwells more upon the triumph of the kingdom of God in the coming age.[84] Closely connected with this hope of the ultimate triumph of God are two other thoughts that are made prominent in Jewish apocalyptic writings, namely, (1) the idea of a world judgment, which will mark the downfall of evil and the exaltation of right, and (2) the hope of a resurrection from the dead, so that even those who have already died may receive their proper dues.

If the book of Daniel is an apocalypse, the absence of the name of the author and the ascription to a prominent person in earlier Jewish history is easily explained, for pseudonymous authorship is another characteristic

---

[83] Hastings, *Dictionary of the Bible*, article "Apocalyptic Literature." A full discussion of "Prophecy and Apocalyptic" is found in the same author's *Eschatology*, 2d ed., pp. 173ff.

[84] Hence the designation "apocalyptic," that is, the literature that "makes known what is hidden" from the eyes of common men.

THE PSALMS AND OTHER SACRED WRITINGS

mark of apocalyptic literature.[85] The author of an apocalypse ordinarily places "in the mouth of some ancient worthy a history of events up to the author's own time, followed by a description of God's judgment on the wicked and deliverance of his people."[86]

While apocalyptic literature seeks to trace the course of events up to the author's own time, the purpose of an apocalypse is not historical but didactic; the author is interested in history only in so far as he can draw from it certain lessons which he desires to teach. This is true of the book of Daniel. Says a recent writer, one who believes that Daniel himself is the author: "It is primarily neither prophetic nor historic. It is designed, rather, to show how God cares for his people even when everything seems against them."[87] The scholars who assign the book to the period between B. C. 167 and 165 are equally positive in their assertion that the primary purpose of the book is didactic: "Its object was to sustain the tried and tempted faith of the loyal Jews under the fierce assaults made upon it by Antiochus Epiphanes. . . . The author reminds his readers that there is a God in heaven, and that he reigns. He bids them lift their eyes to the past and shows them how the fidelity of men like Daniel and his friends was rewarded by deliverance from the lions and the flames. He bids them lift their eyes to the future, the very near future: let them only be patient a little longer, and their enemies will be crushed and

---

[85] Compare, for example, the Apocalypse of Baruch, the Ascension of Isaiah, the Assumption of Moses, the Book of Enoch, etc.

[86] For an explanation of this pseudonymity, see R. H. Charles, *Eschatology*, 2d ed., pp. 196ff.; *The Book of Daniel*, pp. xiv–xvi.

[87] J. W. Beardslee, *Outlines of an Introduction to the Old Testament*, p. 200.

THE BOOK OF DANIEL

the kingdom of God will come—that kingdom which shall know no end."[88]

The classification of the book as primarily didactic suggests a question as to the amount of *historical* material used by the author. On this question scholars differ widely, some holding that the narratives are throughout a work of the imagination, others, that the book rests upon a traditional basis, and that the traditions used by the author contain a substantial historical nucleus. Now, it is undoubtedly true that "fiction, even fiction without any foundation of fact whatever, has played an important part in the education of humanity; and religious fiction, written with a didactic purpose, has in both ancient and modern times been valued by teachers as a powerful instrument of edification, and has won a remarkable amount of popular appreciation." Hence, even if all the narratives in the book were regarded a work of the imagination, it would still be of the highest religious and ethical significance.[89] Nevertheless, it is at least possible that the author depended for some of his information on reliable tradition. "It is probable that Daniel was one of the Jewish exiles in Babylon, who, with his three companions, was noted for his staunch adherence to the principles of his religion, who attained a position of influence at the court, and who perhaps also foretold something of the future fate of the Chaldean and Persian empires. The traditions relating to him were combined with those which reached the author respecting the public events of Daniel's time, and developed by him into the existing narratives, with a special view to the

---

[88] J. E. McFadyen, *An Introduction to the Old Testament*, pp. 329, 330.
[89] See also, above, p. 158; and F. C. Eiselen, *The Minor Prophets*, pp. 318-320; 338-340; F. W. Farrar, *The Book of Daniel*, pp. 3, 4.

THE PSALMS AND OTHER SACRED WRITINGS

circumstances of his own age. . . .[90] The incidents of Daniel's life are not narrated for their own sakes, but for the sake of inculcating certain lessons, to magnify the God of Daniel, and to show that he, by his providence, frustrates the purposes of the proudest of earthly monarchs, while he defends and rewards his servants, who in time of danger or temptation cleave to him faithfully. . . . The general aim of the visions attributed to Daniel in Chapters 7-12 is to show, with increasing detail and distinctness, that as the course of history, so far as it has hitherto gone, has been in accordance with God's predetermined plan, so it is not less part of his plan that the trial of the saints should not continue indefinitely, but that within three years and a half of the time when the persecuting measures of Antiochus first began it should reach its appointed term. God, in other words, was guiding the whole course of history toward the salvation of his people."[91]

Teaching. The principal idea of the book is the ultimate triumph of the *kingdom of God*. "It tells," says Beardslee, "in plainer language than had been used be-

---

[90] Traditions concerning an ancient hero of the faith named Daniel may have constituted another source from which the author derived some material. This Daniel is referred to in Ezek. 14. 14, 20 and 28. 3 as a model of righteousness and wisdom. Since the two chapters are dated in B. C. 594 and 588 respectively, that is, before Daniel's fame could spread far, and since Daniel is named with two patriarchs of antiquity, it is not probable that the Daniel named in Ezekiel is the hero of the book of Daniel, a younger contemporary of the prophet. It may well be that there were current in Israel traditions concerning an early patriarch Daniel, who was renowned for righteousness and wisdom, and that the author of Daniel used some of these traditions. See A. A. Bevan, *The Book of Daniel*, pp. 12, 25; and C. Steuernagel, *Einleitung in das Alte Testament*, p. 653.

[91] S. R. Driver, *The Book of Daniel*, pp. lxviii ff.; G. B. Gray, *A Critical Introduction to the Old Testament*, p. 238.

THE BOOK OF DANIEL

fore, of the subjection of the world to God, and indicates clearly the evidence of the divine rule, and assures us that the progress of God's kingdom is absolutely irresistible and that all things will be ultimately brought into submission to God."[92]

Earlier prophets looked with equal assurance for the establishment of the kingdom of God, when the divine will and purpose would be realized in every detail of life; and, like these prophets, the author of the book of Daniel expected the reign of righteousness to begin immediately after the great crisis during which he lived would be over. However, the description of the kingdom in Daniel differs in some respects from that of earlier writers, as is natural in view of the apocalyptic character of the book as a whole.[93] The kingdom of God for which the earlier prophets looked was an earthly kingdom, "little more than a continuance of the existing state of society, only purged by a judgment from sin, and freed from trouble." The book of Daniel marks a transition from this to the idea of a heavenly kingdom, which appears more prominently in later apocalyptic and New Testament writings.[94]

The teaching of the book of Daniel concerning *angels* marks a distinct advance over teaching found in other parts of the Old Testament, along three lines: (1) The doctrine of guardian or patron angels, determining the destinies of separate nations, appears here for the first time in definite form.[95] (2) For the first time names are

---

[92] *Outlines of an Introduction to the Old Testament*, p. 200.
[93] See above, p. 275.
[94] See especially Dan. 7. 9-14.
[95] The angels of Persia, Greece, and Judah are mentioned in Dan. 10. 13, 20, 21; 12. 1.

THE PSALMS AND OTHER SACRED WRITINGS

given to angels. The guardian angel of the Jews is Michael,[96] who fights for them against the guardian angels of their enemies, and Gabriel appears as a heaven-sent interpreter.[97] (3) Distinction in rank among angels also appears first in Daniel. Michael is called "the great prince,"[98] and "one of the chief princes."[99] The latter expression seems to refer to a group of superior angels, to whom at a later time the title archangels is given.[100]

The hope of a resurrection is the other element in the teaching of Daniel demanding attention. Dan. 12. 2 contains the most definite reference to resurrection in the entire Old Testament. The general Old Testament conception of life or existence after death is hazy, and on the whole, gloomy and full of despair.[101] The dead are represented as gathering in Sheol, where they live a "shadowy, half-conscious, joyless existence, not worthy of the name of life, where communion with God was at an end, and where God's mercies could be neither apprehended nor acknowledged." But here and there rays of light appear. Sometimes the hope is expressed that God will deliver his saints from death;[102] at other times that they will be raised from the dead.[103] To the latter class belongs Dan. 12. 2, which adds two ideas to the earlier teaching: (1) the resurrection of the wicked, which is clearly taught here for the first time; and (2)

---

[96] 10. 13, 21; 12. 1.
[97] 8. 16; 9. 21.
[98] 12. 1.
[99] 10. 13.
[100] Compare Jude 9. In some of the later Jewish writings four such angels are mentioned, in others, seven. The seven angels that stand before God appear also in Rev. 8. 2.
[101] F. C. Eiselen, *The Christian View of the Old Testament*, pp. 184-187.
[102] For example, Psalm 16. 8-11.
[103] For example, Job 19. 25-27; Isa. 26. 19; Dan. 12. 2.

THE BOOK OF DANIEL

the doctrine of future rewards and punishments, though the nature of these rewards and punishments is left indefinite.

But even with these additional elements certain limitations remain: (1) The context makes it doubtful that the author meant to include non-Israelites in the promise of a resurrection. Throughout the book he is concerned with the deliverance and exaltation of the oppressed Jews; hence it is most natural to interpret the references in Chapter 12 also as applying only to the Jews. (2) The expression "many of them that sleep in the dust of the earth shall awake" seems to imply that not even all Israelites will be raised from the dead. As is suggested by several commentators, the writer may have had in mind only "those individuals who had in an extraordinary degree helped or hindered the advent of God's kingdom, that is, the Jewish martyrs and apostates respectively; the great majority of the nation, who were of average character, neither overmuch righteous nor overmuch wicked, remaining still in Sheol."

It may be stated, in conclusion, that the teaching and permanent significance of the book are in no wise affected by any particular view regarding its date or authorship. The testimony of Professor Terry, given after a study of the book during a period extending over more than thirty years, is not without weight in this connection. Speaking of himself in the third person, he says: "He has found few portions of the Holy Scriptures more profitable for devout study, and he here repeats what he had published elsewhere, and uttered time and again, that whatever may be the results of scientific criticism touching the date and authorship of the book, the apocalyptic chapters constitute a most original and important

THE PSALMS AND OTHER SACRED WRITINGS

body of divine revelation. Whether written during the exile or in the time of the Maccabees, they contain a picture of the kingdoms of the world, and their ultimate subjection to the kingdom of God, worthy of rank with any prophecies to be found in Hebrew Scriptures."[104]

[104] *Methodist Review*, January, 1902, p. 128.

APPENDIX TO CHAPTER XI

THE BILINGUAL CHARACTER OF THE BOOK OF DANIEL

DANIEL 1. 1 to 2. 4a and Chapters 8 to 12 are written in Hebrew, 2. 4b to 7. 28 in Aramaic.[105] A similar change in language occurs in Ezra, Ezra 4. 8 to 6. 18 and 7. 12-26 being in Aramaic, the rest in Hebrew. But while in Ezra a change in subject-matter accounts for the change in language, no such explanation can be offered in the case of Daniel. Had the change been introduced at the end of Chapter 6, which marks the close of the narrative section, the difficulty would not be so great, but there seems to be no good reason for the break at the end of Chapter 7.

How is the bilingual character of the book to be explained?[106] The following are the more important explanations proposed:

1. Some have thought that Aramaic was used in the sections dealing with Babylonia because it was the language of that country. But (1) the Aramaic of Daniel was not the language of Babylonia either during the exile or during the decades following; (2) on that basis it would be diffi-

---

[105] A more accurate characterization of the language is that of Steuernagel, who describes the language of 1. 1 to 2. 4a as Aramaicized Hebrew, that of 2. 4b to 6. 29 (in English, 6. 28) as pure Aramaic, that of Chapter 7 as Hebraized Aramaic, and that of Chapters 8 to 12 as relatively pure Hebrew.

[106] That it is not easy to find a satisfactory answer may be inferred from the wide divergence of opinion among scholars. Thus, the view which appeals to a cautious scholar like Driver as "relatively the best" (*The Book of Daniel*, p. xxii) is declared by Steuernagel to be the least satisfactory. (*Einleitung in das Alte Testament*, p. 658.)

THE PSALMS AND OTHER SACRED WRITINGS

cult to explain why Chapter 7, for example, should be in Aramaic and Chapter 8 in Hebrew.

2. Others have explained the difference in language by assuming diversity of authorship. According to Meinhold, 2. 4b to 6. 29 (in English 6. 28) was written in Aramaic about B. C. 300; somewhat later Chapter 7, also in Aramaic, was added as an appendix; during the Maccabean period another writer accommodated the earlier narratives to the needs of his own age, prefixed 1. 1 to 2. 4a as a suitable introduction, and then wrote, chiefly on the basis of Chapters 2 and 7, the visions in Chapters 8 to 12.[107] But (1) is it probable that 2. 4b to 6. 29 ever existed without an introduction? (2) The use of Aramaic in Chapter 7, which is certainly more closely connected with Chapter 8 than with Chapter 6, would remain unexplained; and (3) there are too many bonds of unity between the narrative and the vision chapters to give any degree of probability to the theory of diversity of authorship.

The unity of the book has been questioned also on other grounds, most recently by C. C. Torrey and C. F. Kent,[108] who assign chapters 1 to 6, the narrative sections, to one author and Chapters 7 to 12, the vision sections, to another, for the following reasons: (1) Fundamental differences in diction and style; (2) while Chapters 1 to 6 contain both Persian and Greek words, the remaining chapters have none; (3) differences in the characterization of Daniel; (4) differences in contents: one has stories, the other visions; (5) chronological differences;[109] (6) Chapters 1 to 6 contain no references or allusions to Antiochus

---

[107] *Das Buch Daniel*, in *Kurzgefasster Kommentar;* for other forms of fundamentally the same view, see G. Dalman, *The Words of Jesus*, p. 13; H. Preiswerk, *Der Sprachenwechsel im Buch Daniel.*

[108] The former in *Transactions of the Connecticut Academy of Arts and Sciences*, XV, pp. 241-282; the latter in *Sermons, Epistles, and Apocalypses of Israel's Prophets*, pp. 34, 35.

[109] Compare 1. 21 with 11. 1.

Epiphanes, who is the central figure in the remaining chapters. On the basis of historical allusions in Chapter 2 they assign the narrative portions to the period between B. C. 245 and 225; Chapters 7 to 12 they assign to B. C. 166. These objections are not convincing. That a close connection exists between the two sections is recognized even by Kent, for he admits that the author of the visions made use of the narrative sections, that the visions are distributed through the reigns of the same kings as the stories, and that the later writer deliberately bound the two parts closely together. Moreover, there is no good reason why one and the same author should not employ both stories and visions for didactic purposes; if he did, differences in diction and style might be expected. Besides, there are in both parts the same conceptions of the Median kingdom and of Belshazzar, there is the same underlying purpose, and, with all the minor differences, there is a remarkable similarity of style. "No attentive reader," says Kamphausen, "will allow himself to be misled as to the oneness of the authorship of the book by the fragmentary or detached character of the ten pieces of which it is composed, if he attentively observes how the earlier portions allude to the later, and conversely, how the later portions attach themselves to the earlier, and how the same general manner of presentation, thought and language pervades the whole."[110]

3. A third theory, which is considered by Driver "relatively the best," is expressed by Kamphausen in these words: "In Chapter 2 the author has introduced the 'Chaldeans' as speaking in the language which he believed to be customary with them; afterward he continues to use the same language on account of its greater convenience both for himself and for his original readers, both in the narrative portions and in the following (seventh) chapter, the piece in companionship to Chapter 2; for the last three

---
[110] *Encyclopædia Biblica*, article "Daniel"; compare also G. B. Gray, *A Critical Introduction to the Old Testament*, pp. 236, 237.

THE PSALMS AND OTHER SACRED WRITINGS

visions (8-12) a return to Hebrew was suggested by the consideration that this had been from of old the usual sacred language for prophetic subjects."[111] But, (1) is it conceivable that the author believed western Aramaic to have been the language of the Babylonian court?[112] (2) The use of Aramaic beyond the words of the Chaldeans receives no adequate explanation. (3) If Aramaic was the language of the Jews in the days of the author, why should he introduce it as the language of the "Chaldeans"? (4) The differences between the Aramaic of Chapters 2 to 6 and of Chapter 7 receive no satisfactory explanation.

4. It has been suggested that the narratives were intended for the people, hence they were written in Aramaic, the language of the people; on the other hand, the visions were intended for the learned, hence they were written in Hebrew, the language of the learned. If so, 1. 1-2. 4a would be a translation from Aramaic into Hebrew, and Chapter 7 from Hebrew into Aramaic, which might account for the peculiarities in the Hebrew of the former and in the Aramaic of the latter. The Aramaicized Hebrew of 1. 1 to 2. 4a might have been produced in the course of the translation of the passage from Aramaic into Hebrew, and the Hebraized Aramaic of Chapter 7 in the course of the translation from Hebrew into Aramaic. But (1) why did the translator stop at 2. 4a, and (2), why was Chapter 7 singled out for translation into Aramaic?

5. A still different view, favored by a considerable group of modern writers, is that the entire book was written originally in Hebrew. Since the book was intended, not for a select few, but for the people as a whole, since it was the wish of the author to produce an immediate and power-

---

[111] *Encyclopædia Biblica*, article "Daniel."

[112] Compare 1. 4, "the tongue of the Chaldeans." As has been suggested above, p. 267, the phrase "in Aramaic" is probably a gloss, placed originally in the margin to indicate the beginning of the Aramaic section, and transferred from there by accident to the text.

ful effect, and since Aramaic, not Hebrew, was the language of the people, a translation into the vernacular was made either by the author himself or by one of his associates. Later a portion of the Hebrew text was lost; and since no other Hebrew copy was available in the district where this happened, the missing sections were supplied from the Aramaic translation.[113] This theory also is open to criticism: (1) "It does not account for two facts (which can hardly both be accidental) that the Aramaic part begins in Chapter 2 just where the Aramaic language is mentioned, and breaks off just at the end of a chapter."[114] (2) Neither the differences between the Hebrew of 1. 1 to 2. 4a and Chapters 8 to 12, nor the differences between the Aramaic of 2. 4b to 6. 29 and Chapter 7 receive adequate explanation. (3) The Aramaic of 2. 4b to 6. 29 has no earmarks of being a translation from another language.

6. Over against this view stands the theory that the book was written in Aramaic, and that at a later time the beginning and the end were translated into Hebrew. In support of the theory it is pointed out that, while the Aramaic sections contain no indications of having been translated from Hebrew, the Hebrew portions give evidence of strong Aramaic influence. Moreover, a book written in Aramaic had no chance of being admitted into the canon; consequently, to open the way for the admission of Daniel, the beginning and the end were translated into the sacred language, which put Daniel in a class with Ezra. The contents suggested a suitable stopping place at 2. 4a; and the new beginning at 8. 1 was due to the fact that Chapter 9, which is closely connected with Chapter 8, already contained the prayer of Daniel in Hebrew.[115] With this theory also certain questions remain unanswered: (1) The linguistic dif-

---

[113] A. A. Bevan, *The Book of Daniel*, p. 27.
[114] S. R. Driver, *The Book of Daniel*, p. xxii.
[115] K. Marti, *Das Buch Daniel*, p. x.

THE PSALMS AND OTHER SACRED WRITINGS

ferences between sections using the same language are not explained; (2) the explanation of the beginning of the translation at 8. 1 instead of 7. 1 is by no means satisfactory; (3) it would have been just as easy to translate the entire book. No wonder, Charles, who is inclined to favor this theory, is ready to admit that "it requires to be substantiated by a much larger body of evidence than has yet been adduced."[116]

7. Steuernagel, on the assumption that the author used as a source book the chronicles of the Medo-Persian kings, written in Aramaic, gives this explanation: The author, intending to reproduce, with considerable freedom, the stories of Daniel which he found in his source, started out in Hebrew; when he reached what is now 2. 4 he changed his mind and decided to reproduce his source *verbatim*, in the language in which he found it. That brought him to the close of the narrative sections. He added to these, in Hebrew, the vision which now forms Chapter 7, but later translated it into Aramaic, to bring it in line with the narrative sections. Chapters 8 to 12 he regards as a later expansion, though by the same author.[117] Even Steuernagel is not willing to consider this explanation more than a possibility. Perhaps the only thing to do is to admit, with the author named, that the bilingual character of the book of Daniel is still an unsolved riddle.

---

[116] *The Book of Daniel*, p. xxvi.
[117] *Einleitung in das Alte Testament*, p. 659.

CHAPTER XII

THE BOOKS OF EZRA AND NEHEMIAH

CHAPTER XII

THE BOOKS OF EZRA AND NEHEMIAH

Title and Division. Ezra and Nehemiah are counted two separate books in the English Bible; in reality they are two sections of a single work which, with Chronicles, formed originally a continuous history from creation to the middle of the Persian period, about B. C. 430. The two appear as one book, called Ezra,[1] in the Hebrew MSS., and the Massoretic notes, found at the end of the Old Testament books in Hebrew, treat them as such. The Septuagint also regards them as one book, called *Second Esdras,* that is, the Second Book of Ezra; the *First Esdras* of the Septuagint is, on the whole, a different recension of parts of Ezra and Nehemiah.[2] In the Vulgate they appear as two books, corresponding to the present division in English, under the title *First Esdras* and *Second Esdras,* the *First Esdras* of the Septuagint having become *Third Esdras.* The Latin MSS. contain also a *Fourth Esdras,* an apocalyptic work which, aside from the name, has no connection with the other books bearing the same name. *Third* and *Fourth Esdras* of the Latin Bible are included among the English Apocrypha as *First Esdras* and *Second Esdras.*

Contents and Outline. The books of Ezra and Nehemiah cover a period of a little more than a century, from

---

[1] While Jewish tradition regards Ezra as the author, the title might be interpreted as implying only that Ezra is the hero of the book; compare Ruth and Esther.

[2] See further, below, pp. 313-316.

THE PSALMS AND OTHER SACRED WRITINGS

the decree of Cyrus, in B. C. 538-537, to the second visit of Nehemiah, in B. C. 432. There are, however, a few allusions to later persons and events.[3] The record is not in the form of a continuous narrative: The first part deals with events during the years 537-516; then comes a gap of more than fifty years, which is followed by an account of Ezra's return, which is generally thought to have taken place in B. C. 458.[4] After another break, this time of about fourteen years, there follows the account of Nehemiah's return, in B. C. 445-444. His reform efforts were interrupted for a while by his return to the Persian court; the work closes with a brief description of the reforms he attempted on his second visit to Jerusalem, in B. C. 433-432.

The book of Ezra begins with an account of the edict of Cyrus giving the Jews permission to return to Jerusalem. Many availed themselves of the opportunity. On reaching their old home they erected the altar of burnt-offering, kept the feast of Tabernacles, and, in the second year, laid the foundations of the temple. When they refused permission to the Samaritans and others to cooperate, these interfered with the enterprise, and building operations ceased until B. C. 520, when, following the exhortations of Haggai and Zechariah, the work was resumed with such energy that in 516 the temple was dedicated.[5]

---

[3] In Neh. 12. 11, 22, for example, mention is made of Jaddua, who was the great-grandson of Eliashib, a contemporary of Nehemiah, and who, therefore, must have lived about a century later. According to Josephus, he was high priest in the days of Alexander the Great.

[4] It is said to have taken place in the seventh year of Artaxerxes, who is commonly identified with Artaxerxes I; but see further, below, pp. 308–312, the section dealing with the date of Ezra.

[5] Ezra, Chapters 1 to 6.

THE BOOKS OF EZRA AND NEHEMIAH

Between 6. 22 and 7. 1 is an interval of more than fifty years. In 458 Ezra the scribe received a commission from Artaxerxes to go to Jerusalem, to investigate religious conditions there and to teach the law. Accompanied by a number of faithful Yahweh worshipers, he reached Jerusalem, where the returned exiles offered burnt-offerings and sin-offerings. Complaint came to him that many of the Jews had entered marriage alliances with non-Jews; whereupon Ezra offered a passionate prayer of confession. At a general assembly a commission was appointed to investigate the subject of mixed marriages. The book closes with an enumeration of the guilty men.[6]

The book of Nehemiah opens with an account of Nehemiah's return. Nehemiah, a royal cup-bearer at the Persian court, deeply distressed over the condition of affairs in Jerusalem, had himself appointed governor of the Jewish community there. After his arrival he succeeded in arousing a general interest in the rebuilding of the city walls, which was accomplished in fifty-two days, in the face of most serious opposition. He condemned the treatment of the poor by the rich, and finally persuaded the latter to restore to the poor the property which they had been compelled to mortgage. After the completion of the walls he took steps for adequate protection and for securing a more numerous population.[7]

At a great public gathering Ezra read to the people from the Book of the Law; a deep impression was made, and the people, after humbly confessing their sins, entered into a solemn covenant to abstain from marriages with

---
[6] Ezra, Chapters 7 to 10.
[7] Neh., Chapters 1 to 7.

THE PSALMS AND OTHER SACRED WRITINGS

foreigners, and from trade on the Sabbath, and to support the temple service.[8] The population of the city was increased by lot. Following various lists the narrative continues with an account of the dedication of the walls, the provision for the maintenance of the temple service and officials, and the exclusion of all foreigners.[9] After an absence at the Persian court Nehemiah returned in 432, when he instituted various religious and social reforms.[10]

I. EVENTS CULMINATING IN THE REBUILDING OF THE TEMPLE
(Ezra 1. 1 to 6. 22)

1. Decree of Cyrus (1. 1-4).
2. Return from Babylon under Sheshbazzar (1. 5-11).
3. List of returning exiles (2. 1-70).
4. Rebuilding of the altar of burnt-offering (3. 1-7).
5. Rebuilding of the temple begun (3. 8-13).
6. Building operations discontinued (4. 1-5, 24).
   (4. 6, 7-23, which is out of place here, refers to complaints made to Xerxes and Artaxerxes, resulting in the interruption of the work of rebuilding the city walls.)
7. Rebuilding and dedication of the temple (5. 1 to 6. 18).
8. The great Passover (6. 19-22).

II. THE MISSION OF EZRA (Ezra 7. 1 to 10. 44)

1. Visit of Ezra to Jerusalem (7. 1-11).
2. Letter of Artaxerxes to Ezra (7. 12-26).
3. Thanksgiving of Ezra (7. 27, 28).
4. Companions of Ezra (8. 1-20).
5. Incidents of the journey; arrival in Jerusalem (8. 21-36).
6. Complaint regarding mixed marriages (9. 1-4).
7. Ezra's prayer of confession (9. 5-15).
8. Attempt to suppress mixed marriages (10. 1-17).
9. Men involved in mixed marriages (10. 18-44).

---

[8] Neh., Chapters 8 to 10.
[9] Neh. 11. 1 to 13. 3.
[10] Neh. 13. 4-31.

THE BOOKS OF EZRA AND NEHEMIAH

III. COMING OF NEHEMIAH; REBUILDING OF CITY WALLS (Neh. 1. 1 to 7. 73a)
1. Grief and prayer of Nehemiah (1. 1-11).
2. Commission of Nehemiah (2. 1-8).
3. Decision to rebuild the city walls (2. 9-20).
4. Beginning of building operations (3. 1-32).
5. Opposition and precautions (4. 1-23).
6. Social reforms (5. 1-13).
7. Unselfishness of Nehemiah (5. 14-19).
8. Completion of walls (6. 1-19).
9. Provisions for protection of the city (7. 1-4).
10. List of returning exiles (7. 5-73a).

IV. PROMULGATION OF THE LAW (Neh. 7. 73b to 10. 39)
1. Reading of the Law (7. 73b to 8. 12).
2. Observance of the feast of Tabernacles (8. 13-18).
3. Public confession of sin (9. 1-37).
4. Covenant to keep the Law (9. 38 to 10. 39).

V. OTHER ENTERPRISES OF NEHEMIAH (Neh. 11. 1 to 13. 31)
1. List of dwellers in Jerusalem (11. 1-24).
2. List of towns inhabited by returned exiles (11. 25-36).
3. Heads of priestly and Levitical families (12. 1-26).
4. Dedication of the city walls (12. 27-43).
5. Provision for priests and Levites (12. 44-47).
6. Exclusion of foreigners (13. 1-3).
7. Second administration of Nehemiah (13. 4-31).
   (1) Expulsion of Tobiah from the temple (13. 4-9).
   (2) Provision for Levites and singers (13. 10-14).
   (3) Sabbath-observance demanded (13. 15-22).
   (4) Mixed marriages condemned (13. 23-31).

Manner and Date of Composition. In the study of the composition, sources, and historical value of Ezra-Nehemiah the student is introduced to some of the most perplexing problems of Old Testament research. Any sort of adequate discussion would require more space than is here available; hence the present writer is of necessity confining himself to the setting forth of conclusions which seem to him fairly well established. He does

THE PSALMS AND OTHER SACRED WRITINGS

this with the full realization that even some of these conclusions may have to be modified as the result of further investigation.[11] One point, however, is settled beyond question, namely that the books of Ezra-Nehemiah are in the nature of a compilation. Not only is this established by the fact that the books were originally a part of Chronicles, which gives evidence of compilation on every page,[12] but, in addition, there are certain features of the two books themselves which point in the same direction: (1) The change from the first to the third person in the course of the narrative; (2) the unevenness in the treatment of history; (3) differences in language and style, corresponding with the changes in the pronouns; (4) while some sections make the impression that they are the work of eyewitnesses and participants in the events recorded, other sections present equally strong evidence that they originated a long time after the events had taken place.

The question of date can be considered more satisfactorily in connection with the books of Chronicles; for, in the nature of the case, if Ezra-Nehemiah came from the same author or compiler, their date must be the same, that is, about B. C. 300.[13]

---

[11] A good idea of the perplexing problems presented by Ezra-Nehemiah is given by C. C. Torrey, in his *Ezra Studies*, a volume that represents a most thoroughgoing investigation of the problems connected with Ezra-Nehemiah and with Jewish history in general during the first century of the postexilic period. Though some of Professor Torrey's conclusions may have to be modified, no student of this period can afford to neglect his work.

[12] See Chapter XIII, below, pp. 332-335.

[13] The question of date is discussed more fully in Chapter XIII. Here it may be sufficient to give a brief statement of some of the more important reasons why scholars believe that the two books cannot have been written by the men whose names they bear, but that they

THE BOOKS OF EZRA AND NEHEMIAH

Sources. 1. *Memoirs of Ezra and Nehemiah.* Though Ezra and Nehemiah cannot be considered the authors of the books that bear their names, it is quite generally thought that the compiler had access to autobiographical memoirs of the two men, and that these constituted his most valuable sources of information. In some cases these memoirs—written in the first person—were embodied by him in his own work practically without change; at other times he did not hesitate to introduce

---

originated during the Greek period: (1) The misplacing of Ezra 4. 6-23. These verses refer to events during the reigns of Xerxes and Artaxerxes; Ezra was a contemporary of the latter. Would he insert the verses into an account of events clearly belonging to an earlier period? (2) The use of the phrase "king of Persia," which seems to imply that the kingdom of Persia was a thing of the past. (3) The mention of Jaddua, the great-grandson of Eliashib (12. 11, 22), the latter being a contemporary of Nehemiah (13. 28). (4) The days of Nehemiah are grouped with the days of Zerubbabel as a period in the past (12. 47). (5) The language and style, as well as the character of the ideas, point to a late date.

As soon as Ezra-Nehemiah are regarded as a compilation of material taken from various sources, made a considerable time after the events recorded took place, the more troublesome problems of the book receive a satisfactory explanation. For instance, the gaps in the history: the compiler being interested only in the outstanding events of the age, selects only such material as suits his purpose. Moreover, the compiler being removed from the actual events, might at times arrange his material faultily: this would explain the presence of Ezra 4. 6-23, a passage dealing with the building of the city walls, in the midst of a narrative dealing with the rebuilding of the temple. In the same way may be explained the present position of Neh. 8-10, which at one time may have been the sequel of Ezra 10, as also the reversing of the chronological order of Ezra and Nehemiah, which is assumed by an increasing number of modern writers. The theory accounts also for the change in pronouns: Some of the material used came to the compiler written in the first person, other sources used the third person; in the sections supplied by himself he naturally used the third person in writing of his heroes. The use of the same list in two different places (Ezra 2 and Neh. 7) would also find a satisfactory explanation.

THE PSALMS AND OTHER SACRED WRITINGS

alterations, among other things, changing the pronoun of the first person to that of the third person. The memoirs of Ezra are found in Ezra 7. 27 to 9. 15, and may have included, in addition, the Aramaic document in 7. 12-26, which purports to be a letter from Artaxerxes to Ezra.[14] The memoirs of Nehemiah are found in Neh. 1. 1 to 7. 5—perhaps *plus* the list of names in 7. 6-73, which is duplicated in Ezra 2; 12. 27-43; 13. 4-31.

Sections which may rest on the memoirs of Ezra, but which in their present form are the work of a later writer are Ezra 10 and Neh. 8-10. Some parts of the book of Nehemiah may be based on the memoirs of Nehemiah or, perhaps, upon other contemporaneous documents;[15] but if this is the case, the earlier material was worked over by a later writer, who may have been the compiler of the entire work. In these "modified" sections the hand of the compiler may be seen not only in the modifications introduced into the earlier material but also in the presence of more or less extensive additions coming in their entirety from him.[16]

(2) *Aramaic Documents.* Ezra 4. 8 to 6. 18 and 7. 12-26 are written in Aramaic. These sections contain, embedded in suitable narrative setting, what claim to be five official documents: (*a*) A letter sent to Artaxerxes, charging the Jews with treason;[17] (*b*) the reply to this letter, ordering that the rebuilding of the city be

---

[14] On the genuineness and value of the memoirs of Ezra and related questions, see further, below, pp. 302ff.
[15] For example, several paragraphs in Chapters 11 to 13, such as 12. 12–21; 13. 1–3.
[16] For example, Ezra 7. 1–11; some parts of Nehemiah, Chapters 9, 10; 11. 25 to 12. 11; 12. 22–26, 44–47.
[17] Ezra 4. 11–16.

THE BOOKS OF EZRA AND NEHEMIAH

stopped.[18] (c) An inquiry regarding the authority of the Jews to rebuild the temple;[19] (d) the reply to this inquiry, favoring the claims of the Jews and confirming the decree of Cyrus.[20] (e) The letter of Artaxerxes to Ezra, commissioning him to go to Jerusalem.[21] The last mentioned document is separated from the others by two paragraphs in Hebrew, the one narrating the observance of the Passover,[22] the other furnishing a summary account of Ezra and his work.[23] Both of these appear to be the work of the compiler; some scholars, however, consider them later interpolations.

The compiler may not have had direct access to the official documents or archives. On the contrary, it is very probable that the first four documents *plus* the verses furnishing the historical setting[24] constituted originally a section of an independent work written in Aramaic about B. C. 400, and that this was used as a source-book by the compiler.[25] The nature and original extent of this Aramaic work cannot be determined. Some have thought that it was simply an account of the troubles between the returned exiles and their neighbors, to the end of the reign of Artaxerxes I,[26] while others have thought of it as a more comprehensive history of the postexilic community. In either case its presentation of the course of events may safely be accepted as trustworthy, even

---

[18] Ezra 4. 17–22.
[19] 5. 6–17.
[20] 6. 1–12.
[21] 7. 12–26.
[22] 6. 19–22.
[23] 7. 1–10.
[24] With the possible exception of a few minor additions made subsequently.
[25] The other document may have been taken from the memoirs of Ezra.
[26] B. C. 465–425.

THE PSALMS AND OTHER SACRED WRITINGS

though some portions may have been worked over at a later time from a more rigidly Jewish point of view.

The genuineness of the Aramaic documents has been called in question, chiefly on account of their decidedly Jewish coloring, which, it is claimed, is out of place in documents originating at the Persian court or with Persian officials. The decree of Darius, for example, closes with this recognition of the supremacy of Yahweh: "And the God that hath caused his name to dwell there overthrow all kings and peoples that shall put forth their hand to alter *the same,* to destroy this house of God which is in Jerusalem."[27] Equally strange seems the detailed description of the Jewish sacrificial system in the letter of Artaxerxes to Ezra.[28] However, Eduard Meyer has clearly shown that these peculiar Jewish features by no means disprove the genuineness of the documents; and ever since the publication of his discriminating study[29] there has been a growing tendency among scholars to admit the genuineness of the documents, with the exception of the decree of Cyrus given in Hebrew in Ezra 1. 2-4, which is thought to have been preserved in a more original form in 6. 3-5. Those who accept the documents as genuine explain the Jewish elements as due to modifications by the author of the Aramaic history or by the still later Chronicler, or on the assumption that the documents originating at the Persian court were drafted by Jews and then submitted to the Persian authorities for their approval, while in some instances both influences may have made themselves felt.

How the documents came into the hands of the Jewish writer is not known. It has been suggested that they

---

[27] Ezra 6. 12. [28] Ezra 7. 17.
[29] Eduard Meyer, *Die Entstehung des Judentums,* especially pp. 8–71.

THE BOOKS OF EZRA AND NEHEMIAH

came from "the public archives in Jerusalem, where it would be natural to keep copies of letters sent to, and the originals (or copies) of letters sent from, the Persian court." But, while the prevalence of such a custom throughout the east may readily be admitted,[30] it should be noted that these documents were neither addressed to the community in Jerusalem, nor were they sent from there. It is more probable, therefore, that they were secured from the Persian court-archives, perhaps by some Jew who, like Nehemiah, had risen to a position of prominence at the court of Persia.

(3) *Temple and Government Records.* There are some portions of Ezra-Nehemiah which seem to have been written in their entirety by the compiler of the book; and yet it is by no means certain that in writing these sections he did not make use of earlier material. There is nothing improbable in the view that the compiler, who evidently belonged to the priestly circles, had access to earlier temple records and that he gathered from them information regarding the restoration of worship after the exile, the rebuilding of the temple, and the provisions for the maintenance of the temple service. He may also have had access to records dealing with non-religious community affairs, which may have been preserved in the temple archives or in the archives of the civil government. If such records were used, material from them may be found especially in Ezra 1 and 3 and in the sections of Nehemiah that were added by the compiler.

Historical Value. The preceding paragraphs call attention to the fact that the compiler of Ezra-Nehemiah, though living a century or more after the occurrence of

---
[30] Compare the Elephantine Papyri; on the existence of such archives, see H. Winckler, *Vorderasien im zweiten Jahrtausend, passim.*

THE PSALMS AND OTHER SACRED WRITINGS

the latest events recorded, had access to various earlier sources, in part practically contemporaneous with the events described, in part written within a generation or two following the activities of Nehemiah. If, now, the compiler reproduced, without material alteration, some official documents and portions of the memoirs of Ezra and of Nehemiah, the historical value of the book can hardly be overestimated. If, on the other hand, he misunderstood his sources, took undue liberties with them, failed to arrange them in the proper order, wrote himself what he claims to have received from the past, and in general gave free play to his imagination, little help can be expected from the book in tracing the history of the postexilic community. What, then, is the real situation? (1) There seems to be insufficient reason for questioning the substantial accuracy of the official letters and decrees. (2) In the case of the memoirs of Nehemiah internal evidence is so convincing that few scholars question their genuineness. If so, they must have been written soon after B. C. 432—probably between 430 and 425, and may, therefore, be expected to give a reliable account of the events in which Nehemiah had a part. (3) It is different with the memoirs of Ezra. Their authenticity has been seriously questioned: their similarity in language, ideas, and general interest with sections coming from the Chronicler has led some to suspect that the alleged memoirs are in reality the work of this late compiler. C. C. Torrey, for example, insists that there is no portion of the entire work, including Chronicles, Ezra, and Nehemiah, in which "the Chronicler's literary peculiarities are more strongly marked, more abundant, more evenly and continuously distributed, and more easily recognizable than in the Hebrew narrative

THE BOOKS OF EZRA AND NEHEMIAH

of Ezra 7-10 and Neh. 8-10."[31] Consequently, he is very positive in his assertion that the Chronicler is the real author of the sections known as the memoirs of Ezra.

It is by no means certain, however, that the facts in the case warrant the conclusion. The similarities may indicate that the Chronicler treated the memoirs of Ezra with much freedom, but they do not disprove their authenticity: Ezra was a scribe, a student and lover of the Law, and was permeated by the spirit of ecclesiasticism, which is also characteristic of the Chronicler. Under these circumstances it is only natural that in language, style, and general point of view the work of the Chronicler should resemble more closely the production of the priest-scribe Ezra than that of the layman Nehemiah. Moreover, after recognizing the similarity, the later writer may have felt freer to modify the memoirs of Ezra and even to rewrite them, in part at least, from his own point of view.[32] Without entering into a full discussion, for which there is no room in this connection, the present writer may express his belief that the arguments against the genuineness of the Ezra memoirs are not conclusive, and that, therefore, it is still safe to regard the accounts of events contained in them as substantially accurate and reliable. At the same time he is quite ready to admit that these memoirs have undergone radical modifications at the hands of the compiler.[33]

Without denying the authenticity of the memoirs of

---

[31] *Ezra Studies*, p. 241.

[32] For example, the reference to the immense wealth in Ezra 8. 24-27 may come from the Chronicler, who delights in exaggeration of this sort.

[33] If the documents and memoirs found in Ezra-Nehemiah are authentic at least in essence, the question whether the Chronicler had access to the original sources or only to a work of which they formed a part, becomes of secondary importance.

THE PSALMS AND OTHER SACRED WRITINGS

Ezra or of Nehemiah, some scholars have brought the charge against the Chronicler that, through faulty use of his sources, he misrepresented the course of the history during the postexilic period in three important respects: (1) The return of the exiles in B. C. 537; (2) the attempt on the part of the returned exiles to rebuild the temple soon after the return; (3) the date of Ezra's mission. Regarding the first point, the book of Ezra states that in B. C. 537 a large body of exiles returned from Babylonia. Over against these definite statements stand the assertions of numerous recent writers, following in the footsteps of W. H. Kosters,[34] that practically no exiles came from Babylonia in that year, that the list in Ezra 2 relates to the time of Nehemiah, that the temple was built by the Jews left behind in the land,[35] that Ezra was the first to lead a body of exiles back from Babylonia, which he did, not before Nehemiah, about B. C. 458, but after Nehemiah's first visit, probably about the time of his second visit in B. C. 433-432. The chief argument in favor of the contention that Cyrus issued no decree, and consequently that there was no return in 537, is found in the silence of the prophets Haggai and Zechariah concerning such return. This leaves as the only source of information the books of Ezra and Nehemiah, compiled about B. C. 300 by the compiler of the books of Chronicles. Now, the argument continues, a comparison of Chronicles with Kings reveals the unreliability of the former, which involves the books of Ezra and Nehemiah, coming from the same hand. On reaching this point in the argument Kosters subjected Ezra-Nehemiah to a minute critical analysis, which led him

---

[34] *Die Wiederherstellung Israels in der Persischen Periode*, passim.
[35] 2 Kings 25. 12, 22-26.

THE BOOKS OF EZRA AND NEHEMIAH

to the conclusion that the sections containing the references to the return in 537 are so late that their testimony cannot stand against the silence of the two prophets who prophesied less than twenty years after the date of the alleged return.

Now, it is true that the opening chapters of Ezra reached their present form at a relatively late date and that it is impossible to determine all the sources from which the Chronicler drew information; nevertheless, it is well to bear in mind that undue reliance may easily be placed on the argument from silence. The silence of the two prophets may be accidental; it would assume significance only if it could be shown that there was a necessity for mentioning the return in case it was a historical fact. Such a necessity did not exist; on the contrary, the prophets might feel fully justified not to mention it, since they were addressing people who had participated in the return and, therefore, were thoroughly familiar with it. There certainly is nothing in the utterances of the two men that could be construed as in any way conflicting with the statement in Ezra that Cyrus issued a decree giving permission to the Jews to return to their old home. Nor is there anything inherently improbable in the view that such decree was issued. On the contrary, it is in perfect accord with the inscription of Cyrus, which gives a description of the treatment he accorded to the peoples that had been deported by the Babylonians. Moreover, the historical situation would furnish a strong incentive to the Persian ruler to establish near the borders of Egypt a community that would be bound to the Persian authorities by strong ties of gratitude.[36] From all these con-

---

[36] The Elephantine Papyri, which have thrown such valuable sidelight on conditions during the Persian period, furnish a striking illus-

THE PSALMS AND OTHER SACRED WRITINGS

siderations it would appear that G. A. Smith is right when he says, "We must hold that the attempt to discredit the tradition of an important return of exiles under Cyrus has not been successful; that such a return remains the more probable solution of an obscure and difficult problem."[37]

Closely connected with the denial of a return in 537 is the claim that the book of Ezra is wrong when it asserts that the foundations of the temple were laid by the returned exiles soon after their arrival in Palestine,[38] and the further claim that the temple was rebuilt exclusively by Jews who had been left behind at the time Jerusalem was destroyed.[39] Here, again, appeal is made to the words of Haggai and Zechariah. It is pointed out that these prophets addressed their audiences as "the remnant of the people,"[40] which is interpreted to mean the remnant left behind in B. C. 597 and 586. It is further claimed that the statement concerning the beginning of building operations soon after the return is definitely contradicted by utterances of these prophets which imply that no steps looking toward the rebuilding of the temple had been taken before B. C. 520.[41] By way of explanation it is

---

tration of the kindly policy adopted by the Persian rulers toward the Jews: Cambyses, the successor of Cyrus, spared the Jewish temple at Elephantine at the time he conquered Egypt, in B. C. 525.

[37] *The Minor Prophets*, vol. ii, p. 215.

[38] Ezra 3. 8ff.; 5. 16.

[39] Even some who admit that a few exiles may have returned at various times deny that these played any important part in the building enterprise.

[40] Hag. 1. 12, 14; 2. 2; Zech. 8. 6.

[41] Hag. 1. 2-9; 2. 15-18; Zech. 1. 16; 4. 9; compare also Ezra 5. 2. Some scholars, realizing the difficulty, but unwilling to reject the statements of Ezra as unhistorical, attempt in various ways to harmonize the apparently contradictory statements. Driver, for example, sug-

THE BOOKS OF EZRA AND NEHEMIAH

suggested that the statements in Ezra were inspired by the promise in Isa. 44. 28, that Cyrus would issue an order that the foundations of the temple be laid. The evidence against the reliability of the statement that the foundations of the temple were laid in B. C. 536, while perhaps not overwhelmingly conclusive, is of considerable weight. No doubt the words of Haggai and Zechariah, naturally interpreted, make the laying of the temple foundations fifteen or sixteen years earlier improbable. On the other hand, it can easily be explained why the Chronicler should assign the beginning of the enterprise to an earlier date. In the words of J. E. McFadyen: "To him it may well have seemed inconceivable that the returned exiles should—whatever their excuse—have waited sixteen years before beginning the work which to him was of transcendent importance."[42] He may have found further justification for his view in Isa. 44. 28; at any rate, he seems to have been quite familiar with the prophecies concerning the restoration, for he introduces at the very beginning of the narrative a reference to a prophecy of Jeremiah.[43]

But even admitting that the Chronicler was mistaken when he stated that the foundations of the temple were laid soon after the return of 537, it still remains very probable that the returned exiles had a share in the building enterprise. The terms used by Haggai and Zechariah do not exclude the presence of returned exiles; besides,

---
gests (*Introduction*, p. 547): "The truth probably is that the ceremony described in Ezra 3. 8–13 was one of a purely *formal* character, which Haggai could disregard altogether." It is very doubtful, however, that the explicit statements of the prophets permit this interpretation of their silence regarding the laying of the foundations in 537.

[42] *An Introduction to the Old Testament*, p. 342.
[43] Jer. 25. 12.

THE PSALMS AND OTHER SACRED WRITINGS

it is exceedingly doubtful that the people left behind possessed sufficient spiritual enthusiasm and initiative to carry out the ideas and ideals of the prophets. If there was a return in 537, which to the present writer seems more than probable, a large share of the credit for rebuilding the temple must be given to the faithful Yahweh worshipers who retained their faith in Yahweh during the dark days of the exile and eagerly embraced the first opportunity offered to return to the promised land.

The date of Ezra's mission—assuming that he is a historical character[44]—presents a still more complicated problem. According to Ezra 7. 7, 8, Ezra came to Jerusalem in the "seventh year of Artaxerxes the king." For centuries this king was commonly identified with Artaxerxes I;[45] consequently, the journey of Ezra was dated in 458, that of Nehemiah in 445-444,[46] Ezra being considered the forerunner of Nehemiah. Van Hoonacker was the first to attack this interpretation seriously;[47] and he suggested that Ezra was a contemporary, not of Artaxerxes I, but of Artaxerxes II.[48] This would bring the journey of Ezra down to B. C. 397, the seventh year of Artaxerxes II, and Nehemiah would become the forerunner of Ezra. Since then many other scholars have become convinced that Nehemiah reached Jerusalem before Ezra, but differences of opinion have arisen regarding the exact date of the latter's coming. Some, following van Hoonacker, accept the date 397; others, agreeing with Kosters, connect him with the second visit of Nehe-

---
[44] See further, below, pp. 310, 311.
[45] B. C. 465-425.
[46] Neh. 2. 1.
[47] *Néhemie et Esdras*, published in 1890; some questions had been raised previously.
[48] B. C. 404-359.

THE BOOKS OF EZRA AND NEHEMIAH

miah, in 432 or soon after; while still others, like Torrey, deny the historical character of Ezra and look upon him as a personification of the spirit of later Judaism. The following are the principal reasons for placing the coming of Ezra after the first visit of Nehemiah: (1) The situation which, according to the book of Ezra itself, confronted Ezra on his arrival, implies an orderly, settled life, such as was impossible until after the city walls had been built and the city had been well fortified. (2) The prayer of Ezra[49] seems to imply that the building of the walls was an accomplished fact. (3) Nehemiah's memoirs are silent concerning the reforms alleged to have been undertaken by Ezra; nor are any of the reformers who are said to have accompanied Ezra named as cooperating with Nehemiah. (4) The reform work of Nehemiah has the appearance of being preliminary to that of Ezra; at any rate, the measures of Nehemiah are less radical than those of Ezra.[50] All these facts, it is pointed out, would find a satisfactory explanation on the assumption that at least the earlier reforms of Nehemiah preceded the mission of Ezra.

If the statements in Neh. 8. 9; 10. 1 are accepted as in any sense reliable, it follows that Ezra and Nehemiah were in Jerusalem at the same time. Those who believe these statements to be correct naturally hesitate to carry Ezra down to the fourth century; but feeling the force of the facts noted above, they are unwilling to place him earlier than Nehemiah's administration; hence they connect him with the second visit of the latter. On the other

---
[49] Ezra 9. 9.
[50] For example, whereas Ezra demands the putting away of non-Jewish wives (Ezra 10. 11, 12), Nehemiah is content with forbidding mixed marriages for the future (Neh. 13. 25).

THE PSALMS AND OTHER SACRED WRITINGS

hand, those who hold that the connection of Ezra with Nehemiah is due to a mistake of the Chronicler, have no hesitation to date him later; and, accepting the ambiguous statement that Ezra came to Jerusalem in the seventh year of Artaxerxes, as referring to the second king bearing that name, they assign his journey to B. C. 397. The advocates of this view claim that they make only one assumption, namely, that the Chronicler failed to arrange his material in the right order; and they point to the misplacement of Ezra 4. 6-23 as an exact parallel. If the later date is accepted, it becomes necessary to arrange the material in the two books somewhat after this fashion: Ezra 1. 1 to 4. 5; 4. 24 to 6. 22; Neh. 1. 1 to 6. 19; Ezra 4. 6-23; Neh. 7. 1-69 (Ezra 2); Neh. 11. 1 to 12. 47; 13. 4-31; Ezra 7. 1 to 8. 36; Neh. 7. 70 to 8. 18; Ezra 9. 1 to 10. 9; Neh. 13. 1-3; Ezra 10. 10-44; Neh. 9. 1 to 10. 39.

Professor C. C. Torrey takes a more radical position than any discussed in the preceding paragraphs,[51] when he denies the historical character of Ezra himself, whom he regards merely a reflection of Nehemiah or a personification of the spirit and ideals of later Judaism. According to this view, the creation of the character of Ezra and the composition of the memoirs of Ezra were inspired in large part by a desire to correct the impression made by the memoirs of Nehemiah that the reestablishment and purification of Judaism were the work of a layman, a view which would appear intolerable to the Chronicler and to the *priestly* circles in which he moved. The arguments in favor of this contention may be summarized as follows: (1) The religious, intellectual, and ecclesiastical

---

[51] *Composition and Historical Value of Ezra-Nehemiah,* especially pp. 57-62; and *Ezra Studies,* pp. 238-248.

THE BOOKS OF EZRA AND NEHEMIAH

atmosphere in which the Chronicler found himself practically compelled him to create such a character. (2) The striking similarities between the hero of the Ezra memoirs and the Chronicler find their only natural interpretation in such a theory: "If we have any definite knowledge at all of this 'Ezra,' we know that he was a man precisely like the Chronicler himself. . . . There is not a garment in all Ezra's wardrobe that does not fit the Chronicler exactly. To suppose that the latter could have *rewritten* the words, and twisted the ideas, of this kindred spirit, whose testimony was of such importance to all his own special interests, is out of the question; his intelligence was not of such a low order as this; and we know, besides, that his habit was directly opposed to any such proceeding, even when the material was not exactly suited to his purpose."[52] (3) Ezra and the Ezra tradition are unknown to later Jewish writers. For instance, Ecclesiasticus, who speaks in the highest terms of Nehemiah, makes no mention of Ezra.[53] A moment's thought will show that arguments like these can do no more than establish the *possibility* of Torrey's conclusion; it would be too much to say that they do or even can establish its probability; and, certainly, they fall far short of establishing it as a fact. Unless more convincing arguments are presented, the student will be justified in retaining the belief that Ezra was a real person, who played a prominent role in the development of postexilic Judaism.

In the absence of all external evidence the various problems raised by the books of Ezra and Nehemiah and outlined in the preceding paragraphs cannot be definitely

---

[52] C. C. Torrey, *Ezra Studies*, pp. 243, 244.
[53] Compare also 2 Maccabees 2. 1ff.

settled. No doubt the advocates of each of the several modern positions may discover certain facts which seem to favor their contention; but it is equally true that the older view, which accepts the chronology of the Chronicler, is not without support. Most of the elements upon which the reconstruction theories are based can be explained as introduced, perhaps more or less unconsciously, by the Chronicler, who, writing when conditions were far different from what they were in the fifth century, could not remain uninfluenced by the environment in which he lived. And there is abundant evidence to show that he frequently modified his sources from the standpoint of his own age.[54] But even if it were admitted that the compiler disarranged his material, and that he introduced various modifications, he has preserved his sources with sufficient faithfulness to make them historical documents of the highest value. Especially the memoirs, proceeding as they do from the chief actors in the events described, are of the greatest significance for an adequate understanding of a period in the life of the postexilic community, which in turn is of very great importance for the whole subsequent history of Judaism.

[54] For the bearing of this whole discussion on certain questions connected with the literary history of the Pentateuch, see F. C. Eiselen, *The Books of the Pentateuch*, p. 311.

APPENDIX TO CHAPTER XII

THE FIRST BOOK OF ESDRAS

In the Septuagint the canonical Ezra-Nehemiah, called Second Esdras, is preceded by a book called First Esdras, which in its present form—it is incomplete, for it ends in the middle of a sentence—consists of parts of Chronicles and Ezra-Nehemiah, and of one section not found elsewhere:

1 Esdras 1 = 2 Chron. 35. 1 to 36. 21.
2. 1-15 = Ezra 1.
2. 16-25 = Ezra 4. 7-24.
3. 1 to 5. 6 = Not found elsewhere.
5. 7-70 = Ezra 2. 1 to 4. 5.
6. 1 to 9. 36 = Ezra (4. 24) 5. 1 to 10. 44.
9. 37-55 = Neh. 7. 73b to 8. 13a.

The section peculiar to First Esdras, 3. 1 to 5. 6, relates how three pages of Darius agreed to a test of their wisdom in the presence of the king by a discussion of the question, What is the strongest? One defended the proposition, "Wine is the strongest"; the second, "The king is the strongest"; the third, "Women are the strongest, but, above all things, truth beareth away the victory." The third, Zerubbabel, was declared the winner, and Darius promised to grant him anything he might desire. In reply he reminded the king of a vow he had made at the time of his accession to restore the Jews to their old home. Whereupon Darius issued a decree giving permission to the Jews to return and to rebuild their temple, granting them at the same time other privileges. This story, then, would give the

THE PSALMS AND OTHER SACRED WRITINGS

credit for the restoration of the Jews, not to Cyrus, but to Darius.

The source from which the new material was taken cannot be definitely determined; but a theory advocated by C. C. Torrey has much in its favor. Calling attention to the fact that Ezra 3. 7[55] seems to contain an allusion to 1 Esdras 4. 48, which allusion cannot be explained by anything in the present book of Ezra, and to the other fact that certain sections of the narrative found only in 1 Esdras reveal the same interests as the Chronicler,[56] he suggests that 1 Esdras 4. 47[57] to 4. 56, and 4. 62 to 5. 6[58] once stood in the work of the Chronicler, immediately after Ezra 1. 11 and immediately before Ezra 2. 1. If this theory is correct, the story of the three pages, 1 Esdras 3. 1 to 4. 42, must be regarded as an interpolation from an unknown source, and verses like 4. 43, 44, 57-61; 5. 6a, the words "the same is Zerubbabel" in 4. 13, and the substitution of Cyrus in 4. 47 and 5. 2 as harmonizing modifications by the interpolater.

There is considerable difference of opinion regarding the relation of First Esdras to the canonical Ezra-Nehemiah:

1. Mention may be made, in the first place, of the view ably developed by Sir Henry Howorth that First Esdras represents the original Septuagint translation of the Hebrew Ezra-Nehemiah, while Second Esdras[59] represents the translation of Theodotion. From this he draws the further conclusion that First Esdras is in every respect superior to and of greater value to the Old Testament student than the canonical Ezra-Nehemiah.

---

[55] The same as 1 Esdras 5. 55.
[56] For instance, 1 Esdras 4. 52-56, 63; 5. 2.
[57] Beginning with "wrote," the subject in Chronicles having been Cyrus.
[58] Omitting, "who spoke wise sentences before Darius the king of Persia."
[59] That is, the canonical Ezra-Nehemiah.

THE FIRST BOOK OF ESDRAS

2. There is another view which regards First Esdras as a secondary, but independent compilation, written for a specific purpose. The motive for this compilation is variously interpreted. Driver, for example, suggests that "the writer wished partly to stimulate his countrymen to a more zealous observance of the Law, partly by the example of the munificence of Cyrus and Darius to gain for them the favor of some foreign ruler—perhaps one of the Ptolemies."[60]

3. A still different theory is worked out by Torrey, which is summed up by him in these words: "It is simply a piece taken without change out of the middle of a faithful Greek translation of the Chronicler's History of Israel in the form which was generally recognized as authentic in the last century B. C. This was not, however, the original form of the History, but one which had undergone several important changes."[61]

4. S. A. Cook, after a lengthy discussion of the whole subject, advocates a still different view: "All the data suggest that E. [First Esdras] and E. N. [the canonical Ezra-Nehemiah] represent concurrent forms which have influenced each other in the earlier stages of their growth. They are rivals, and neither can be said to be wholly older or more historical than the other. The endeavor was made to correct E to agree with the Massoretic Text, ... and the presence of such efforts and in particular the doublets are of essential importance in indicating that E's text does not precisely represent a Hebrew-Aramaic work, and that when all allowance is made for correction and revision of the Greek, problems of the underlying original text still remain. But it was impossible to make any very satisfactory adjustment, E diverged too seriously from the Massoretic Text, which had cut the chronological knot by the

---

[60] *Introduction to the Literature of the Old Testament*, p. 554.
[61] *Ezra Studies*, p. 18.

THE PSALMS AND OTHER SACRED WRITINGS

exclusion of the story of Zerubbabel, and we may suppose that this facilitated the desire for the more literal translation of Theodotion."[62]

It is not possible to go into a detailed discussion of the complex problem in this place; but evidently criticism has not spoken the last word on the subject, and Cook is right when he admits that any explanation must be a provisional one. In the nature of the case, the same uncertainty exists regarding the date of First Esdras, because the question of date is closely bound up with the question as to its relation to the canonical books.

---

[62] In R. H. Charles, *The Apocrypha and Pseudepigrapha of the Old Testament*, p. 19.

CHAPTER XIII

THE BOOKS OF CHRONICLES

CHAPTER XIII

THE BOOKS OF CHRONICLES

Name and Place in Canon. Originally, the two books of Chronicles in the English Bible formed one continuous work called in Hebrew דִּבְרֵי הַיָּמִים, *Dibhrē Hayyāmîm,* which may be translated "Acts" or "Annals of the Days." The early Greek translators introduced the division and called the two books Τὰ Παραλειπόμενα, *Ta Paraleipomena,* which may be rendered "The Things Omitted" or "Passed Over"; that is, the things which were omitted in the other historical books, especially in Samuel and Kings.[1] Jerome adopted the division as also the Septuagint title, *Paralipomenon,* but suggested as a more satisfactory equivalent of the Hebrew the title *Chronicon,* from which is derived the English *Chronicles.*

In its original form the work included also Ezra and Nehemiah; but these two books, covering a period not dealt with in the other historical books and thus having a value of their own, were separated from Chronicles before the extent of the Jewish canon was finally fixed. As a result they have had a history of their own and must be studied by themselves.[2] The English Bible, following the Latin Vulgate, which in turn is dependent on the Greek Septuagint, places Chronicles after Kings

---

[1] As will be seen, this view is not correct. Chronicles is not a continuation or supplement of the other historical books, but runs parallel with them.

[2] See Chapter XII.

THE PSALMS AND OTHER SACRED WRITINGS

and before Ezra-Nehemiah, thus recognizing the fact that Ezra-Nehemiah are the continuation of Chronicles. But this is not the order in the Jewish canon. The Massoretic lists and the MSS. written in Spain put Chronicles first among the books in the third division of the Jewish Canon, while they assign last place to Ezra-Nehemiah. On the other hand, the Talmud, most of the Hebrew MSS. written in Germany, and the early printed editions of the Hebrew Bible place Chronicles at the end of the list, following Ezra-Nehemiah; which has been interpreted to indicate that when Ezra-Nehemiah were first separated from Chronicles it was the intention to admit only the former into the canon, because, unlike Chronicles, they dealt with an important period in the life of the postexilic community, which was not described in any other Old Testament book, and to exclude Chronicles as a "superfluous and inferior variant of Kings." With this interpretation it is further assumed that at a later time, but before the extent of the third division of the canon was finally fixed, Chronicles was admitted, probably because of its emphasis on religious institutions and practices, which were so highly prized in the later postexilic period; but it had to be content with the "ragged end" of the collection, either at the beginning or at the close.[3]

Contents and Outline. Chronicles is neither a continuation of nor a supplement to Samuel and Kings, but a parallel to the historical books from Genesis to Kings: it covers the period from Adam to the issuing of the edict by Cyrus, in B. C. 538 or 537, granting permission to

---

[3] It has been suggested that the Massorites assigned first place to Chronicles, because it places so much emphasis on temple worship and various ceremonial institutions. This explanation is possible, but there is no evidence to prove the assertion.

THE BOOKS OF CHRONICLES

the exiled Jews to return to Jerusalem.[4] The two books fall naturally into four parts: I. Genealogies, intended primarily to trace history from the creation of man to the reign of Saul, though some of them are carried down to late postexilic days;[5] II. The reign of David;[6] III. The reign of Solomon;[7] IV. The history of Judah, from the division of the kingdom under Rehoboam to the restoration from exile.[8]

I. GENEALOGIES—*Principally from Adam to Saul* (1 Chron. 1. 1 to 9. 44)

1. From Adam to Isaac (1. 1-34a).
2. Descendants of Isaac, through Esau (1. 34b-54).
3. Descendants of Isaac, through Israel-Jacob (2. 1 to 9. 44).
   (1) From Israel-Jacob to the age of David (2. 1-17).
   (2) Descendants of Caleb (2. 18-55).
   (3) Davidic line from David to Anani (3. 1-24).
   (4) Descendants of Judah (4. 1-23).
   (5) Descendants of Simeon (4. 24-43).
   (6) Descendants of Reuben, Gad, Manasseh—east of the Jordan (5. 1-26).
   (7) Descendants of Aaron (6. 1-15, 49-53).
   (8) Levite singers and priests (6. 16-48).
   (9) Priestly and Levitical cities (6. 54-81).
   (10) Descendants of Issachar, Benjamin, Naphtali, Manasseh—west of the Jordan, Ephraim, Asher (7. 1-40).
   (11) Descendants of Benjamin—line of Saul (8. 1-40).
   (12) Returned exiles (9. 1-34).
   (13) Family of Saul (9. 35-44).

II. REIGN OF DAVID (1 Chron. 10. 1 to 29. 30)

1. Death of Saul and of his sons (10. 1-14).
2. Anointing of David (11. 1-3).
3. Capture of Jebus—Jerusalem (11. 4-9).

---

[4] Some of the genealogies continue far into the postexilic period.
[5] 1 Chron., Chapters 1 to 9.
[6] 1 Chron., Chapters 10 to 29.
[7] 2 Chron., Chapters 1 to 9.
[8] 2 Chron., Chapters 10 to 36.

THE PSALMS AND OTHER SACRED WRITINGS

4. David's heroes and their exploits (11. 10-47).
5. David's adherents (12. 1-40).
6. Attempt to bring the ark to Jerusalem (13. 1-14).
7. Defeat of the Philistines (14. 1-17).
8. The ark in Jerusalem (15. 1 to 16. 43).
9. David's purpose to build the temple (17. 1-27).
10. David's victories (18. 1 to 20. 8).
11. Census and consequent pestilence (21. 1-27).
12. Preparations for the building of the temple (21. 28 to 22. 19).
13. Provisions for the temple service (23. 1 to 26. 28).
14. Civil and military officials (26. 29 to 27. 34).
15. Instructions with reference to the building of the temple and its service (28. 1 to 29. 22a).
16. Accession of Solomon; death of David (29. 22b-30).

III. REIGN OF SOLOMON (2 Chron. 1. 1 to 9. 31)

1. Solomon's sacrifice at Gibeon and choice of wisdom (1. 1-13).
2. Solomon's wealth (1. 14-17).
3. Building and dedication of the temple (2. 1 to 7. 22).
4. Various enterprises of Solomon (8. 1-18).
5. Visit of the queen of Sheba (9. 1-12).
6. Solomon's wealth and power (9. 13-31).

IV. HISTORY OF JUDAH FROM THE DIVISION TO THE RESTORATION (2 Chron. 10. 1 to 36. 23)

1. Division of the kingdom (10. 1-19).
2. Reign of Rehoboam (11. 1 to 12. 16).
3. Abijah (13. 1-22).
4. Asa (14. 1 to 16. 14).
5. Jehoshaphat (17. 1 to 20. 37).
6. Jehoram (21. 1-20).
7. Ahaziah (22. 1-9).
8. Usurpation of Athaliah (22. 10-12).
9. Death of Athaliah; crowning of Joash (23. 1-21).
10. Reign of Joash (24. 1-27).
11. Amaziah (25. 1-28).
12. Uzziah (26. 1-23).
13. Jotham (27. 1-9).
14. Ahaz (28. 1-27).
15. Hezekiah (29. 1 to 32. 33).
16. Manasseh (33. 1-20).
17. Amon (33. 21-25).
18. Josiah (34. 1 to 35. 27).

THE BOOKS OF CHRONICLES

19. Jehoahaz (36. 1-4).
20. Jehoiakim (36. 5-8).
21. Jehoiachin (36. 9, 10).
22. Zedekiah and the fall of Jerusalem (36. 11-21).
23. Decree of Cyrus (36. 22, 23).

Date. 1. *Relation of Chronicles to Ezra-Nehemiah.* That Chronicles, Ezra, and Nehemiah are the work of one and the same author is made practically certain by the following considerations: (1) Not only are Ezra-Nehemiah the direct continuation of Chronicles, but the closing verses of Chronicles are identical with the opening verses of Ezra.[9] (2) There is a striking similarity in style between those parts in Chronicles, Ezra, and Nehemiah which were not taken *verbatim* from earlier sources. (3) The interest of all three books centers in the same things—the temple and its service, the priesthood, the law, statistics, and genealogies. (4) Internal evidence in Ezra-Nehemiah points to the same date for these books as that to which Chronicles must be assigned. Consequently, in discussing the date of Chronicles evidence furnished by the other two books may also be considered.

2. *Evidence supplied by Chronicles..* If Ezra-Nehemiah and Chronicles were written by one and the same author, Chronicles cannot be earlier than the activity of Nehemiah, about B. C. 450-430; but even when considered by itself, the available evidence points to the late postexilic period: (1) The fact that the narrative is continued to the first year of Cyrus[10] shows that it was written not earlier than B. C. 537. (2) The reckoning in *darics*,[11] which is a Persian coin named after Darius I,[12]

---
[9] Compare 2 Chron. 36. 22, 23 with Ezra 1. 1-3a.
[10] 2 Chron. 36. 22.
[11] 1 Chron. 29. 7.
[12] B. C. 522-485.

THE PSALMS AND OTHER SACRED WRITINGS

implies that the coin was well known, not only to the writer, but also to the reader; otherwise the statement would have been unintelligible; but this presupposes a date not earlier than the middle of the fifth century. (3) The compiler knew the Pentateuch in substantially its final form; for he uses material from both the earliest and the latest documents;[13] which suggests a date not earlier than the closing years of the fifth century. (4) In 1 Chron. 3. 19-24 the Hebrew text traces the genealogy of David to the sixth generation after Zerubbabel, who was prominent about B. C. 520.[14] The early Greek, Syriac, and Latin translations, which may have preserved the original reading, carry it on to the eleventh generation; but even the Hebrew text would point to a date not earlier than B. C. 350.

3. *Evidence supplied by Ezra-Nehemiah.* The testimony of Chronicles finds corroboration in the books of Ezra and Nehemiah: (5) The book of Ezra cannot have been written by Ezra himself but must come from an author living subsequently to Ezra; for at times he introduces Ezra as the narrator,[15] while at other times he writes about him.[16] Indeed, the author seems to have lived after the fall of the Persian power, that is, after B. C. 332; at any rate, such inference may be drawn from the use of the phrase "king of Persia,"[17] which seems to imply that the kingdom of Persia was no longer in existence. Documents coming from the Persian period

---

[13] 1 Chron. 1. 5-7 = Gen. 10. 2-4 (P.); 1. 8-16 = Gen. 10. 6, 7 (P.) *plus* 10. 8, 13-18a (J.); 1. 17-23 = Gen. 10. 22, 23 (P.) *plus* 10. 24-29 (J.), etc.
[14] Hag. 1. 1, 14; 2. 2, etc.
[15] 8. 1ff.
[16] 10. 1ff.
[17] Ezra 1. 1; 4. 5, 24; 7. 1, etc.

THE BOOKS OF CHRONICLES

name simply "the king."[18] (6) The book of Nehemiah cannot come from Nehemiah, because in it reference is made to Jaddua, the great-grandson of Eliashib,[19] the contemporary of Nehemiah;[20] according to Josephus,[21] this Jaddua was high priest in the days of Alexander the Great, that is, about B. C. 330; moreover, the "days of Nehemiah" are referred to as a period in the past.[22] (7) The language and style, as also the general point of view,[23] point unmistakably to a late date.[24] All the evi-

---

[18] 4. 8, 11, 23; 5. 6; 6. 3; 7. 11. The difference may be noted also outside of Ezra. Hag. 1. 1, 15 and Zech. 7. 1 speak of Darius, the king, without adding the name of the country, because in the days of these prophets Persia was still in existence. The same practice prevails in the Elephantine Papyri, written in the fifth century B. C. On the other hand, these papyri refer to the kings "of Egypt," because when the letters were written the native kingdom was a thing of the past. With this may be compared the reference in Ezra 5. 12 to Nebuchadnezzar "king of Babylon," because the statement was written after the downfall of Babylon.

[19] Neh. 12. 10, 11, 22.
[20] Neh. 13. 28.
[21] *Antiquities*, XI, viii, 4.
[22] Neh. 12. 47.
[23] See further, below, pp. 331, 332.
[24] For a more detailed discussion of the linguistic evidence, see S. R. Driver, *Introduction to the Literature of the Old Testament*, pp. 535ff. Hastings, *Dictionary of the Bible*, article "Chronicles"; and especially E. L. Curtis, *The Books of Chronicles*, pp. 27-36. Curtis sums up the whole situation in these words: Chronicles "exhibits many peculiarities of phraseology and syntax. Many old words are made to do service in new ways either rare or unknown in the older language, and new words, the product of the late religious organization and viewpoint, appear frequently. Also the incoming Aramaic, already a well-known language, had its influence on the Hebrew of the Chronicler, as is shown both by the presence of Aramaic loan-words and by many common Aramaic constructions. The many peculiarities of syntax, which are against the common usage of the earlier writers, indicate that the compiler and author, who was bilingual, either used Hebrew with some difficulty or that the language itself was decadent in his day. In ad-

THE PSALMS AND OTHER SACRED WRITINGS

dence, therefore, seems to favor a date during the later postexilic period, following the time of Alexander the Great, or about B. C. 300.

Scope and Purpose. Chronicles, including Ezra-Nehemiah, is clearly in the nature of a compilation. The material used by the compiler was derived, in part from the canonical books Genesis to Kings, in part from other sources.[25] The compiler treated this earlier material with considerable freedom; and the scope and purpose of the entire work can, perhaps, best be determined by a study of the excerpts from other Old Testament books and of their treatment by the Chronicler. Much may be learned, for instance, from the omissions in material taken from other books, as also from the additions made by the Chronicler, whether these additions were derived from other sources or supplied by him. Even a superficial comparison of Chronicles with other canonical books brings out the fact that some important persons and events treated at length in Samuel and Kings are passed over entirely in Chronicles or receive but slight consideration. Thus, there is almost complete silence concerning the northern kingdom, which involves the omission of the extensive Elijah and Elisha narratives in the books of Kings.[26] The life and reign of Saul receive scant consideration; only the story of his death is told;[27] and

---

dition to its common late characteristics, this group of writings (Chronicles, Ezra, Nehemiah) has marked peculiarities of style and vocabulary. Words and phrases not found at all elsewhere are met frequently both in passages from older sources which have been worked over and, particularly, in additions bearing the certain marks of the compiler. No O. T. writer reveals himself more certainly" (p. 27).

[25] See further, below, pp. 332-335.

[26] Elijah is alluded to in 2 Chron. 21. 12, not derived from Kings, while Elisha is not mentioned at all.

[27] 1 Chron. 10. 1-12 = 1 Sam. 31.

THE BOOKS OF CHRONICLES

this apparently for the sole purpose of pointing a moral.[28] Saul being a wicked king, the saintly David could have no affection for him; hence no reference is made to David's grief over Saul's death;[29] nor is there any mention of the facts that for several years the rule of David extended only over the south, or of the efforts of Adonijah to make himself king. It seems that, as far as possible, nothing is told of the good kings that could or would in any wise weaken the force of their good example. This tendency is especially noteworthy in the case of David: the incidents of Uriah and Bathsheba, of Amnon, Tamar, and Absalom, all described at length in Samuel, are all passed over in silence. There is no reference to the idolatry of good King Solomon, or to the tribute of silver and gold paid by Hezekiah, another pious ruler, to Sennacherib of Assyria. Some of the stories centering around prophets were either omitted or greatly abbreviated.[30] These and other omissions of a similar nature cannot be explained on the ground that the stories were known to the people who had access to Samuel and Kings, and therefore might be excluded from the new work, because the same statement might be made regarding many sections that are repeated word for word.

The additions made by the Chronicler consist, partly of altogether fresh material, partly of expansions of brief accounts taken from earlier sources, and partly of short additions to longer narratives found also in Samuel and Kings. However, all of these additions, long and short, reflect one and the same spirit and point of view, evidently

---

[28] 1 Chron. 10. 13, 14.
[29] Compare 2 Sam. 1. 17-27.
[30] For example, the story of Nathan, 2 Sam. 12, and the incidents in which Isaiah had a prominent part, 2 Kings 18-20.

THE PSALMS AND OTHER SACRED WRITINGS

the spirit and point of view of the compiler. In the opening chapters the additions consist in large part of statistical matter, such as genealogies and lists of names; but even these are significant as indicative of the writer's chief interest—nearly one half of the genealogical introduction is devoted to Judah and Levi, and it is around the same two tribes that the rest of the book centers. The narrative sections reveal numerous additions relating to the organization of public worship, with special reference to the part taken by Levites and singers.[31] A good illustration of this tendency may be seen in the story relating the bringing of the ark to Jerusalem.[32] In 1 Chron. 15. 13 David is introduced as explaining why the first attempt had proved a failure; there were no Levites to carry the ark; hence he summons Levites to assist in the ceremony. Again, the long section 1 Chron. 22. 2 to 29. 30, largely in the nature of an addition, deals almost exclusively with plans for the building of the temple and with Levites, priests, and other persons needed in the temple service. Levites also occupy a prominent place in the narratives of Jehoshaphat's reign.[33]

Many of the additions manifest a pronounced didactic aim. Indeed, the whole book makes the impression that the principal purpose of the Chronicler from beginning to end was, not to write history, but to teach a great truth, namely, that both right doing and wrong doing receive their proper reward. "Kings had not always recorded the sins which involved a disastrous close to the reigns

---

[31] The interest in music is so pronounced that it has been conjectured that the compiler was a Levite, a member of one of the guilds of temple singers or musicians.

[32] Compare 1 Chron. 15. 1-24; 16. 4-42 with 2 Sam. 6.

[33] 2 Chron., Chapters 17, 19, 20; compare also 1 Chron. 13. 1-5; 2 Chron. 8. 13-15; 13. 2-22; Chapters 29, 31, 35, etc.

THE BOOKS OF CHRONICLES

of good kings, or the misfortunes which punished the wickedness of bad kings. The Chronicler, as far as his source permitted, supplied these defects."[34] Thus Uzziah was stricken with leprosy because he insisted on offering incense in spite of the earnest protest of the priests;[35] Josiah's defeat and death were a punishment for disobedience;[36] the long reign of the wicked Manasseh could be explained only on the assumption that he turned to Yahweh in heartfelt repentance.[37] The same didactive motive appears in the introduction of certain stories in which prophets play a prominent role; for, while some of the prophetic stories in Samuel and Kings are omitted or abbreviated by the Chronicler, others are added. Prophets are brought into relation with kings, to whom they predict prosperity as a reward of good conduct and adversity as a punishment for bad conduct. Thus Shemaiah announces the invasion of Judah by Shishak as a punishment for disloyalty to Yahweh, but promises a modification of the punishment when king and princes humble themselves.[38]

Of interest are also some of the minor changes and modifications in material derived from earlier sources. For example, the Chronicler, believing that all temple

---

[34] Bennett and Adeney, *A Biblical Introduction*, p. 115.
[35] 2 Chron. 26. 16ff.
[36] 2 Chron. 35. 21ff.
[37] 2 Chron. 33. 11ff. Other illustrations may be found in 1 Chron. 10. 13, 14, Saul's death; 10. 10, Uzza's death; 2 Chron. 12. 2, Shishak's invasion; 21. 10, failure of Jehoram; 22. 7, destruction of Ahaziah; 24. 24, defeat of Joash; 25. 20, defeat of Amaziah; 28. 4, 5, defeat of Ahaz; 36. 12, troubles of Zedekiah, etc.
[38] 2 Chron. 12. 5-8; compare also 15. 1-15, cause of Asa's prosperity; 16. 7-10, cause of Asa's partial failure; 19. 1-3, rebuke of Jehoshaphat; 20. 14-17, promise of victory; 20. 37, prediction of shipwreck; 21. 12-15, Jehoram's sickness, etc.

THE PSALMS AND OTHER SACRED WRITINGS

priests belong to a single family of the tribe of Levi, cannot admit that at any time in the past a member of any other family or tribe filled the priestly office; consequently, the sons of David, who, according to Samuel, were priests, are said to have been "chief about the king."[39] In 1 Kings 8. 22 the statement is made that Solomon stood before the altar while he offered the dedicatory prayer; according to the Chronicler's view that place was reserved exclusively for the priest; hence he makes the king construct a special "brazen scaffold,"[40] upon which to stand. According to 2 Sam. 21. 19, Elhanan slew Goliath; according to 1 Chron. 20. 5 he slew the brother of Goliath. According to Kings, Josiah undertook his work of reformation in the eighteenth year of his reign, subsequently to the finding of the Law of Yahweh;[41] Chronicles, in order to show the devotion of the king in early youth, places the reform movement in his twelfth year;[42] then, strange to say, six years later the Book of the Law is discovered.[43] Since the Chronicler describes both Asa and Jehoshaphat as good kings, he believes that they should have removed the high places, consequently he states that they did so;[44] afterward, following the account in Kings,[45] he represents them as allowing the high places to remain.[46] In 2 Sam. 24. 1 Yahweh is

---

[39] Compare 1 Chron. 18. 17 with 2 Sam. 8. 18.
[40] 2 Chron. 6. 13.
[41] 2 Kings 22. 3ff.
[42] 2 Chron. 34. 3.
[43] Verses 8ff.
[44] 2 Chron. 14. 5; 17. 6.
[45] 1 Kings 15. 14; 22. 43.
[46] 2 Chron. 15. 17; 20. 33. In view of the almost complete silence of the Chronicler concerning the northern kingdom "Israel" in 15. 17 must be understood as equivalent to "Judah," compare 11. 3. Other-

THE BOOKS OF CHRONICLES

introduced as causing David to number the people; but, in view of the sequel, the introduction of Yahweh in this connection involved a conception of his character not in accord with the more ethical ideals of the Chronicler's age; hence he substitutes Satan for Yahweh.[47]

These and other similar changes introduced by the Chronicler reveal the scope and purpose of the entire work: Chronicles must be regarded as an "Ecclesiastical" History of Israel, a history written from the point of view of the Priestly Code,[48] a point of view that dominated the whole religious thought and life of the later postexilic period. The compiler knew the Priestly Law and was in entire sympathy with it; moreover, accepting its Mosaic origin, he believed that its authority had been recognized and its provisions had been observed by all the God-fearing kings of Israel. With this view of the influence exerted by the Priestly Code, it is not strange that he should represent the good kings David, Solomon, Jehoshaphat, Hezekiah, and Josiah as worshiping Yahweh with a full accompaniment of ritual, priests, Levites, and choirs, and according to all the ceremonial laws of the Pentateuch. Naturally, this view of the earlier history determined in large measure the selection of the material to be used in the new work. But, as has already been suggested, the Chronicler was dominated by another motive; he had no interest in history as such, but only in the religious lessons that might be learned from history.

---

wise it would have to be regarded as an editorial addition for the purpose of harmonizing 15. 17 with 14. 5. No such addition is made in 20. 33, and as a result the contradiction remains.

[47] 1 Chron. 21. 1; compare also 2 Sam. 24. 24 with 1 Chron. 21. 25; 1 Kings 11. 11 with 2 Chron. 8. 2; 1 Sam. 28. 6 with 1 Chron. 10. 14; 1 Kings 3. 4–13 with 2 Chron. 1. 3–6.

[48] See F. C. Eiselen, *The Books of the Pentateuch*, pp. 247ff.; 308–312.

THE PSALMS AND OTHER SACRED WRITINGS

His chief aim appears to have been to teach that virtue and vice, in private life and in national affairs, would sooner or later receive their dues; and he selected from the sources at his disposal only such material as could be used to illustrate or give added emphasis to this fundamental idea.

The "ecclesiastical" interest of the compiler explains the almost complete silence concerning the period before David and concerning the northern kingdom. The age of the Judges was an age of anarchy, during which the Law was forgotten. The northern kingdom had revolted from Yahweh and from Judah, it had fallen into sin and idolatry; hence Yahweh was in reality absent from Israel,[49] and allowed it to be taken into exile, from which there was no return. Judah, on the other hand, was the people of Yahweh's choice, Jerusalem was the holy city, and the center of it all was the temple, the dwelling place of Yahweh. It is for this reason that even in the genealogies in the opening chapters a disproportionate amount of space is given to Judah and to the "ecclesiastical" tribe Levi.

Sources. A comparison of Chronicles with the other historical books of the Old Testament shows that it consists to a considerable extent of extracts, more or less modified, from the books of Samuel and Kings, and that it is dependent, though to a less extent, upon the Pentateuch and Joshua.[50] The compiler himself cites a number of sources, or one source under a variety of titles, which, he states, furnish additional information concerning the events narrated. These sources are: (1) The book of

---

[49] 2 Chron. 25. 7.
[50] E. L. Curtis, *The Books of Chronicles*, pp. 17-19; S. R. Driver, *Introduction to the Literature of the Old Testament*, pp. 519-525.

THE BOOKS OF CHRONICLES

the kings of Judah and Israel;[51] (2) the book of the kings of Israel and Judah;[52] (3) the words (acts) of the kings of Israel;[53] (4) the words (acts) of Samuel the seer;[54] (5) the words (acts) of Nathan the prophet;[55] (6) the words (acts) of Gad the seer;[56] (7) the words (acts) of Shemaiah the prophet and of Iddo the seer;[57] (8) the words (acts) of Jehu the son of Hanani;[58] (9) the words (acts) of Hozai, or, of the seers;[59] (10) the vision of Isaiah the prophet;[60] (11) the visions of Iddo the seer;[61] (12) the Midrash of the book of kings;[62] (13) the Midrash of the prophet Iddo;[63] (14) the words (acts) of Uzziah, written by Isaiah the prophet;[64] (15) the prophecy of Ahijah the Shilonite.[65] These fifteen sources are introduced with very much the same formula;[66] and though the language used suggests primarily

---

[51] For Asa, 2 Chron. 16. 11; Amaziah, 25. 26; Ahaz, 28. 26. There is a difference in the Hebrew construction between 2 Chron. 16. 11, on the one hand, and the remaining passages on the other.
[52] For Jotham, 2 Chron. 27. 7; for Josiah, 35. 26, 27; see also the Septuagint translation of 1 Chron. 9. 1.
[53] For Manasseh, 2 Chron. 33. 18.
[54] For David, 1 Chron. 29. 29.
[55] For David, 1 Chron. 29. 29; for Solomon, 2 Chron. 9. 29.
[56] For David, 1 Chron. 29. 29.
[57] For Rehoboam, 2 Chron. 12. 15.
[58] For Jehoshaphat, 2 Chron. 20. 34.
[59] For Manasseh, 2 Chron. 33. 19.
[60] For Hezekiah, 2 Chron. 32. 32.
[61] For Solomon, 2 Chron. 9. 29.
[62] For Joash, 2 Chron. 24. 27.
[63] For Abijah, 2 Chron. 13. 22.
[64] For Uzziah, 2 Chron. 26. 22.
[65] For Solomon, 2 Chron. 9. 29.
[66] Reference is made, but in a different manner, to "the chronicles of King David," 1 Chron. 27. 24; "the last words of David," 1 Chron. 23. 27; "the lamentations" (concerning Josiah), 2 Chron. 35. 25; "genealogies," 1 Chron. 5. 17.

THE PSALMS AND OTHER SACRED WRITINGS

that in them further information concerning the persons and events described may be found, it may be safe to infer also that the compiler made use of them in the production of his work.

It is by no means certain that the fifteen titles enumerated refer to fifteen distinct sources. There can be little doubt that 1 and 2 are identical; 3, though spoken of as the acts of the kings of Israel, is cited for Manasseh, a king of Judah; perhaps it also is simply a variation of 1. Source 8 is said to have formed a part of the book of the kings of Israel, and source 10 a part of the book of the kings of Judah and Israel. All this may mean that 1, 2, 3, 8, 10, that is, five of the fifteen titles, refer to one and the same source or to different parts of the same. If this conclusion is warranted, may the further inference be drawn that the other prophetic sources cited —Samuel, Nathan, Gad, Shemaiah, Iddo, Ahijah—are parts of the same continuous work, each part taking its name from its central prophetic figure? In other words, is there adequate reason for believing that the fifteen titles refer, not to fifteen separate sources, but to one single source, called, perhaps, "the book of the kings of Israel and Judah"? This question cannot be definitely settled; it must be admitted, however, that there is nothing inherently improbable in the view that all the references are to one and the same historical work.

If so, was this "book" the canonical book of Kings, perhaps, *plus* the story of the United Kingdom as recorded in Samuel? Now, it is beyond doubt that both these canonical books were in existence when Chronicles was compiled, and, moreover, that the compiler made extensive use of them; nevertheless, the source book of the Chronicler cannot be identified with the canonical

THE BOOKS OF CHRONICLES

book of Kings, for the simple reason that it must have contained information not found in Samuel and Kings.[67] But if the source book of the Chronicler, referred to under a variety of names, may be called "the *Midrash* of the book of Kings,"[68] the conclusion may be warranted that, though it cannot have been the canonical Kings, it was a Midrash, that is, an edifying commentary, on the canonical book. It may be, therefore, that in addition to the canonical sources[69] the Chronicler used "a work based on the canonical book of Kings, and amplified by exegetical inferences and edifying details, or stories told to enhance the glory or the moral significance of some of the persons or events in the original work."[70]

Value and Significance. In estimating the value of the books of Chronicles the scope and purpose of the compiler, as discussed earlier in this chapter, must be kept in mind. A comparison with the other historical books of the Old Testament reveals the fact that its historical value is inferior to that of the canonical books from which much of its material is drawn. True, it offers a parallel text, which in some cases may have

---

[67] For example, there is nothing in the story of Jehoshaphat as narrated in Kings that could be called "the words of Jehu the son of Hanani," 2 Chron. 20. 34; the prayer of Manasseh is not a part of the canonical Kings, 2 Chron. 33. 18; nor are the genealogies referred to in 1 Chron. 9. 1. For further information regarding Jotham the reader is referred to the book of the kings of Israel and Judah, but Chronicles tells more about him than the canonical Kings (2 Kings 15. 32-38).

[68] Source 12 above; compare 2 Chron. 24. 27.

[69] The question has been raised whether the Chronicler availed himself of the canonical books at all, or depended exclusively on a Midrash. Though the question cannot be settled with absolute certainty, the theory that he used both the canonical books and the Midrash offers the most satisfactory explanation of all the facts in the case.

[70] G. B. Gray, *A Critical Introduction to the Old Testament*, p. 96.

THE PSALMS AND OTHER SACRED WRITINGS

preserved a more original reading; but, since the Chronicler did not hesitate to modify his sources to suit his own ideas, the testimony of the other books is on the whole to be preferred. It has also been suggested that the compiler had access to sources other than the canonical books[71] and older than the Midrash, but this is by no means certain. If such sources were accessible to him, he may have derived from them some items of information not found elsewhere in the Old Testament. Thus the genealogies in 1 Chron., Chapters 1 to 9, when freed of later additions, may rest on reliable early authorities; as may also be the case with the information regarding several interesting incidents in Hebrew history narrated in Chronicles, and nowhere else in the Old Testament.[72] However, on the whole, the judgment of Professor Sayce as to the historical character of Chronicles is well founded: "The consistent exaggeration of numbers on the part of the Chronicler[73] shows us that

---

[71] Perhaps sources used in the compilation of these books.

[72] For example, 2 Chron. 11. 5–12, the fortifications of Rehoboam; 2 Chron. 27. 3, 4, the building enterprises of Jotham; 2 Chron. 26. 5–15, Uzziah's enterprises in peace and war; there is also additional information relating to wars carried on by some of the kings, 2 Chron. 14. 9–15; 17. 11; 21. 16; 26. 7; 28. 17, 18.

[73] The Chronicler resembles in this respect the Priestly Code. As illustrative of this tendency to exaggerate, attention may be called to facts like these: The Chronicler credits David with preparing for the building of the temple 100,000 talents of gold and 1,000,000 talents of silver (1 Chron. 22. 14), and with contributing out of his own personal resources 3,000 talents of gold and 7,000 talents of silver (29. 4); the officials are said to have contributed of gold 5,000 talents and 10,000 *darics*, of silver 10,000 talents, of brass 18,000 talents, and of iron 100,000 talents. Sacrificial animals are numbered by the thousands (1 Chron. 29. 21; 2 Chron. 29. 32, 33; 30. 24; 35. 8, 9), and the numbers of warriors are in many instances incredibly large. On all these points and others of a similar nature a comparison with the older narratives in Samuel and Kings is exceedingly suggestive.

THE BOOKS OF CHRONICLES

from a historical point of view his unsupported statements must be received with caution. But they do not justify the accusations of deliberate fraud and 'fiction' which have been brought against him. What they prove is that he did not possess that sense of historical exactitude which we now demand from the historian. He wrote in fact with a didactic and not with a historical purpose. That he should have used the framework of history to illustrate the lessons he wished to draw was as much an accident as that Sir Walter Scott should have based certain of his novels on the facts of mediæval history. He cared as little for history in the modern European sense of the word as the Oriental of to-day, who considers himself at liberty to embellish or modify the narrative he is repeating in accordance with his fancy or the moral he wishes to draw from it."[74]

The religious teaching of Chronicles gives evidence of the limitations of the age in which the book was written. Though there are some expressions of intense religious fervor, the book defines religion largely in terms of ritual and ceremonial, and never loses an opportunity to emphasize external observances. Its attitude toward the moral problems of life is superficial; there is no sign of perplexity such as troubles the author of Job. The author believes without question in a mechanical correspondence between conduct and destiny. The reward of piety is prosperity, while prosperity is an infallible proof of piety; in the same way, the punishment of sin is adversity, while adversity is an infallible proof of sin. No doubt, in its own day the book served an important didactic purpose, of encouragement and of warning; but to the modern student its chief value lies in the fact that it en-

[74] *Higher Criticism and the Monuments*, p. 464.

INDEX

INDEX

I. Subjects Discussed

Accent in Meter, 13, 21, 22
Acrostic, 31, 201
Agur, 103, 104
Allegorical Interpretation of Song of Songs, 166-169
Angels in Book of Daniel, 279, 280
Antithetic Parallelism, 17
Apocryphal Additions
  To Daniel, 252, 253
  To Esther, 235
Apocalyptic Literature, 274-276
Aramaic
  In Daniel, 258, 269-271, 283ff.
  In Ezra, 298-301
Arrangement of Psalms, 71
Artaxerxes, 308
Artificial Devices in Poetry, 29ff.
Ascending Rhythm, 18
Azariah, Prayer of, 252

Bel and the Dragon, 252
Bilingual Character, Book of Daniel, 258, 283-288
Blank Verse, 14

Canon
  Chronicles, 319, 320
  Daniel, 251, 252
  Ecclesiastes, 228, 229
  Esther, 235-237
  Song of Songs, 166
Chronicles, Books of, 319ff.
  Additions, 327-329
  An Ecclesiastical History, 331, 332
  Canonicity, 319, 320
  Contents, 320-323

Date, 323-326
Historical Significance, 336, 337
Modifications, 329-331
Name, 319
Omissions, 326
Relation to Ezra-Nehemiah, 323
Religious Significance, 337, 338
Scope and Purpose, 326-332
Sources, 332-335
Classification of Psalms, 71ff.
Climactic Parallelism, 18
Compilation of Psalter, 64ff.
Date of, 69-71

Daniel
  Author of Book, 256-274
  Historical Character, 277, 278
Daniel, Book of, 251ff.
  Apocryphal Additions, 252, 253
  Bilingual Character, 258, 269-271, 283-288.
  Canonicity, 251, 252
  Contents, 253-256
  Date and Authorship, 256-274
  Historical Character, 277, 278
  Historical Inaccuracies, 265-269
  Of Maccabean Origin, 263-274
  Significance, 273-277
  Teaching, 278-282
  Theology, 271, 272
David
  Character, 55, 56
  Founder of Psalmody, 43
  Musical Skill, 51, 52
  Writer of Psalms, 42, 47ff.
Davidic Psalms, 49ff., 57, 58
Deborah, Song of, 50

INDEX

Development of Hebrew Religion, 55, 56
Devotional Value of Psalms, 78–80
Distich, 25
Divine Names in Psalms, 67, 68
Doxologies, 42
Dramatic Poetry, 31–33

Ecclesiastes, Book of, 213ff.
  Canonicity, 228, 229
  Contents, 214, 215
  Date and Authorship, 222–228
  Greek Influence, 225–227
  Inconsistencies, 216–218
  Interpolations, 219–221
  Literary Form, 215–221
  Meaning of Term, 213
  Postexilic, 224–228
  Significance, 228–231
  Unity, 215–221
Ecclesiastical History, 331, 332
Ecclesiasticus, 61, 62
Elihu, Speeches of, 133, 136, 143–146
Emotion in Poetry, 13, 15
Epic Poetry, 31, 32
Esdras, First Book of, 313–316
Esther, 235
Esther, Book of, 235ff.
  Canonicity, 235
  Contents, 237, 238
  Date, 246–248
  Historical Character, 238–245
  Mythological Elements, 243, 244
Ezra, 293
  Date, 308–311
  Historicity, 310, 311
  Memoirs, 297, 298, 302, 303
  Mission, 308–311
Ezra and Nehemiah, Books of, 291ff.
  Contents, 291–295
  Date, 295–301

Division, 291
Historical Value, 301–312
Manner of Composition, 295–301
Relation to Chronicles, 323
Sources, 297–301

False Wise Men, 86
Friends of Job, 132, 136

Gnomic Poetry, 34
Greek Influence
  Proverbs, 109
  Ecclesiastes, 225–227

Hebrew Language, 29, 30
Hebrew Poetry, Characteristics, 15
Hexastich, 27
Historical Situation Reflected in Psalms, 53, 54, 72ff.
Holy Children, Song of the Three, 252

Imagination in Poetry, 13, 15
Individual Psalms, 75–78

Jeremiah, Author of Lamentations, 202–207
Job, 125, 126, 136
  Character, 140
  Folk Tale of, 139–143
  Friends, 132, 136
  Historical Character, 158, 159
Job, Book of, 33, 125ff.
  Contents, 125ff.
  Date and Authorship, 151ff.
  Historical Character, 158, 159
  Home, 160, 161
  Literary Form, 130–132
  Original Extent, 138ff.
  Problem, 132–137
  Prologue and Epilogue, 135, 136, 139–143

INDEX

Job, Book of (continued):
  Religious Solution, 137
  Soliloquy on Wisdom, 149, 150
Jotham, Fable of, 34

Ḳînah, 22, 23, 199
Ḳînah Meter, 22, 23, 201
Kingdom of God, in Daniel, 278, 279

Lamentation, 22, 23, 199
Lamentations, Book of, 199ff.
  Contents, 199, 200
  Date and Authorship, 202-207
  Dates of Individual Poems, 208, 209
  Literary Form, 201
  Significance, 209
  Unity, 207, 208
Lemuel, 104
Literary Dependence, 53-55
Lyric Poetry, 31, 33, 34

Maccabean Crisis, 273, 274
Maccabean Psalms, 60-63
Megilloth, 165, 203
Meter, 13, 21ff.
Monostich, 25
Moses, Author of Job, 151, 152

Nehemiah, 293, 294
  Memoirs, 297, 298, 302

Parallelism of Members, 15ff., 24
  Babylonian, 19
  Egyptian, 19
  Kinds, 17, 18
  Origin, 19, 20
Pentastich, 27
Pessimism, 134, 229, 230
Philosophy
  Of Calamity, 89, 90
  Of Evil, 90-92
  Of History, 89

Poetic Books, 12
Poetic Units, 13, 24ff.
Poetry
  Characteristics, 12
  Definition, 12, 13
  Kinds, 31ff.
Poetry, Hebrew
  Extent, 11, 12, 50, 51
  Secular, 34, 35
Prayer, 39
Pre-exilic Psalms, 58-60
Proverbs, 88
  Definition, 95, 96
  Definition of Religion, 121
  Greek Influence, 109
  Postexilic, 108-112
  Practical Teaching, 120, 121
  Pre-exilic, 112-114
  Religious Basis, 120
  Value, 119, 120
Proverbs, Book of, 95ff.
  Compilation, 113ff., 115
  Contents, 96-102
  Date and Authorship, 105ff.
  Value, 119, 120
Psalms, Book of, 39ff.
  A Priori Evidence Regarding Dates, 50-52
  Arrangement, 71
  Authors, 42, 43
  Classification, 71ff.
  Compilation, 64ff.
  Date and Authorship, 47ff.
  Dates of Individual Psalms, 63, 64
  Davidic, 49ff., 57, 58
  Devotional Value, 78-80
  Division, 40, 41, 65ff.
  External Evidence Regarding Dates, 52, 53
  Internal Evidence Regarding Dates, 53-58
  Interpretation, 75ff.

INDEX

Psalms, Book of (continued):
  Maccabean, 60–63
  Number, 40, 41
  Pre-exilic, 58–60
  Speaker in, 74ff.
Psalm Titles, 42ff.
  Additions to, 44
  and Contents, 45
  and Language, 45
  Attitude toward, 46
  Origin, 46
  Significance, 43ff.
Purim, Feast of, Origin, 244–246

Rebuilding of Temple, 306, 307
Religious Development, 55, 56
Resurrection, 275, 280, 281
Return from Exile, 304–306
Rhythm, 13, 14
  Ascending, 18
Rime, 14, 30, 31
Ruth, Book of, 189ff.
  Aim, 190–193
  Contents, 189, 190
  Date and Authorship, 193–195

Secular Poetry, 34, 35
Skepticism, 134, 229, 230
Solomon, Author of Ecclesiastes, 222–224
  Author of Job, 153
  Author of Psalms, 42, 43
  Author of Proverbs, 105ff., 118
  Author of Song of Songs, 182
  Hero of Song of Songs, 169–174
Song of Songs, 33, 165ff.
  Allegorical Interpretation, 166–169
  Authorship and Date, 182–185
  Canonicity, 166
  Collection of Love Songs, 174–176, 180, 181

Dramatic Interpretation, 169–174
Lyric Interpretation, 174–176, 180, 181
Name, 165
Song of the Sword, 12
Speaker in Psalms, 74ff.
Speculation, 89–92, 132–137, 216–218
Stanza, 25
Stichos, 22, 24ff.
Strophe, 27ff.
Suffering, 132–137
Susanna, 252
Synonymous Parallelism, 17
Synthetic Parallelism, 17

Tetrastich, 26
Theological Ideas reflected in Psalms, 53–55
Thought Lyric, 34
Tristich, 26

Verse, 24

Wars of Yahweh, Book of, 11
Wedding Songs in Palestine, 175, 180, 181
Wisdom, 98
  and Philosophy, 83
  Growth of Movement, 87ff.
  and Speculation, 89–92
Wisdom Literature, 83ff.
Wisdom Movement, 87ff.
Wise Men, Aim and Function, 84–87
  Characteristics, 85
  False, 86
Writings, 7

Yahweh, Speeches of, 136, 146–148
Yashar, Book of, 11

INDEX

II. BIBLICAL PASSAGES

	PAGE		PAGE
Gen. 4. 23, 24	30, 35, 51	2 Sam. 24. 1	330
36. 13	125	1 Kings. 1. 3ff	173
46. 13	125	3. 16–28	105
49. 2–27	35, 51	4. 29–34	105
Exod. 15. 1–18	16, 35, 50	4. 32	165
15. 11	68	8. 22	330
15. 18	25	10. 1	106
20. 2	68	2 Kings. 25. 27	243
Num. 21. 14, 15	35	1 Chron. 10. 1–12	326
21. 17, 18	35, 51	10. 13, 14	327
21. 27–30	35	15. 13	328
24. 8	27	20. 5	330
Deut. 22. 13ff	174	21. 1	156, 331
25. 9, 10	193	23. 5	43, 52
32	16	25. 1–7	43
33. 2–29	35	2 Chron. 12. 5–8	329
Josh. 10. 12, 13	35	21. 12	326
Judg. 5. 2–31	35, 50	25. 7	332
9. 8–15	34, 35, 87	26. 16ff	329
14. 14	30	29. 25	52
14, 15	35	2 Chron. 33. 11ff	329
Ruth 4. 7	193	35. 21ff	329
1 Sam. 10. 12	87	35. 25	203
16. 1–13	190	36. 22, 23	323
16. 18	51	Ezra 1. 1–3	323
18. 7	35	3. 8ff	306
22. 3, 4	191	4. 6–23	297
31	326	4. 17–22	299
2 Sam. 1. 17	50	5. 6–17	299
1. 19–27	35, 327	5. 16	306
3. 33, 34	35	6. 1–12	299
5. 8	87	6. 12	300
12. 1–7	88	6. 19–22	299
20. 18	87	7. 1–10	299
21. 19	330	7. 7, 8	308
22. 1	52	7. 12–26	299
23. 1	51	7. 17	300

INDEX

	PAGE		PAGE
Ezra 8. 24–27	303	Psa. 3. 7	26
9. 9	309	4. 1	26
Neh. 2. 1	308	5. 11	26
8. 9	309	8. 5	153
10. 1	309	9	31, 40
12. 11	292, 297	10	31, 40
12. 22	292, 297	14	68
12. 47	297	18	48, 52
13. 23–29	191	18. 1	25
Esth. 1. 3	240	19	40
1. 4	241	19. 7–9	25
1. 19–22	241	20	45
2. 6	240	21	45
2. 17	241	24	40
3. 7	238	24. 7–10	32
4. 14	236	25	31
9. 19	246	25. 1–3	34
10. 1–3	242	27	40
Job 1. 9	132	27. 1	44
2. 9	142	29. 1	18
3	154	34	40
7. 17	153, 157	36	31
19. 23–27	136, 157, 280	37	31
26. 5–14	150	40. 13–17	68
27. 7–23	150	42	40
28	149	43	40
31. 35–37	144	44	62
32. 1–5	143	45	35
38. 1, 2	144	50. 7	68
38. 2	140	53	68
40. 2	140	57. 7–11	40, 68
42. 7	134, 140, 142	59. 1	45
Psa. 1	28	60. 5–12	40, 68
1. 1	71	71. 19	68
1. 2	17, 71	72. 20	39
1. 3	26	73. 1	44
1. 6	25	74	62
2	28	76. 1	44
2. 1	71	80	28
2. 2	26	80. 1	44
2. 6	17	96. 1	44
2. 12	71	103	45

INDEX

	PAGE
Psa. 107	28
108	40, 67
111	31
112	31
119	28, 31
121. 1-4	18
122	53
122. 1	45
129	77
133	28
134	28
137	53
137. 4	59
139	55
144	45
145	31
Prov. 1. 1	105
8	98, 150
10. 1	17, 105
15. 17	17
19. 7	99
22. 17	105
24. 23	105
24. 30-34	86
25. 1	102, 117
26. 4	18
30. 1	103, 105
31. 1	104, 105
31. 10-31	105
Eccl. 1. 1	222
1. 2	214
1. 12	222
1. 16	223
7. 16-18	225
12. 8	214
12. 13, 14	218, 219
12. 13	229
Song of Songs 1. 1	165
Isa. 5. 1-7	88
5. 21	87
9. 8-21	90
13. 17	267

	PAGE
Isa. 15. 1	17
26. 19	157, 280
44. 28	307
Jer. 8. 8-13	87
9. 23	110
10. 1	113
Jer. 18. 18	112
20. 14-18	154
25. 1	113, 265
25. 12	307
31. 29	87
36. 9	265
51. 11	267
Lam. 1. 1	23
1-4	31
Ezek. 14. 14	125, 278
14. 20	125, 278
16	88
17	88
23	88
28. 3	278
Dan. 1. 4	286
2. 4	267, 286
2. 18	272
3. 5	270
4. 26	272
8. 14	273
10. 13	279
10. 20	279
10. 21	279
11. 25-39	268
11. 45	273
12. 1	279
12. 2	157, 280
Amos 3. 6	89
4. 6-11	90
5. 23	58
Nah. 1	31
Hab. 1. 1 to 2. 5	90
3. 17	27
Zech. 3	141, 156
Mal. 2. 17	92, 114, 156

INDEX

	PAGE		PAGE
Mal. 2. 17 to 4. 3	91	John 9. 2	114
3. 7–12	92	2 Thess. 2. 1–12	259
3. 13 to 4. 3	92	Heb. 11. 33, 34	259
3. 14	156	Jude 9	280
Matt. 25. 15	259	Rev. 8. 2	280

www.ingramcontent.com/pod-product-compliance
Lightning Source LLC
Chambersburg PA
CBHW050430240426
43661CB00055B/2327